Damaged

Bullied, Volume 3

Vera Hollins

Published by Vera Hollins, 2020.

Edited by: Bethany Salminen
Cover Design by: Rasha Savic
Cover Girl Art photo by: annamile from Depositphotos

To Milica. Thank you for everything. You rock!

Prologue

THREE AND A HALF YEARS AGO

"Did you know that ninety nine percent of our solar system's mass is the sun?" Kayden asked me, pausing the movie on his laptop to look at me.

We sat on the floor next to each other as we watched a sci-fi movie called *Sunshine*, but unlike Kayden, I wasn't excited about it. Personally, I thought it was rather dull. From time to time, he paused the movie to tell me some facts about space, most of which weren't relevant to the movie at all.

One of the first things I'd learned about Kayden was that he was a space geek. He was obsessed with everything that had to do with space, unlike me.

"No."

"Yes. Its mass is 330,000 times bigger than Earth's, and when it dies, it will become a red giant and envelop Earth."

I was totally lost. I had no interest in the sun and our apocalyptic future, but I figured I should show at least some interest. "What is a red giant?"

"It's a dying star in the last phase of stellar evolution. This won't happen for another five billion years, but just thinking about Earth being gone gives me chills."

He grinned, his dark brown eyes glimmering with excitement and joy, and I wondered how he could be so excited about something so depressing. That was Kayden, though. I'd known him for more than a month now, and if I could describe him with a single word, it would be *cheerful*. He was always so positive—so unlike me—and I often felt unusual next to him, like there was something wrong with me because I didn't share the same sentiments. Most of the time I was gloomy, and I tried to act like a normal teenager in front of him, hoping not to seem like an awkward creep.

I had to pee badly, and I squirmed. The toilet in Kayden's bathroom wasn't working, so I had to go downstairs, but I didn't dare. I'd only been in Kayden's house a few times so far, and each time I came over, his twin brother, Hayden, treated me horribly. So I didn't want to risk seeing him. Hayden was an absolute jerk, and I completely disliked him. Every time I saw him, my skin would crawl and heart beat faster in fear.

"What's wrong?" Kayden asked me after a minute and stopped the movie again.

"Um, nothing."

He chuckled. "Look, if you want to go to the bathroom, just go."

My cheeks reddened as his lips curled into a grin. "How do you know?"

"You've been squirming for the past thirty minutes." His smile widened, eliciting a stronger blush from me.

"Okay. Fine. I want to go to the bathroom."

"Then I officially give you permission to go."

He burst out laughing, and I pouted. I wasn't used to being this relaxed with someone, and I'd never had a male friend, so Kayden's nearness and friendly attitude made me uncomfortable.

Now I needed to put some space between us until my shame subdued. "Fine," I said as I got up.

"You know where the bathroom is. Or do you want me to be your guide?" He was still grinning, enjoying teasing me immensely.

"I know where it is," I muttered, lacking any good comeback, and left his room.

My eyes immediately darted to Hayden's door, and my pulse picked up. He wasn't supposed to be home, but I was afraid of stumbling across him anyway. He was an awful person, and his humiliation and mean remarks constantly hurt me. He treated me like I was a lesser human, and even though he was the most beautiful guy I'd ever seen, he was so ugly on the inside.

I went downstairs and halted when I heard sobs coming from the living room. *Sobs?*

Wait. This wasn't a woman crying.

My heartbeat sped up once more. Was this Hayden?

A male voice mumbled something through tears, and I stopped breathing. No. This wasn't Hayden. Or was it?

"Hurts...," the guy said.

I tiptoed to the wall separating the living room from the hallway and froze when what was clearly Hayden's voice said, "I understand." My breathing faltered.

The other person mumbled something in response. Then he asked, "Why?"

"I don't know, man," Hayden replied. "Life is shit."

I reached the doorway on my toes and peeked into the room. A pang spread through my chest when I saw Hayden and his friend Blake seated on the floor next to each other with their backs turned to the back of the couch. Blake held his head between his knees with his arms encircling his legs, while Hayden held his arm across Blake's shoulders. He looked at him with worry written all over his face.

I inhaled sharply and whipped my head back, my heart hammering against my rib cage. I couldn't believe what I just saw. Blake was crying and Hayden... I'd never seen Hayden look like that before... He was worried.

What was going on?

"She was..." More sobs and murmurs filled the air. I strained to hear Blake better, but it was impossible.

"I wish I could help you, man," Hayden said softly, and my breath caught in my throat. A sprout of warmth unfolded in me.

I'd never heard him speak like this. *Never.* His voice was always cold, derisive, or emotionless, as if it was impossible for him to care for anyone, but now he was this kind stranger, looking after his friend who was suffering, and I was stunned.

I knew it wasn't right of me to eavesdrop and I should leave right away, but I couldn't. I was glued to the spot as I listened to Hayden's soothing words, "I'll be with you through everything, man. I'll help you get through this."

I clutched my throbbing chest. This was impossible. He was an evil, heartless person who didn't even love his own brother. He couldn't be this supportive. He was incapable of caring.

"It was my fault!" Blake cried and burst into more tears.

"No, it wasn't your fault. It was the fault of those—"

"It was!" He muttered something I couldn't catch, his voice laced with bitterness. "Emma..."

Emma? I risked another glance at them, and all air left my lungs when I saw Hayden's face. He was *crying*. His eyes were red, and the tears created glistening paths down his face. It tugged at something deep within me.

"I'm here for you," he said. "You'll be okay."

He hugged him and patted his back as Blake continued to sob. I clenched my hands, battling with the revelation that Hayden wasn't who I'd projected him to be.

"You'll be okay," he repeated tenderly, and to my utter surprise, something changed in me. "You can always count on me. You'll get through this."

My heart expanded with a potent emotion, which was equally dangerous and life-giving. I stared at the wall across from me, but I didn't see anything. My knees grew weak and my head swarmed with so many questions as the realization settled in my mind.

Hayden Black cared. He was capable of being there for others, and despite all his cruelty, he had something good deep inside of him... He was much more than what I'd thought.

And just like that—in a matter of a few fleeting seconds—I started to *like* him.

Chapter 1

PRESENT (DECEMBER)

The distant, incessant beeping of the heart monitor slowly penetrated into my mind, loosening my nightmare's clutches. I blinked a couple of times and squinted, disoriented at the outright change in surroundings. My mind was still focused on that road from my dream where Kayden's dead body transformed into Hayden's unconscious form, which caused me darkness and pain that bordered on agony.

The world of nightmares had become an almost daily occurrence since Hayden's accident. It clashed with an equally dark reality that overlapped with my biggest fears, and it wore me down physically and mentally. I was so exhausted I dozed off as soon as I got here.

I ignored the pain in my back from the uncomfortable sleeping position as I sat up and looked at Hayden. The hope in my chest turned to ashes, replaced by a myriad of emotions that hit me each time I expected to see him awake.

He lay unconscious in a single-bed room in the ICU, surrounded with machines that kept him alive. His pale face displayed vulnerability and exhaustion, which made my heart ache. It was dark outside, so the hospital lights cast a sickly yellow light on him that added to his haggard appearance.

An IV drip was attached to his right arm, and it sickened me to look at the intravenous line ending at his elbow. He'd fractured his left elbow, so his arm was in a cast, and his previously bruised ribs were now broken. He slipped into a coma after his surgery nine days ago, and each new day brought more anguish as we waited for him to wake up.

I bit my lip and ran my fingers over the stubble on his cheeks. My gaze swept over the lines of his face for the umpteenth time, briefly halting on his scar that seemed more pronounced than ever. It was a tragic echo of the accident that almost took his life, which now told a story full circle. He'd had a breathing tube in his mouth until a few days ago when his physician determined he was able to breathe on his own. This was a sign of improvement I was clinging onto, along with his doctor's words that he was young and strong so he had a good chance of making it.

It was absurd how easy I could lose myself in doubts and fear. Nine days felt like nine years. They represented an endless cycle of hope, anxiety, and despair, and it was almost impossible for me to focus on anything but Hayden.

I was barely able to make it through midterms, but extensive studying had been my only way of escaping reality for a short while. My every waking thought was about the uncertainty of his condition, which could last for one more day or forever.

I shuddered. No. I refused to think about that bleak possibility. He would wake up. *He will.*

This time I didn't let myself fall into another "what if" phase. I had to be stronger than before, for me *and* Hayden. He needed us to believe in him and support him. I couldn't let those old, negative thoughts trap me, so I'd decided to stay positive.

Hayden and I were together now, but our fight from nine days ago showed that we both needed to work on understanding and readjust the way we perceived each other and our actions. Things had escalated so fast I sometimes wondered if I imagined them or not, and it was hard to accept.

That Tuesday morning brought too many emotions colliding together. Everything was supposed to be good after Brad, my mother's ex-boyfriend from New Haven, had gotten arrested for what he'd done to my mother and me. He was sent back to prison, and our attorney assured us he wouldn't get out anytime soon after the kidnap and assaults. My mother was in a stable condition, and I'd been discharged from the hospital, on my way to create a brighter future with Hayden.

But then that morning happened, representing black and white outcomes at their finest. One minute, everything was wonderful. I could still feel tingles whenever I remembered Hayden's kiss that pervaded all my senses, right before my heart melted when he gave me the most invaluable thing: his diary. I was amazed that he wanted to show me the deepest parts of himself despite his fears and insecurity. He even begged me not to leave him after I read it.

Then, Hayden got a call from one of the guys in the gang, and the cruel twist happened. He became uncontrollably enraged, which was further fueled when he misinterpreted my worry for him.

I didn't want him to fight anymore. I wanted him safe, away from pain and that dark world, but he thought I wanted to control him. He lashed out at me and told me things I'd rather bury in the deep corners of my mind and never remember again, before he left me alone in front of the hospital.

And then... And then history repeated itself. By the time I noticed he was going to get hit, it was too late, and the car ran into him and sent him flying through the air. Hayden lost consciousness right away.

I closed my eyes. I couldn't help but envision the image of his immobile body interlaced with the dark image of Kayden and his dead eyes, both accidents coming together as one. Hayden had survived that first accident thanks to Kayden, but there was no one to take the hit for him this time. It was as if this accident was his punishment for cheating death back then, and I was afraid. A powerful fear haunted me in my dreams—the fear of definitely losing him this time.

I let out a shaky breath and shook my head to dispel these thoughts.

I looked at Hayden's diary that lay in front of me on his bed. It was a precious piece of him I'd kept by my side since the morning he gave it to me. It was my treasure and undoing because it brought pain along with answers and understanding. I had a full insight into who he was, and just like he'd said, in some moments it was too intense and raw, while others displayed fragility that shattered me. I needed a distraction from my nightmare, so I turned the page and started reading a new entry.

"Date: October... Does it matter which day?

Here I am. Trying to sort out my emotions. Fucking impossible.

For as long as I can remember, I've been different. I think differently. I feel differently. I act differently. I've always known there was something wrong with me. Something that makes me feel like I don't belong anywhere. Like no one can understand me. Fuck, even I can't understand myself. Wherever I go, there is that emptiness inside of me that paints the world black.

I have so many scars. There are so many things I'm scared and ashamed of, and if people knew even a fragment of who I am, they would run away from me like I was some contagious disease or worse.

Actually, yes. I'm a disease. There is nothing good about me. And even if I do something remotely good, I destroy it the next day so that it can never be recovered.

I'm sick and tired of it.

I'm sick and tired of this cycle.

Enough.

But it's never enough, is it?

I see myself as those damaged goods sold in stores. Their flaws are so perfectly hidden, and when you finally see them, it's too late. And what do you do with damaged goods? You throw them away.

I'm damaged. And I'll always be thrown away."

"Hayden, no."

My heart beat fast in my chest, its pounding loud in my ears. *Damaged.* It sounded horrible. It sounded unacceptable, disposable. He was anything but that. He was a wonderful being who was worth much more than he would ever give himself credit for. He was caring, emotional, passionate, fierce, desolate, insecure... He was so many things, and I loved every single thing about him, even the bad ones, because they made him *him.*

Then again, I found a bitter truth in this single word. Now, brain damage had led him into a coma, which posed a crucial question—would he suffer serious consequences after he woke up?

The chances for a good outcome were slim to none. According to his neurologist, there was a variety of traumatic brain injury effects: paralysis, change of any of the five senses, memory problems, mood changes, difficulties with concentration and attention, irritability, aggression, and so much more. It would be a miracle if he woke unchanged, and the difference between what they showed us in movies and reality broke my heart.

The first thing his doctor told us was not to expect him to open his eyes and act like usual, which terrified me. What would he be like when he woke up? Would there be any significant change in him? How long would his recovery last? When would he wake up? So many questions.

I tightened my jaw as I looked at him, refusing to cry. I told myself I wouldn't ever cry here, no matter how hard it was to handle my emotions. The doctors had told us to treat him like he could hear us because it could help him recover, which was a comforting thought. I was grasping it with both hands, so I always spoke positive things to him. I talked about my feelings. I assured him he wasn't alone and unloved. I made sure to mention Carmen, Blake, and Masen, who were beyond themselves with worry.

"I love you, Hayden. You're going to be all right."

I took his hand into mine and followed the contours of his long fingers with my forefinger, marveling at the difference in the size of our hands. I loved his hands. I loved how strong they felt compared to mine. The bulging veins on his arms, the muscular neck and shoulders, his plump lips... There was no physical part of Hayden I didn't like.

"You'll wake up soon, and we'll have a lot of fun together." I fought so hard not to let my voice crack. I had to keep my tone cheerful and encouraging. "I want us to do so many things. I want to know more about you. I want us to laugh together... Soon."

I pursed my lips and inhaled deeply through my nose. I flicked my eyes to his face, checking for any reaction, but I found none. His unmoving face brought a new wave of dull pain that worked hard to crush my hope. Waiting was the worst.

"Midterms were so exhausting. Jessica was panicking all the time because she thought she hadn't studied enough, and it was funny. I'm sure she did better than me. Melissa was so cool about it. Seriously, she never looks like she cares about her grades, but she always manages to get top marks."

I glanced at the heart monitor, but the stats remained the same. There was no reaction from him. I often wondered if he was dreaming or experiencing anything in this state. Was he in his own world, or would these days seem like a fleeting moment once he woke up?

"She doesn't need to study much to memorize things, almost like you. She's clever and able to adjust to any situation."

Despite the difficulties her family faced in the midst of her parents' divorce, she was always strong and lively, and I truly admired her. Steven, their mom, and she were going to move into her grandparents' house next week, and her move to Enfield was one of the rare things that were a consolation lately.

"She's going to transfer to our school next Wednesday." His face didn't move an inch, and I sighed. I had to believe he'd heard and understood everything. "It's a bit unusual since holidays start next week, but I'm so glad."

Holidays. I didn't want to think about spending them without Hayden. I turned another page and read another entry.

"Date: One of those days.

I hate it. This anger. This rage. This madness that makes me speak and do things I regret and hate myself for. I can't stop it. They told me to note down how I feel in the moment and try to figure out what triggers it, but it's so fucking difficult. I'm frustrated that sometimes I can control it, but some other times I screw everything up, and I hate myself.

She understood it. I saw it in her eyes in that moment. She completely understood those words came from somewhere I'm ashamed of. She understood I don't want her to go. When I tell her I'll always throw her away, I actually need her more than my next heartbeat. And then she said I couldn't push her away anymore, and she completely trapped me.

Fuck. I thought my madness rules over me, but more than this madness, she's the one I can't ever resist.

Shit. Why can't I be normal for her?"

I snapped his diary shut as a stream of sorrow poured over me. I wanted to tell him so much, but the words didn't come out easily.

I put the diary back into my bag and took out my notebook, glancing at the graphite drawings of Hayden I made these days, which were now spread on the table. After the initial shock had passed, I had an idea to communicate with Hayden through writing. I struggled to find the right words to express my emotions, but I wanted to share all my feelings with him from the previous days, so I decided to write letters to him; letters he would hopefully be able to read soon.

Since the silence of this room filled the long hours I spent here with unease, I drew Hayden for the most of my time. It was my refuge. Sometimes I just reproduced what I saw, but other times I drew from my memory, depicting him in a different way each time. They were my gifts for him, since I wanted to give him something as thoughtful as the art supplies and diary he'd given me.

"Here goes another letter. I already told you this a few days ago, but I'm not as good with words as you are, so don't laugh at me, okay?"

I swallowed the lump in my throat, imagining his reaction. He would probably roll his eyes or snort and reply sarcastically, and I missed it so much.

I cleared my throat. I was going to read loudly as I wrote, which I did with every letter.

"Nine days have passed since you got hit. Every day is a paradox because it feels like an eternity, but the time flies by. Just like every other day, I rushed in here after school with a crazy heartbeat and tingles in my chest, hoping I'd finally see you awake. Then..."

Then a heavy weight, my closest companion during these last nine days, returned to my chest, and I had to feed myself with an almost fruitless hope that you'd wake up soon—that you would be one of those who managed to pull out...

No, I couldn't write that. I had to stay positive and write only positive things. If he could hear everything we said, I had to focus on soothing and nice things. I crossed out "Then" and continued writing.

"But I'm sure you'll wake up soon. And I want us to do so many things together and visit many places. Maybe we can go to the river again. I would probably be freezing since it's so cold and snowy, and you'd think it was funny or something. I miss that. I miss you teasing me."

I closed my eyes and took a deep inhale. An insurmountable pain crushed my chest. My lip quivered, and the tears threatened to spill, but I closed my eyes and focused on suppressing them.

"Anyway, I hope you're not in pain. I hope that if you're dreaming or experiencing anything right now, it's all nice."

My hand shook hard, and I fisted it, unable to write anything anymore. The more I wrote, the more the wound in my heart opened because the words were too painful. I decided to end it here.

"I'm waiting for you. We all are. I love you, Hayden. I love you so much."

The beeps in the room quickened, and I snapped my gaze to the heart monitor. Did he hear me? I desperately waited for him to move... Waiting...

Waiting...

Come on, Hayden.

His heartbeat returned to its previous rate, and I had to press my hand against my mouth to stifle a whimper. *It's okay. It's going to be all right.*

I folded the paper and put it on top of all the previous letters I wrote. He'd have quite a lot to read once he woke up because this was the seventh letter I wrote. I stood up and pressed my lips to his, giving him a lingering kiss, wanting to pour all my feelings into this touch. Once more, his heartbeat quickened and mine followed, each inch of me filled with tension and hope...

Was he feeling this? Would he finally wake up?

"Hayden?" I whispered.

Nothing. There was no reaction.

I suppressed my hurt. This would have to be enough. I had to believe he'd felt my kiss.

"I love you so much, Hayden."

The door opened, and Blake and Masen came inside. They were the only ones beside Carmen and me who were allowed to visit him in the ICU, thanks to Carmen pulling some strings.

"Hey, Sarah," they greeted me. Even now, I couldn't get used to the new way they spoke to me.

They were still bullies, and they treated others however they wanted, but they didn't mock me anymore. In fact, they made sure everyone knew they would personally deal with them if they bullied me, and it was difficult to wrap my head around the change in their behavior. I didn't know why, but they finally accepted me as the girl Hayden loved.

"Hey," I said and stood up. I was going to go for a walk to clear my mind.

"Is there any change?" Blake asked. He stopped next to Hayden and fist bumped his shoulder. "Hey, buddy. You're still looking as good as ever. I'm sure the nurses are all crazy about you." He smirked at me.

I didn't smile. "Everything's pretty much the same. I'm going outside now. See you later." Leaning in, I kissed Hayden's forehead. "I'll be back soon," I whispered to him.

I snatched my bag and rushed outside. If I hadn't left, I would've burst into tears, and I didn't want anyone to see that. I moved through the endless hallways aimlessly, sick and tired of the same depressive environment I'd been seeing day after day. My heart was beating too fast, and it was impossible to even my erratic breathing.

Hayden had to wake up. He had to. He was strong, and he had our support. It was just a matter of time until this nightmare was over.

It was just a matter of time...

Chapter 2

"OH GOSH, I'M LATE!" I exclaimed and sped toward the theater.

"Hey, relax. We're nearby anyway," Kayden tried to reassure me.

"Yeah, but I was late the last few times. Christine is going to kill me!"

"I hope she will. There would be one less moron in the world." Hayden's harsh voice was like a slice of a knife to my fragile heart. It was ridiculously easy for him to send me spiraling into darkness.

My anxiety proliferated. I started crossing the street, typing a text for Christine to tell her I would be there in a few minutes, when a car horn ripped through the night air. I knew what I was going to see next. My chest filled with horror.

Two bright flashes of light blinded me before the car swerved to the side, heading for Hayden. Kayden moved to shield him, but he wasn't quick enough, and they got both hit and crashed to the ground.

The sight put shackles of pain on my heart and mind, and my world crumbled. They didn't move, both lying in a pool of their blood. I approached them in daze of desperation, noticing how the night changed into the day, and the scene transformed into a more recent one.

My gaze flickered between them before it settled on Kayden, whose limbs were spread at odd angles. His empty eyes drowned me in despair, and I burst into tears, dropping to my knees. I grabbed his arm to shake him and called his name repeatedly, but it was useless. I saw this moment many times, but it was always the same. Kayden would never come back. He was dead.

Dead.

Dead.

Never coming back...

"You killed him," Hayden accused me, and I whipped my head at him, quivering in wrenching tears. He now stood right next to me, with the crimson blood surrounding the scar on his face. His cold eyes that were so similar yet so different than Kayden's warm ones bore into me, reminding me I had done this. "This is all your fault."

"I'm sorry," I cried out. I clutched my chest and bent over when fresh pain hit me. "I'm so sorry, Hayden. It was just a mistake... I was careless."

"It was a stupid mistake! We got into an accident because you didn't pay attention, and now he's dead! I'll hate you forever!"

I jumped to my feet. "Fine! Then I'll hate you too because you did the same thing! You were blaming me all this time, but you made the same mistake. How could you be so careless?! You went into the street without even looking!" I let out a wail, unable to control myself anymore.

Everything was silent. All the people around us were frozen in time and space, reminding me of my mistakes and regrets.

"Now I don't know if you're ever going to wake up again..." My voice broke, and I reached out to him, but he began fading away.

"And now you're going to lose me too. I'm not coming back."

NO. No, no, no.

Don't leave me!

"NO!" I rushed to him, but he was already gone, leaving devastation in his wake. My blood ran cold as I looked back at Kayden...

Only he wasn't Kayden anymore. He was Hayden, who lay unconscious on the street in front of the hospital. A huge wound opened in me, and there was nothing I could do about it...

I fell to my knees and grasped his shoulders. "Please, wake up. Wake up, Hayden."

Please, wake up.

Wake up...

I snapped my eyes open. I was panting and covered in sweat. I tried to erase the horrible scene from my mind as I blinked to clear my vision, relieved that it was just a nightmare. It wasn't real.

It wasn't real.

I got out of my bed when my pulse got back to normal, reminding myself that Hayden was going to be all right. He was going to wake up any moment. I checked my phone for any messages or calls from Carmen, but there were none. She was in the hospital all the time these days, and she'd promised me she would notify me if there were any changes. I moved quickly as I got ready for school, impatient to get out of here.

Everything had changed in such a short period of time. I didn't consider this house my home anymore, and the room that had been my only sanctuary now felt like a confinement. It served as a reminder that I was stuck in this house with my mother, and I was counting the months until I could get out of here and live my life the way I wanted, starting with college.

I took off my pajama top and looked routinely at the bullet graze wound on my right upper arm in the mirror. It didn't hurt anymore and was healing quite nicely, so there wouldn't be much scarring, much to my relief. The memories of Brad were scarring enough. Satisfied, I dressed and went downstairs.

I ran into Lydia, Patricia's caregiver, on my way to the kitchen. We hired her soon after Patricia got out of the hospital because she had casts on both legs and needed assistance. "Good morning," I said.

"Good morning, Sarah." She gave me a beaming smile, but I found no strength to return it.

She was a charming lady in her fifties who always smiled, so I wondered how she endured my mother's moodiness. Patricia wasn't exactly happy-go-lucky. She was more surly than usual these last few days, mostly because she couldn't have any alcohol. I didn't hang around her. I wanted to avoid her as much as possible, especially after how she treated me during and after Brad's kidnapping.

The kidnapping was the final straw, and I'd stopped trying to make things right between us. She showed she didn't respect me or care about me, and I had enough. I'd let her selfishness win too many times. I wasn't going to let her ruin my life just because she was my mother. I had my own life to live, which didn't include her anymore.

"I was just going to see if your mother woke up. Are you going to school?"

"Yes. My friend is about to pick me up."

"Have a good time."

Absolutely. She had no idea. "Thank you."

She headed upstairs as I continued to the kitchen. I made a sandwich and forced it down, grimacing because I had no appetite, as usual, and all food was tasteless. My life took a turn for the worse with Hayden's distressing condition, my mother's bad temper, and midterm anxiety, so it didn't come as a surprise that I had recurring nightmares and couldn't eat well. It was hard for me to smile, and I had difficulty focusing on anything other than Hayden.

Mel and Jess were trying to cheer me up, sending me funny texts all the time, but it felt empty. Everything felt empty when Hayden was in that hospital bed, trapped in a coma.

My phone vibrated, and I opened a text from Jess.

"I'm waiting in front of your house."

"I'm coming."

I texted her back and went to grab my jacket, feeling grateful because I could rely on her.

We had to sell our cars so we could pay for Lydia and our other expenses. My mother took a sick leave, but since she wasn't able to work for at least a few more weeks, we were badly strapped for cash. She even suggested that I start working full-time, which was out of question. I wasn't able to get angry at her anymore; I was already used to her outrageous propositions.

Mrs. Black offered me money, but I didn't want to accept it. Still, she insisted on helping me, so I came up with a win-win solution. She was spending all her time in the hospital, so she needed someone to take care of the housekeeping. I told her I would only take her money if she let me help with the cleaning a few days a week, and she reluctantly agreed. She couldn't know how much I needed this as a distraction. It was too cold and snowy for me to run, so work relieved me from the pent-up stress.

"Hey," Jessica greeted me when I got in her car.

"Hey," I replied and put on my seat belt. I was already shaking from the cold. A thick blanket of snow had covered the streets and houses, and its glimmering white matched the depressing gray of the morning sky. We hadn't seen the sun for the last few days, which was seriously affecting my mood.

Jess started the car and turned on the radio. "How did you sleep?"

"I had another nightmare."

She glanced at me before she headed down the street. "I'm sorry. I know we talked about this and you refused, but are you sure you don't want to take any pills? They could help you—"

"No. No pills. I can handle this."

"I get that you're against them, but they can help you—"

"As I already told you, Jess, I don't want to take those things."

"Okay. I understand you. You remember what I told you about my therapist? She can recommend a therapist to visit—"

"I know, Jess. You don't have to remind me," I interrupted her again and regretted it immediately. I wasn't being fair. She didn't have to put up with me. "I'm sorry, Jess. I'm not a great company at the moment but still... I'm sorry. Besides, you know I'm hard up these days. More than usually, anyway."

She heaved a long sigh, casting me a worried glance. "Yeah, I know. Sorry. And I know you won't accept my offer to help you pay for a session, so I won't ask you again."

A couple days ago, Jessica had offered to pay for me in case I wanted to start therapy, but I couldn't accept something like that. I hated being treated like a charity case.

I appreciated that she wanted to help me. My social anxiety had become worse, and I was more withdrawn, so there was no way I could allow anyone to examine me like I was some experiment. I refused to think about this possibility. I was stressed out just imagining it.

"Thanks, Jess."

"So how's Hayden?"

"Same. I keep reminding myself that's a good thing because it means his condition didn't deteriorate."

"I wonder if he's dreaming. I read a little about comas last night, and I found some pretty interesting stories."

"Yes?"

She turned onto a new street. "Some patients experienced strange dreams or nightmares during their coma. They saw some unimaginable things. Others saw flashes of light. And some people could hear people next to them, but the real voices were mixed with the twisted reality of their own world."

"I've read something like that too."

"It's fascinating."

"Yeah, but it's also scary. Imagine being able to hear everything or *feel* everything, but you can't wake up."

"Maybe Hayden will wake up but won't remember anything that happened during his coma. Maybe he'll feel like only a moment has passed."

"I hope so."

The snow started falling again, forcing the vehicles to slow down. The cheerful sounds of the indie pop, Jess's favorite, coming from the radio did nothing to improve the way I felt. In fact, I needed silence, but I was already hard to be around enough, so I didn't say anything. She'd told me once that music was a cure for her problems, but I couldn't relate. Right now, the artist's words about her undying love only brought heart-rending thoughts, so I shut her voice down and focused on the snowy canvas outside.

The nightmares sucked the last ounce of positive energy out of me, and all that remained was a depressed shell clinging desperately onto hope that Hayden would wake up and get out of this without major consequences.

The somber atmosphere between Jess and me was too heavy for us to pretend everything was okay, so we remained silent for the rest of our drive.

• • • •

SCHOOL WAS A COMPLETELY different experience now that I wasn't bullied anymore. It was unusual, and I had yet to come to grips with the fact that I was able to walk through the school without anyone attacking me. People didn't stop gossiping about me, though; their curiosity was boosted by Masen's and Blake's change of heart, and I knew better than to hope they would stop.

As for Masen and Blake, they didn't change their attitude toward Jessica and other "less privileged" students. Masen wasn't as much of a problem as Blake, so when Jess and I reached the lunch line in the cafeteria, I looked around for any sight of him. These days, he tended to let out his frustrations by bullying various students, usually in the school's backyard, and Jess was one of them.

Just as Jess and I took our trays of food, Blake and Masen passed us, and Blake bumped into her with his shoulder before she could see him. Some contents of her tray fell to the floor, instantly making her the main attraction of the lunchroom. She bent her head and hid her red face behind her hair, frozen in place.

"Oops. My bad." He sniggered and continued to the lunch line.

I glared at his back, about to tell him off, but then he stopped at the end of line, and I was finally able to see his face. He looked horrible. The shadows beneath his dull gray eyes were a clear sign of a sleepless night, and it was painful to see.

I was supposed to be mad at him for how he treated Jess, but the longer I watched him stare at some spot on the ground, the more my anger dissipated. The tormented look shadowing his face twisted my stomach. He didn't even try to hide it, and I couldn't help but pity him. He and Masen were constantly visiting Hayden, and my heart broke a little each time they cracked some joke for his benefit with eyes that showcased their pain.

Jessica looked like she was about to start crying, but I hugged her and whispered into her ear, "Everything is going to be all right. Don't pay attention to them. This is nothing."

She nodded. I helped her pick up the food from the floor and threw it into a trash can. She repeated her order to the young counter attendant who looked warily between her and Blake.

"Go to our table. I'll come in a minute," I told her and marched over to Blake.

He raised his gaze from the floor and frowned at me. "Sarah?"

I ignored the mad pounding of my heart. "What you just did isn't right. I know you feel bad because of Hayden, but Jess doesn't deserve this."

My anxiety rose, just like it always did during confrontations. People near us broke into hushed whispers, and I tried my best to ignore them.

"I already told you once that what I do with her is none of your business."

"It *is* my business. I can't just stand aside while you harass my friend. Stop doing that to her—"

He took a menacing step toward me; his face was a mask of rage he always carried when I made his hackles rise. "Sarah, I don't want to do this with you right now. You're Hayden's girlfriend, and I agreed to start treating you differently, but don't think for a second you can tell me what I can or can't do. Now be a good girl and go to your table before I snap and do something Hayden would beat me for."

I swallowed and glanced at Masen who observed our exchange silently. He just shrugged his shoulders like he wanted to say "You better listen to him." A hint of sympathy crossed over his face, but it did nothing to soothe my frayed nerves.

"Look. I don't know you, but I respect you as Hayden's friend, so I'm going to say that what you're doing to Jessica is disgusting. You don't know what she's going through because you don't see further than the end of your nose.

I just hope that one day when you finally realize how wrong you are, it won't be too late." I turned on my heel and strode to my table, not giving him a chance to reply.

There were so many things I could tell him, but I felt conflicted. He was Hayden's friend and they cared about each other, but Jess was my friend, and I was right in the middle of this unexplainable mess.

"Why did you talk to him?" Jess asked me when I took my seat, looking in Blake's direction with a deep frown.

"Because I'm tired of his bullying. You didn't deserve that."

"I don't want you to get in trouble because of me. I already told you that you don't need to speak up for me."

"But Jess, I can't just stand and watch—"

"You only make it *worse*," she gritted out, and I winced. She looked away, trying to hide her face from me, but I didn't want to drop this that easily.

"What? Why?"

She cast a glance at Blake and then looked back at me with dread filling her eyes. "I... It's nothing."

"It's not nothing, Jess. Tell me."

"It doesn't matter. Things won't change if I tell you." She fiddled with the ends of her long hair.

"Jess? Please. Is he... Is he bullying you more because of me?" Her eyes fell to her lap, and she gave me a terse nod. Fear pierced me. "How... What is he doing to you?"

"It doesn't matter," she replied in a clipped tone, and I knew she wouldn't tell me. I understood her attitude because I was the same when it came to divulging things.

"Okay. Just know I'm sorry. I don't want to make it worse, so..." My voice trailed off when a student I'd never seen before entered the cafeteria.

He was tall and scrawny, and he wore stone washed jeans and a blue plaid shirt that looked baggy on his thin body. The black framed glasses and styled wavy hair suited his cute boyish face perfectly, completing his hipster look. His blue eyes darted around as he walked, revealing insecurity and shyness, and a bad feeling filled my chest.

"Who is he?" some people around us asked.

"A new transfer student," someone said.

"He's weird."

"So skinny."

"He looks like he's going to shit himself."

A relentless round of giggles ensued. Some students pointed at him, while others just stared at him the same way they stared at me. He was fresh meat. It was sickening.

And it was like a cruel reminder of Jessica's first day in this Hellhole.

I snapped my head to Hayden's table, and my heart leapt to my throat. Blake, Masen, and two guys from the football team stood up and headed to the new student with menacing steps. The attention of the whole cafeteria was on them now. A few students had already prepared their phones, standing close to the boy.

"What do we have here?" Masen said with a smirk.

"I'm not sure if he's a guy or a girl. He looks girly to me," Blake said, scratching his chin. "Does he look girly to you, Mace?"

"Totally. Look at that shiny hair and those girly glasses. What, your mommy picked them for you?" Masen grabbed the boy's glasses and snatched them off his face. The boy paled, hunching as he took a step backward. Bile rose in my throat, and my limbs went cold. Blake and Masen followed him, refusing him the distance.

"P-Please. Give them b-back," he stuttered, his voice high-pitched and soft. The students around them snickered.

Blake snorted. "Of c-course. You'll get them b-b-back," he mocked him, and I clenched my jaw. *Jerk.* "*If* you tell us your name first."

He lowered his head and began twisting the hem of his shirt. "Kevin. Now, give them b-back."

"Kevin what?" Masen asked.

"Kevin Burks."

"We want to throw you a welcome party, Burks," Masen told him. *Not again.* No.

My stomach twisted, and I looked at Jessica. Her eyes filled with tears. "I can't believe they're doing this again," she whispered.

Kevin was rooted to the spot, gaping at Masen and Blake. "Th-That won't be necessary. Now, I'd like to eat. P-Please."

Blake and Masen erupted into chuckles. "Did you hear him?" Blake asked Masen and the guys from their football team. "*Please*. So sweet." His eyes narrowed as he looked back at Kevin. "I think it *is* necessary, Kevin. You see, we can't let you start your new life at East Willow High without a party, right, everyone?" He looked at the students around them for support, who, as expected, inched closer to Kevin, preparing to throw whatever they had on their trays.

"What do you mean?" Kevin was visibly shaking, and I grew more restless.

"You won't need these for now," Masen said and let Kevin's glasses slip from his hand. As soon as they hit the ground, Masen stomped on them, breaking them into pieces. Kevin cried out, looking in horror at Masen and Blake.

I jumped to my feet; every inch of my body buzzed with adrenaline.

"Sarah?" Jessica mouthed.

"This is so wrong," I told her in a shaky voice.

"Yes, but—"

"No," Kevin shouted, and I turned my head to find the first projectiles landing on his chest. He bent and tried to cover himself, but it only encouraged more students to join this abuse. Kevin fell to his knees and shielded his head, whimpering after each hit.

No, no, no. I looked around the cafeteria, waiting for anyone to interfere, but all people stared at them mesmerized—some of them amused, some of them with blank faces, but *no one* moved. Pain, fear, and rage amalgamated into a burning ball that shot through my veins and reached its bursting point. Damn it!

I was already half way there before I realized I'd moved, sensing Jessica right behind me. Just like that day when Blake threw the "welcome party" for Jessica, I stopped right in front of Kevin and protected him with my body as I faced Blake, Masen, and their friends.

"Stop! No more!" I glared at each of them with my heart pumping furiously. I trembled hard, barely able to stand with all those eyes on me. My chest rose and fell quickly with increasing fear as I waited for Blake and Masen to react.

"What the fuck?" Blake spat out and took a step toward me. "Step aside."

Masen stopped next to Blake with arms crossed over his chest. "Sarah, get out of here. This is none of your business."

"Can you stand up?" Jessica asked Kevin in a tiny voice, and I looked over my shoulder to see her helping him up. He looked at her with a mix of awe and gratitude, his cheeks slightly colored as she held his upper arm for support.

"Th-Thank you," he muttered to her.

I took in all those phones directed at me. I didn't want to think how many times the videos or pictures would be shared online or what kind of comments they would post. I fixed my gaze on Blake.

"This is inhumane and completely wrong," I said, hoping my voice didn't reveal how shaken I felt. "He doesn't deserve this."

Blake took another step to me. "Step aside if you don't want to get hurt. If you think you can suddenly play tough just because you're Hayden's girlfriend, you can forget it. You can't order us around, so *step aside*." His eyes were full of venom, and the message was more than clear. If I didn't move away, I would pay for it.

"*No*." It was Jessica who answered him this time, leaving me flabbergasted. "We won't let you hurt him anymore." Her wavering voice complemented the fear on her face, but I was so proud of her for standing up for Kevin. "Come on, Kevin. Let's get you out of here."

She moved, but Blake was quicker. He grabbed her arm and pulled her against him. "Step away from him!"

"Let me go," she shrieked.

"You're going to pay for this, Fats. You'll regret the moment you opened your ugly, fat mouth—"

"Get away from her!" I pushed him away with all my force, managing to make him stumble because he wasn't expecting it. I stepped between them, shielding both Jess and Kevin. "I won't let you lay a finger on her!" I motioned to Jess and Kevin to follow me. "Let's go."

"You're not going anywhere," Blake hissed.

"The hell we aren't," I growled and grabbed an orange from the floor next to my foot. I swung it at his head hoping to distract him long enough for us to leave.

I glanced at Masen and noticed something in his eyes that was close to wonder, but I didn't wait for it to soak in. I swiveled around and headed to the exit, followed by Jess and Kevin, and as if someone had pressed a switch, the whole cafeteria erupted into laughter and shouts.

"Sarah, the savior!"

"Jessica, the savior!"

"Call Sarah Decker when you need help!"

"We don't need Batman! We have Sarah! And Jessica!"

"Batman v Sarah!"

Geez. They were nuts.

We rushed through the empty hallway, trying to put as much distance between us and the cafeteria as possible. For some miraculous reason, Blake and Masen didn't come after us. We actually managed to get out of there unscathed.

A part of me was terrified at the prospect of getting punished by Blake and Masen, but this time I refused to let it rule me. I would definitely regret it when they retaliated, but now I had to be strong for Jess and Kevin.

No one uttered a word until we reached the second floor. I took a good look at Kevin, saddened to see him in this condition. His shirt was completely ruined, covered with multi-colored splashes, and his face was smeared with liquid that slid from his hair down his cheeks. He was squinting slightly, and I assumed his vision was blurry without his glasses.

"I'm so sorry you had to go through this," I told him, offering him a soft smile. "This isn't about you. They're just jerks who like messing with everyone."

He looked furtively between Jessica and me. Even though he was much taller than my 5' 9" frame, he seemed like a lost little boy. "Th-Thank you. You two are amazing." He was speaking to both of us, but his gaze was solely on Jess.

"It's nothing. Are you hurt?" Jessica asked him, inspecting his body for injuries. "Can you see without your glasses?"

He sighed and looked down his shirt. "Everything is b-blurry, but it's not like walking-into-walls blurry, s-so don't worry. I'm fine. However, my ego is not."

"They did the same thing to me, so I feel you."

Kevin gaped at her. "They did?" She nodded. "But why? You're s-so perfect!" I was a second away from a huge smile. He blushed, which only made
him look cuter.

Jess blushed too, smiling at him as she stared at the floor. "Yeah, well,
that monster doesn't feel that way," she muttered. Her smile dropped, and my
heart dropped too.

Monster. Once upon a time, I thought the same of Hayden, and it was
something I wanted to erase from my memory. Had Blake gotten under her
skin that badly?

Kevin looked befuddled. "Monster?"

"It's a long story," I replied instead of her. "Anyway, I'm sorry. We didn't
even introduce ourselves. I'm Sarah."

"And I'm Jessica." His smile matched hers, and I was glad to see him a bit
calmer. He looked all too innocent, which made him a perfect target, and my
chest ached because he had to go through this too.

"I'm Kevin." He scratched his head. "I think I should go. I..." He pointed
at his clothes. "I can't walk around like this, can I?" He chuckled, but the
sound was empty, and a heavy silence settled between us.

"Yes, of course," I answered. I could see we were making him uncomfortable, which was understandable after what he'd just gone through. "Are you
sure you aren't hurt? If you are, we can take you to the school nurse."

"No, I'm okay. Th-Thanks."

"You know...," Jess started, glancing at me. "You can hang out with us if
you want." Her voice revealed her insecurity, and I was surprised but all the
more glad she'd suggested it. He was new and already bullied, so he needed
our support and friendship. Besides, he seemed like a good kid.

"Yeah. That would be great," I added, feeling excited for the first time after a long time about making new friends.

Kevin clearly hadn't expected this, but he looked at us with gratitude, his
eyes lingering on Jess. "Th-Thank you. I think so too."

Chapter 3

I'D SPENT COUNTLESS hours on forums since the day of Hayden's accident, trying to find a solution to a challenge that was dating someone with borderline personality disorder, burning to get some answers. That was why I was going to Hayden's DBT therapist, Ms. Kishimoto, tonight.

I was more than lucky to get an appointment with her seeing that I'd called to schedule it only a few days ago. I'd expected to wait for weeks.

"I appreciate that you found some time in your busy schedule to talk with me."

"I'm pleasantly surprised that you came, Sarah. I wish the partners of my patients came to see me more often. A successful, healthy relationship with someone with BPD takes commitment from both partners." She offered me a polite smile to assuage me. I was shifting in my seat too often, and I didn't know what to do with my hands. I disliked therapists, but I had to do this for Hayden and our relationship.

"I just want to know what I'm doing wrong. I want to help him, not make things worse."

"Of course. Did anything specific happen between Hayden and you?"

I took a deep breath, hoping my voice wouldn't betray how nervous I felt. "You're aware that Hayden is... He's in a coma now."

She nodded, her beautiful, young-looking face expressing sympathy. "Mrs. Black called me and notified me of the latest events. He is young and strong, Sarah. He doesn't quite believe it, but he's a fighter. His strong will always amazed me."

"Yes, well... Thank you."

I didn't know how to approach the issue, since there was a part of me that blamed myself, despite knowing I hadn't done what he accused me for. My mistake was not being able to read the signs and react accordingly, so I hoped to learn what I could do the next time Hayden became enraged and started arguing with me.

"How are you holding up?"

I shrugged. I didn't have the slightest desire to talk about myself. "I'm okay."

She nodded, taking the hint. "Is there something else you wish to tell me?"

"Yes." My cheeks colored under her intense stare, and I hated being observed like this. I had a feeling she was already constructing my diagnosis in her head, and I didn't like it one bit. "We had a fight that morning. He... He got so mad. He said some hurtful words and left me. I didn't notice in time that he wasn't paying attention to the traffic, so... He got hit and... Now he's in a coma."

She mulled over these words for a long moment, and I almost expected her to write them down in the notebook that lay in front of her on her desk. "Do you blame yourself for his accident?"

A jolt unfurled through my chest because her words hit the nail on the head. I swallowed past the sudden dryness in my throat. "N-No." *It's pointless to lie, Sarah. You need to be honest if you want your relationship with Hayden to work.* "A little."

"I see. And why do you blame yourself?"

"Because I didn't react properly. I'm afraid I just made his anger worse."

"Can you describe that argument?"

I tried to recollect every detail as I recounted that fight, avoiding mentioning what the call Hayden received was about, since she would then know he was dabbling in criminal activity.

"You told me you've been studying BPD."

"Yes."

"Then you're aware that many things they do or say during their rage episodes may not be the display of their real thoughts?" I nodded. "Honesty, trust, and communication are important in a relationship. Has Hayden opened up to you about his feelings so far?"

I called to mind each time he spoke about his feelings and revealed his deepest fears and thoughts. "Yes. He even gave me his diary."

Her eyebrows shot upward. "His diary?"

"Yes. Um, he said he wasn't able to express himself fully when he talked to me, so he gave me his diary. He thought it could help me understand him better."

"I see. I must say that is a huge progress."

I twiddled my thumbs in my lap. A part of the suffocating weight lifted off my chest. "Really?"

"Yes. A lot of their problems come from their insecurity and trust issues, so giving something so personal to another person to read represents a huge step. It's a clear sign that he cares about you deeply. How long have you two been together?"

I blushed. "Eleven days." And he was in a coma for ten of those days. The irony.

This time her whole face twisted with surprise, and I blushed harder. "Eleven days?"

"Yes." I resisted the urge to squirm on my chair again.

She regained her blank expression in a second. "Based on your determination to make things work with Hayden, I was under the impression that you were together for a much longer period of time."

"We knew each other well before we started dating." I didn't want to elaborate on our complicated past.

She nodded. "I see. As I mentioned, the major disturbance in their behavior comes from their unstable self-image, which induces a potent emotion—fear. Since they have low self-esteem, they fear that others would perceive them in the same way. They fear of being abandoned or betrayed, they fear of not being worthy of love, they fear loneliness and emptiness... So many fears that are a constant in their life. This constant brings them a lot of stress, which is why they are faced with emotional instability each day. A relationship with them can be a real roller coaster ride."

A roller coaster ride. Yes, it had been a hell of a roller coaster ride, which confused me to no end. Hot and cold, love and hate, anger and joy, all of these emotions impeding our happiness and mutual trust.

"So how can I help him with his fears?"

"First of all, you need to assure him that he is safe with you and that you won't leave him. It takes a lot of patience and effort on your part. Take his feelings seriously. Validating his feelings is extremely important. He needs to know that you care about how he feels and that you understand how difficult his feelings could be."

"I get that, but sometimes it's too hard. Just when I think I understand him, he does something that completely astounds me. He becomes so angry with me, and I'm no closer to understanding what I did to get treated that way. And I don't know how to deal with his tantrums."

"Here are a couple of suggestions. Don't try to solve issues during arguments. It would be best to solve the problem after you both calmed down. Secondly, your tone during arguments is extremely important. Don't raise your voice. You need to be conflict-capable and emotionally stable. You have to be able to confront him firmly and bear with the extreme changes in his behavior. This means that understanding his feelings during such an episode can help you deal with it, and you'll avoid reacting to triggers and prolonging your argument instead of resolving it."

"You mean that instead of defending myself, I should try to approach the core of the problem?"

"Exactly. The more you defend yourself, the more he'll believe that his suspicions or accusations are correct. So arguing back in a gentle way, without becoming offensive, and maintaining simple communication is imperative. Ignoring his claims or adding sarcasm and insults can only hinder your communication process. Also, pay attention to your facial expressions and body language because they send a clear message too."

"I see. I'll work on that."

"And remember: if, let's say, he tells you that he hates you or something along these lines, there is some underlying cause, which doesn't have to do anything with you. So don't take it personally. The best thing to do in order to discover the real source of his discontentment is to communicate and validate his feelings."

"Thank you for your suggestions. I hope in time I'll learn to read the situations properly." If he wakes up...

No. Stop thinking like that, Sarah. He will wake up.

"Hayden is a surprising young man that has more potential than he's aware of. If you're both able to meet in the middle and compromise, communicate your needs and troubles, and also work on understanding each other, then you have a better chance at a long-lasting relationship."

I glanced at the clock on the wall and saw we were running out of time. "Once more, thank you, Ms. Kishimoto, for your time and suggestions. I believe that Hayden and I will be able to solve our problems in time." I truly did. I was learning more and more about him and his issues, along with ways to deal with them.

Maybe love wasn't enough to make things work, but it certainly gave a good boost for people to try working out their issues. It was a fruitful ground for building trust, reconciling differences, and flourishing understanding.

Hayden had never had anyone by his side, not even Kayden, who hadn't been able to cross the gap between them and settle their disputes, and he had been hiding his real self all this time. He'd gotten so used to wearing his masks, always pushing everyone away, that him opening up to me felt like a miracle.

This accident reminded me how short our life was. We didn't have many chances. It reminded me that holding grudges only filled our life with bitterness and misery.

He'd done so many despicable things, but they were in the past. There was no point in building our future if I couldn't fully give myself to him.

So I'd forgiven him. I'd forgiven him for everything, even the cruelest, most devious acts. I'd forgiven him because, despite everything, he wanted to change. He suffered on the inside, and he wanted to escape his darkness. He'd always been trapped in his world, dealing with his version of reality the only way he knew. I could always hold it against him, but what was the point of staying in the past? People changed, and if he regretted everything, he deserved a second chance. So I decided to be a better person and get over his bullying.

And I felt at peace. There was no holding back; my heart and mind were ready to embrace everything that awaited us.

"I want you to know there is an option of couples counseling," she said. "It could help you establish effective communication and make your relationship more stable and functional."

I'd never considered going to therapy with Hayden, but I had to if that could help us. "I'll think about it." She nodded. "Is there anything else we can do to make our relationship work?"

She cracked a smile. "Yes. Laugh."

"Laugh?"

"Yes. Always try to have time for each other and do something that will make you happy. Hayden needs happiness more than anything, so find things that you both enjoy and do them together."

My heart fluttered at the image of a smiling Hayden, which was so rare. All I wished for was to see him smile more.

I stood up and took my backpack and jacket. "Thank you. I won't take more of your time."

"One more thing, Sarah." Her face grew serious. "Please, take care of yourself. It would be ideal if both of you can equally give and take in your relationship, but there is always a possibility that you'll end up giving more. If that happens, you'll overtax yourself. Create healthy boundaries and make sure your needs are fulfilled too. Do you understand what I mean?"

"Yes. I'll keep that in mind." She stood up too, and we shook hands.

"Good. If it becomes too hard, it's better to leave sooner rather than later, for both your sakes."

I was already at the door, itching to get going. "Yes. Thank you."

"Sarah." Her smile was professional this time. "I know some good therapists. So if you ever decide to consult a therapist for your own needs, do let me know. I'll be more than happy to recommend someone to you."

• • • •

I FELT EXHAUSTED AFTER another Krav Maga training session, and all my muscles screamed in pain and begged for some form of relief. Liam and Trevon taught us two new moves, and we had to repeat them over and over, but I wasn't complaining. This class was another stress reliever, and I welcomed anything that would take the edge off the anguish taking root in me.

Mel was supposed to visit Hayden with me, but her mom called after the class and asked her for help with something, so she was just going to drop me at the hospital. I had to hand it to Mel because she was doing her best to understand and accept Hayden. She'd promised me she would treat him better from now on and support us, which I appreciated a lot.

"We've arrived to your destination, ma'am," Mel said and gestured at our surroundings, acting like she was my chauffeur. I giggled. I could almost imagine her wearing a black suit and driver cap.

I returned her amused stare. "You could totally pass as a chauffeur. It suits you."

"Why, thank you. It's always been my dream to drive those spoiled rich assholes around while they screw each other behind me."

I snorted. Her silly imagination knew no limits. "You forgot they're also drinking champagne in formal wear," I added, playing along.

"Yes. And throwing cash at me as they flash their intimate parts at the people outside, with 'Gangnam Style' playing in the background."

I was in fits of uncontrollable chuckles that went on as I walked through the hospital hallways. I entered Hayden's room with a rush of exhilarating hope that he was finally awake, but all my positive feelings vanished when I found Blake and Masen seated next to his bed. I'd hoped I wouldn't have to see them so soon, but luck was not on my side.

My eyes landed on Hayden's unmoving, painfully frail form, and my hope dwindled to nothing, leaving bitterness in its stead. Blake's eyes zeroed in on me, telling me this wasn't going to end well.

"Hey," I greeted them weakly, my eyes on Hayden's pinched face. A flicker of sorrow fused with the bitterness, but I refused to let it overcome me. He would wake up soon. Just a little bit more.

"Hey, Sar," Masen said, calling me by a regular nickname instead of the one he'd often used—Sars. "Have you saved anyone since lunch? Some other nerds or hobos?"

I didn't want to talk about it in front of Hayden in case he could hear us. It might upset him to hear his girlfriend went against his friends because of their bullying.

"I can't even count how many," I mumbled.

"I want to have a word with you outside," Blake said and strolled out of the room without waiting for my answer.

I looked at Masen with raised eyebrows, surprised by Blake's request. I was reluctant to talk with him.

"He won't eat you. Come on. Don't be a pussy." His eyes glimmered mischievously, and I already knew what kind of words would come out of his mouth next. "Although, your pussy—"

"Okay, Masen! Enough." I raised my hands in the air and squeezed my eyes shut, shaking my head. "Save those obscene words for the girls you hang out with."

I left the room before he spurted out more nonsense. His laughter followed me until I closed the door behind me and turned to Blake, who was leaning with his shoulder against the wall across from me.

"You and I go back a long time, Sarah," he began, no hesitation whatsoever. "I have to admit I really disliked you." The feeling had been mutual. "But you're with Hayds now, and you went through a lot of shit, so I don't want to do something I'll regret later. Don't interfere in what isn't your business. Mace and I won't bother you anymore, but if you keep pulling the shit you pulled today, I'm not sure we'll be able to tolerate it."

I was livid. "You expect me to stand aside and let you abuse innocent people?"

"As I said, what we do isn't your business. We have the right to do whatever—"

"No, you don't." My heart was beating overly fast, my palms clammy. I wasn't as brave as I sounded, and I expected him to hurt me at any moment.

He stepped away from the wall, reaching me in an instant. "Careful, Sarah. My patience with you can quickly reach its limit. I'm telling you this for your own good. You don't have a say in what Masen or I do. Either you'll stay out of our business, or you'll get hurt too."

I bristled at his words. How could he be so blind and unfair? How could he be so inconsiderate of others?

"But that guy did nothing to you. It's sick and wrong that you tortured him just because of, what? Your own issues?"

I didn't notice when he moved, but the next moment he was in my face, gripping my arm. His steely gray eyes bore into me, increasing my fear of him. "I won't repeat myself, Sarah. I would hate to be forced to go against you."

He dropped my arm and returned to Hayden's room, leaving me in a state of disarray. What was I going to do now? I was right in the middle of two worlds, and I didn't know where my next step would lead me. If I went against Hayden's friends, I would protect people like Jess, but Hayden would be caught in between. If I stayed out of it for Hayden's sake, Jess would suffer.

I couldn't return to the room and pretend everything was all right when Blake had been clear on how everything would work from now on. Maybe Hayden was changing, but that couldn't be said for Blake and Masen, and expecting them to act mature just because I asked them to would be pushing it. So I waited in the hallway for them to leave, using the time to compose myself.

They left twenty minutes later, and I was finally able to get alone time with Hayden. The regular beeping reminded me that Hayden's situation was uncertain and could last indefinitely, but once more, I pushed the depressing thoughts aside. I wouldn't let my optimism dissolve so easily.

I placed my backpack on the chair and used the anti-bacterial cream in the dispenser above the bedside table, following the instructions of the staff who had instructed me to take care of hygiene around Hayden.

"Hey, Hayden. I missed you." I kissed his forehead. The creases around his mouth and eyes emphasized how weak he was, and my chest ached for him. I smiled at him, my hand reaching out to caress his cheek. "This has been a long day. It's Thursday, by the way. December fifteenth. You're in the ICU and currently in a coma, but you'll get better soon," I informed him in a reassuring tone, just like his doctor had advised me.

I took a seat next to him and caught his hand. If only I could get a slightest response from him, even a tiny twitch of his fingers. I stared at his hand as I imagined it, but it only brought me more grief.

"I just had another Krav Maga class, and it was brutal. If my instructors keep up this tempo, I'll be a killing machine in a month."

This was my first class after I got out of the hospital. I'd debated with myself whether I should continue training since it was expensive, but Melissa had managed to convince me not to give up on it. I just had to cut some other things I wanted so I could afford to pay for it, which wasn't such a big deal, considering I'd been sacrificing like this my whole life.

"Melissa says hi. She also wanted to visit you, but you know her parents are in the middle of a divorce, so they're busy moving."

I mentioned my visit to his therapist, babbling continuously for the next few minutes. The silence fell on us like a heavy burden, and I reached for his diary. I opened it to an entry I hadn't read before, and my pulse kicked up.

"Date: Let's just say today is one of those days I'm really pissed off.

Why do you always leave so easily? I need you to stay and say "I'm not going anywhere." I need to see that you care. So why do you promise so much one moment and do so little the next? If I ripped my heart out for you and put it into your traitorous hands, would that be enough for you? If I bled out after I took a fucking bullet for you, would that be enough for you? If I became the version of me you created, would that be enough for you?

No? Then what the fuck do you want?

Do you even love me?

Why is it so hard for you to stay?

Unless I'm just a shadow of a man, and you're about to find a real version, someone who will treat you million times better than I ever will."

My heart gave a shudder, and my eyes sought his face. "You're perfect, and I love you. I love you so much, Hayden." I kissed the back of his hand, relaying my love for him through that soft touch.

My hand shook as I turned the next page.

"Date: It's still the same. More shit piles up.

This scar is fucking me up. It's like it exists to remind me how fucked up everything is, and I can't stand looking at it.

Why did he have to be such an idiot? Why couldn't he just let me die? I deserved to die. I deserved to be in that coffin, not him.

But I can't even hate him anymore. I want to hate him. I want to keep hating him because of every single shit I went through, but I. Fucking. Can't.

I can't because deep down I know it's my fault. Just like always."

"No. Don't say you deserved to die. It was never your fault." I ran the back of my fingers across his scar, hurt by the raw emotions seeping out of his pages. I finally knew how he felt when he looked at it, and it was too painful.

I was on the verge of tears, but I didn't want to lose it. My body felt cold as his pain reverberated through me, his vulnerability and reproach resembling my own. We were both broken, and I wished I could wipe our issues away.

My hand trembled harder as I continued to the next page. The pressure in me soared when I spotted the words written in capital letters.

"Why do I exist? I don't understand.

I DON'T FUCKING UNDERSTAND.

Everything I touch, I destroy.

Everything I see, I destroy.

Everything I want, I destroy.

SO WHY DO I FUCKING LIVE???

She rejected me. That bitch rejected me. She broke me. She completely smashed me, and I HATE her.

I want to inflict the same pain on her. No. EVEN WORSE. I want her to cry and suffer until she vomits from all that pain. I want her to crawl on the floor and beg me to accept her, but I'll never accept that selfish, lying bitch ever again. Fuck. I'm so mad!! If I were to see her now, I would've done some nasty shit to her, and it wouldn't be even close to satisfying me.

Payback's a bitch.

She'll pay.

She'll pay for making me fall in love with her.

She

The page was ripped in the middle, but the entry didn't end there.

Why? Why can't anyone love me? Why can't she be mine?

WHY DO I NEED HER SO MUCH WHEN I HATE HER?

I HATE HER.

SARAH.

Sarah, Sarah, Sarah, Sarah, Sarah, Sarah...

Shit.

I'm not drunk enough. I'm never drunk enough. I can never drown these suffocating thoughts. All I feel is this gaping hole in my chest that grows bigger fast, and there's nothing that can fill it.

She's gone and along with her, my hope for salvation is gone too."

I clamped my hand against my mouth with a whimper. One tear escaped and fell on the page. When I refused him in the hospital three months ago, I opened some wounds that still hurt.

"I love you, Hayden," I repeated my earlier words. "I'm yours." I caressed his hand, hoping with all my might that he could feel it and hear me. "You're capable of so many things, and I believe in you. One day, you'll achieve great things." My voice wavered, and I closed my eyes, fighting against the powerful rush of tears. "I'm sorry for all the pain I caused you. I'm here now. I'm not going anywhere."

I placed his diary into my bag and took a new piece of paper, planning to put these words into a letter. I wiped off my tears and focused on the influx of thoughts that poured out of me, speaking them as I scribbled. I tried to keep my voice as steady and calm as possible.

Exhaustion took over my body when I finished the letter, so I rested my head on his bed, right next to his hand.

"I'm not going anywhere, Hayden," I mumbled and closed my eyes, slowly dragged into the world of dreams.

· · · ·

THE BEEPING FILLED my ears, and confusion veiled me. The surroundings in my dream changed, turning into a mixture of white and gray, and I felt someone shifting next to me. I looked around, but I found no one.

I heard distant groans, and then they shifted again, pulling me back into reality. I moved, my eyes fluttering open, becoming aware of the heavy breathing on my left. My head snapped upward, and I met Hayden's dazed eyes.

Oh my God.

He... He's awake!

"Hayden!" Euphoria and disbelief clashed in my chest, but then he frowned and looked around him in confusion. I stilled. "Hayden?"

His eyes seemed unfocused as they darted around the room, telling me there was something terribly wrong. The beeps of the heart monitor became more frequent, matching my rising heartbeat.

His eyes finally returned to me, and he grimaced. "*Sarah?*"

Chapter 4

IN THE FIRST FEW DAYS following Hayden's accident, the hospital staff explained what we might encounter once he woke up. They couldn't be certain about whether he would be confused, disoriented, agitated, or if he would manifest some defect from his brain injury, but they all agreed on one thing—waking up would be a difficult process for both the patient and his loved ones.

I'd thought I was prepared for everything, but I was wrong. As I watched him breathe more rapidly and his face twist in fear, panic gripped me, pushing away the joy of seeing him awake.

"Hey, Hayden. It's all right. You're fine. You're in the ICU, and you just woke up from a coma—"

"What?" His forehead creased, and his eyes focused and unfocused constantly as he looked around. "What is... What is this shit?" I took his hand gently, but his eyes widened. His hand didn't respond to my touch at all. "What is this shit?!" His heart rate was too high. His movements were uncoordinated as he tried to move, and he cried out.

"Please don't move, Hayden. Your ribs are broken, and moving will only hurt you..."

I pressed the nurse call button hoping someone would arrive as quickly as possible because he was growing more agitated with each second. His eyes were unusually wide now, and his face was much paler than just a minute ago.

"Hayden, you're in the hospital. You just woke up after ten days. You've been in a coma all this time—"

"Why are the walls shrinking?!"

"What?"

"Why am I tied down?!" I looked down his body, confused because he wasn't in any way restrained, but before I could assure him that he wasn't tied down, he started thrashing against the bed. "Let me go!" He groaned in pain, but he didn't stop his frantic movements. "Fuck! Where does this pain...? Let me go!"

"Hayden!" I grasped his upper arm and tugged it gently. I hoped to get his attention and calm him down, but he didn't react to me.

"I'm not in the hospital!" His breathing quickened when he spotted the cast on his left arm, and he growled, flailing his injured arm.

"Hey!" I tried to stop him from moving it, but he jerked away from me and gaped at his right hand and then at his left that was covered with a cast.

"Why can't I feel my hands?"

No.

The door flew open, and the nurse finally entered the room. Her eyes flashed with surprise at seeing Hayden awake before she took him in and turned serious. She rushed to him.

"Mr. Black. I'm Nurse Robinson. You may hurt yourself if you keep doing that since you suffered broken ribs and—"

"Let me go!" The beeping of the heart monitor was so loud and fast I feared his heart wouldn't endure all this exertion. He writhed madly as he tried to pull away from her, and she had to fight to keep her hands on his shoulders.

She reached for her phone in her pocket and tapped the screen. "Nurse Olivia, call Dr. McConnor. The patient in the room thirty-seven is conscious, but he's agitated, and I need assistance."

"What's happening with him?" I asked.

She barely spared me a glance. "Please, leave the room. He's overreacting to sudden stimuli, and your presence will only upset him more."

I took a shaky step backward, wishing nothing more but to stay next to him, but I didn't want to make his condition worse. "I'll be right outside, Hayden. I'm not going anywhere."

"NO! Don't go!"

His frightened eyes bore into me, rattling me from the inside out, as he fought against the invisible shackles while trying to reach for me. Terror enveloped me, and I grew cold. I wanted to tell him so many things. I wanted to hug him and chase away his nightmare, but this was out of my hands.

"Leave the room *now*," the nurse repeated.

"Okay."

I backed away to the open door, never breaking my eye contact with Hayden. "I'm right outside. Don't worry," I mouthed to him. My heart broke when he let out a shout of horror.

"SARAH!"

Doctor McConnor and two nurses almost collided with me when they sprinted into Hayden's room, but before I could apologize for blocking their way, one of the nurses faced me and said, "Please get out of the room."

"Yes, I'm sorry." I stepped out and flinched when she shut the door in my face before I could look at Hayden one last time.

I clenched my hands, staring at the number on the door. My heart thumped fast against my rib cage. I was shaking terribly, and I had to sit down so my knees wouldn't give out on me.

I slumped down on the chair and fumbled to take my phone out of my pocket so I could call Carmen. She picked up after the second ring. "Sarah?"

"Hayden woke up. His doctor is with him now, but he's not well. He was all confused and mad and—"

"I'll be there in a minute," she interrupted me and ended the call.

I sighed and looked at the cracks on my screen. A dull pain flooded my chest because they brought me to a time three months ago when Hayden and I were enemies. I closed my eyes and threw my head back, mentally and physically exhausted. The pressure in my head mounted as I replayed the last couple of minutes, trying to make sense of what had happened.

I pressed my hand against my lips to stifle a cry. I was terrified. I was terrified because of the unknown. I was terrified because I didn't know if I had it in me to erase his sorrows. Hayden had woken up after ten days, but the fight hadn't finished yet, and the obstacles we had to cross were formidable.

A nurse passed next to me with a tray of medication and syringes and entered Hayden's room. I jumped up and started pacing up and down the hallway, too restless to continue sitting. What were they going to do?

Mrs. Black darted around the corner, and I rushed to her, meeting her half-way. "Sarah!" She caught my hands. "Tell me what happened."

"I was sleeping when I felt someone moving next to me. I woke up and found Hayden looking at me, but he wasn't himself. He was confused, and he claimed the walls were shrinking and he wasn't in the hospital. He also said he was restrained..." My voice betrayed my distress, and I had to take a deep breath before I continued. "He went off the deep end, and I couldn't calm him down. Then the nurses and his doctor came, but another nurse entered his room with some medicine just a minute ago, and I don't know what that was for," I rambled, close to crying.

My voice and body shuddered, and it felt like all these days of suppressed worry and fear came right back to me with full force.

"It's okay, Sarah," she said and pulled me into a hug, allowing me to weep into her shoulder. "It's going to be okay."

She caressed my hair, but it only made me feel worse. I couldn't believe I was losing it in front of her. She was his mother, and I was sure she had hard time handling this situation herself, yet I troubled her with my emotional outburst.

"I'm sorry." I sniffed and moved to step away from her, but she didn't let me, keeping me close to her.

"Don't be. You're human, and it's only normal that you feel this way." She patted my shoulder. "We have to look on the positive side of this. He woke up. What you just described tells me he's experiencing hallucinations, which can happen to patients who wake up from comas."

I stepped back to look at her with a small frown. "Hallucinations?"

"Yes. Some patients experience hallucinations after waking up or confuse reality with their dreams. He's agitated and confused because he was unconscious for a longer period of time, so his brain is reacting to a sudden, drastic change."

"So his reaction was *normal*?"

"I wouldn't call it normal, but it's nothing unusual. It can happen. I know it's very difficult to witness it, but it will be better in a few days. That nurse probably brought the sedatives, which will calm him down if he's too upset to do it himself."

"But won't sedatives cause more damage in his condition?"

"Based on what you said, he's already confused enough, and sedatives aren't something we give lightly. We give them in small amounts and only when absolutely necessary." She stepped closer to Hayden's room and sighed. I had to give it to her because she was so strong and composed. "If they are administrating them now, it may be because he can't be reasoned with and can hurt himself."

"Does this have anything to do with his BPD?"

She turned around to face me. "No. This aggressive reaction can happen to anyone. Whatever he experienced after waking up has most likely everything to do with his brain injury and not his disorder."

She took a seat and motioned to me to do the same. I glanced at his door, wondering what took them so long. There were no sounds coming from his room, so there was no way for us to know if they managed to resolve the situation or not.

"We need to be calm and patient during his recovery. He survived the worst, so now we have to work on whatever issue he has at the moment," she said.

I sat next to her and winced, remembering one more thing. "He said..." Something cold passed through me. "He said he didn't feel his hands. Was that... Was that a hallucination?"

She whipped her eyes at me, fear taking over her features, but it passed as quickly as it came, and her composed mask returned to her face. I gaped at her, surprised at how much this was like Hayden. Hayden could always throw masks onto his face easily, deft when it came to hiding his emotions. Now I knew who he'd gotten that from.

"Let's wait and see what his doctor will say, okay?"

Doctor McConnor and the nurses came out five minutes later and informed us they had sedated him and he shouldn't wake up until tomorrow. He confirmed that the worst had passed and Hayden was out of danger, but he still couldn't tell how serious his condition was without conducting some tests.

"He is possibly going to be confused and angry the next few days. Also, he may experience more hallucinations. We'll monitor him closely to see if there are any other symptoms. I couldn't talk with him much since he wasn't cooperative, but I will try again as soon as he wakes up."

Mrs. Black nodded. "Did he show any abnormalities beside hallucinations?"

"I can't say that without running some tests first. It's clear that he can't keep attention and isn't able to process new information. Also, we have to check if there is any memory damage."

"Memory damage?" I asked.

"Yes. He may not be able to recollect some events or parts of his life. It is possible that the memories of the last days before the accident or the very day of the accident aren't clear, but I can't say anything for certain without speaking with him."

I shifted on my feet anxiously as countless questions twirled through my mind. "How about his hands? He told me he couldn't feel them."

His face grew forlorn. "I don't want to give any diagnosis, but it's possible that he suffers from hand paralysis."

I pressed my hand against my mouth. No.

Carmen pulled him to the side, and they spoke in hushed voices for the better part of a minute. I strained to hear them, but I couldn't understand the half of their conversation with the vast amount of medical expressions they used. All I could make out was that Hayden in all likelihood had hand paralysis and a few more defects. I clasped my cold hands together, willing myself to accept the situation and find a way to deal with it.

"Sarah?" I tore my gaze from my feet to look at Carmen, who had already entered Hayden's room. Doctor McConnor and the nurses had left.

I joined her and closed the door behind me, examining Hayden's slightly gaunt face. "Will he wake up again for sure? He won't slip into a coma again?"

She sat next to his bed and gave me a reassuring smile. "Don't worry. You heard the doctor. The worst has passed. We have to believe in him, Sarah. We have to be strong and help him."

We sat in silence, both of us lost in our thoughts. She left after a while, reminding me to get some sleep, but there was no way I could fall asleep. I was too tense, and I feared I might miss something important if I let myself close my eyes even for a moment.

I caught Hayden's hand, and my throat closed up because of the numbness in it. Would his hands stay paralyzed forever? Was there anything else that was paralyzed? Would he—

Enough with these questions, Sarah. You heard Mrs. Black. Believe in him.

I focused on the fact that he woke up from the coma and let relief push away all doubts. The worst had passed.

"You're going to be all right, Hayden. All of this will be over soon."

I grabbed my sketchbook and started working on my new drawing of Hayden. These days, I was able to draw only him, so I hadn't posted anything on my art accounts. As much as interacting with my followers helped me take my mind off the depressing reality, it was just a weak illusion that reminded me that nothing mattered if Hayden wasn't okay.

I didn't have inspiration to draw, and whenever I tried creating something on my laptop, I ended up deleting it. Even now, as I sketched Hayden meticulously, I was making many mistakes and had to erase some parts repeatedly.

It was past midnight when I stopped drawing, my vision too blurry to focus on the lines. I was worn out, but I couldn't sleep, so I decided to read Hayden's diary again.

I opened it at a random page, letting his words pull me into his world again, enabling me to feel closer to him.

"Date: You know what? Fuck dates.

I struggle with words. I struggle to explain what it feels like when I'm completely calm one moment and the next I'm fucking boiling. It's a sudden overload of emotions. My head feels like it's going to explode, and I can't deal with that suffocating tension. Most of the time, I can't control it. My heart beats fast, my blood boils, my breathing accelerates, and it gets worse and worse until it just erupts. And then... And then comes self-destruction. It's a fucking mess of epic proportions.

Anger is everywhere. It owns me. It courses through my blood and turns me into this pain, static noise, and suffocation.

Fear and shame... They are muffled in the background under the spreading darkness that makes me turn my worst nightmare into reality.

I'm so afraid of it. I'm afraid of the consequences. I know it will come sooner or later. It always comes, and there is nothing I can do about it. I lash out. I hurt people. I'm blinded with rage... All those bottled up emotions just erupt out of me, and it's frightening.

I don't want to hurt anyone. I hate it. But I can't do anything about it. I spurt out all those terrible words, and most often I don't even mean them. I don't mean a single thing, but it doesn't matter, because the damage was already done.

Damage.

I hate that word. It's everywhere. I'm damaged, and I damage you. Ironic. And I still want to give love and make people happy. I want to be so much more than this... Emptiness.

I'm still struggling with DBT. My therapist told me it takes time and lots of practice, but it's frustrating when I stay stuck in that same vicious circle. I want to break out of it. So I fight again. And again. And again.

And again.

Take deep breaths. Recognize your anger. Leave. Don't explode but leave. Focus on letting your emotions out in a healthy way. Write. Go outside. Exercise. Repeat. Repeat. Repeat.

It's so fucking exhausting.

But one day I'll get there."

Chapter 5

ONCE MORE, MONDAY PROVED to be the worst day of the week with the freezing temperature and accumulated snow, which I had more than enough of. Quick to escape the terribly cold afternoon, I rushed into the hospital and headed to the second floor.

Hayden had been transferred from the ICU to the general ward, and he was slowly showing more signs of improvement. He woke up three days ago, and for the most part, he was silent or confused, with occasional anger outbursts. It was painful to see him unable to focus or keep his attention on our words, but Carmen assured me we had to give him some time and it would get better.

We were next to him as much as possible, and we tried to cheer him up, but it didn't always work. I was happy all the more when Masen and Blake managed to make him laugh for the first time with some dirty joke only they understood, and I clung onto that single ray of hope.

His hallucinations decreased, but he still couldn't feel his hands, and that terrified me the most. Doctor McConnor told us it could be temporary, but I couldn't help but doubt it, having read about the coma patients who were paralyzed for life one way or another.

I'd planned to skip school and visit Hayden early in the morning, but he told me last night he knew how important school was for me.

"You're already doing so much for me. I don't want your life to stop just because I'm stuck here. Go to school, I'll be fine," he'd said, taking me completely by surprise. His understanding showed me once more just how special he was.

I drew up when I spotted Blake and Masen in front of Hayden's room, their faces wearing a look of concern. They masked it the moment they saw me, which only scared me more. If they hid their real emotions that could only mean something serious was happening.

I reached them in two quick strides. "What's going on? Why are you standing here?" I glanced at Hayden's door. "Is Hayden okay?" I moved to his room without waiting for their answer, but Blake grabbed my arm and pulled me back.

"Don't go in there."

"What? Why?"

"He has visitors." Blake averted his gaze, as if he was hiding something. I glanced at Masen, but his face didn't tell me anything.

"Okay. Who are they?" Blake looked aside, letting me go.

"It would be better if you take a walk," Masen said and offered me a half-hearted smile that failed to douse my unease.

"No. What's wrong? Who's inside? What are you hiding from me?"

They glanced at each other, and Masen shifted on his feet. "They're some guys from our gang," he said unwillingly.

What? All the hairs on my neck stood up. "Why?"

"They wanted to check up on Hayden."

This was bad. "When you say check up on him... Do you mean check if he's well or—"

"As in check if he really has brain injury and can't fight anymore as he claims," Blake interjected, and my gut churned.

I glared at them. "Why did you let them inside? Hayden shouldn't get disturbed—"

"It's not like we could stop them," Masen interrupted me. "They always get what they want, and we would make things worse if we tried to get in their way."

I shook my head as I stared at them in disbelief. This was a hard pill to swallow.

"What do they want from him? He's not well, and they can't seriously expect him to fight." I couldn't hide frustration from my rising voice, feeling helpless because I couldn't do anything to help Hayden get out of the mess he got himself into a long time ago.

Bitterness spread through me when I thought about our falling-out before his accident. Did he want to get out of it? What would happen once he recovered? Would he continue fighting? We didn't have a chance to talk about it and clear the issue, so I couldn't know if he planned to return to fighting after he recovered or not.

"They don't care if he's well or not," Masen replied, talking to me like I was a child. "They only care about whether he's able to bring them money or not."

"That's horrible," I bit back.

"That's life," Blake said flatly. "And for Hayden's and your own good, you'll stay out of it."

"You're seriously expecting me to stand aside and let Hayden get hurt because, what? Because those criminals want it?!"

"Keep your voice down," Blake hissed into my face, glancing at Hayden's door. "You can't get him out of there. Not even Hayden can do that."

My heartbeat ran rampant, and I felt as if everything was spiraling fast. "Why?" I whispered helplessly.

"When you have a certain status that entitles you to some benefits, you can't expect to give it up without paying a price."

A certain status? "A price? Like the Yakuza members cut off their fingers?"

"Not quite, but the principle is the same; you can't expect to get out just like that."

My mind reeled with so many questions, but I didn't have a chance to ask any, because the door opened and three guys in black leather jackets and dark jeans left Hayden's room, sporting intimidating scowls. Blake and Masen inched closer to me in a protective manner, which surprised me.

The shortest guy had a burly build, and I assumed he was the highest ranking out of the three. He closed the door and nodded at Blake and Masen before his emotionless hazel eyes found mine. They flickered with interest, and he checked me out slowly, making my skin crawl by the time our eyes met again.

My breathing picked up its pace. I was frightened to move even an inch in order not to provoke them. All of them wore scary tattoos that crept up their necks. They had shaved heads and earrings of various sizes and shapes, which instigated fear and disgust in me.

"Your girlfriend, Jones?" He motioned with his head at Blake's arm he'd placed in front of mine. It almost looked as if Blake and I were holding hands.

"Just a friend, Miller," he said firmly. His face donned a casual expression, but I could feel the aggression his body gave out.

Miller looked at Masen. "Yours?"

Masen rolled his eyes. "What? Are you interested in banging her? She's my cousin's girlfriend, so back off."

I gaped at Masen, thankful he'd come up with a quick lie. Miller didn't respond, and the tension became almost palpable in the air as the guys glared at one another. I just hoped this wouldn't escalate into something ugly.

Miller shook his head and smirked, his eyes holding mine. "Tell your cousin he has a terrible taste. He should find something more fuckable next time."

Hurt and shame gripped me, but I managed to keep my face expressionless. Miller and his cronies walked away, sniggering on my account. I took a deep breath and pressed my hand against my raging heart, hoping to steady my nerves before I entered Hayden's room. I was worried that these bastards had upset him, and I didn't know what his mood would be when I saw him.

"Don't listen to him. The day he says something nice would be the day I grow a second dick," Masen told me. It felt weird that he was helping me after all those insults he'd thrown at me before, but I was done questioning positive changes in my life.

"Don't worry about me. It's not like I didn't hear something like that before." I sounded resentful, so I threw a smile on my face. "Thank you for helping me."

"If they heard you were Hayden's girlfriend, they would use it against him sometime, so we can't take any chances. You're welcome. Now let's see him."

We entered Hayden's room and found him looking at my drawings that were on his lap. He raised his head and smiled when he saw me. His bleak eyes immediately lightened, but I was barely aware of it because my focus was on his hand that held one of my drawings...

He's moving his hand!

"Hayden?!" I rushed to him. The sight of his now mobile hand brought me tremendous relief. "You can move your hand!" I was astonished because he wasn't able to feel it last night. "When did this happen?"

"In the middle of the night. I'm surprised myself."

I was about to grab his hand, but I halted, afraid to hurt him somehow. Noticing my hesitation, he grinned and took my hand, his fingers wrapping smoothly around it. "Take it, silly. It won't melt if you touch it."

His hand was warm, and the feel of his skin against mine enthralled me. I never knew one simple touch could mean so much. I never knew how important it could be, always taking for granted my ability to feel and move.

The unshed tears messed with my vision, but I didn't want to turn into an emotional mess now, especially not with Masen and Blake around.

"You feel this?" I squeezed his hand.

"Yeah. It's still a bit weird, and my reactions are slow, but it's something at least. Doc told me that was normal, so I guess I can't bitch about it too much."

"That's awesome, man," Masen said with a smirk. "Now you can jerk off." He winked, and I frowned at him, wondering if his dirty jokes ever had a limit.

Hayden burst out laughing, cursing in between the fits because of the pain from his broken ribs. I studied his face closely, more than glad to see him in a good mood after those guys' visit. I was worried that they might've threatened him or something else to get what they wanted.

"Hayden, what did those guys want?" I asked.

Hayden's expression hardened. He looked at Blake. "T is crazy. He insists I fight and can't understand I can't fucking do it. He sent those mofos to check if I was as crippled as he'd heard."

I frowned. Hayden mentioned the mysterious "T" when he received that phone call before his accident. "Is T one of the guys who visited you?" I asked.

"No. Those were his thugs."

I moved my fingers over his, wishing I could protect him. "Did they hurt you?"

"No. We just talked. They were weird, though." He looked at Masen and Blake. "They said I agreed to fight Axel, but I never did that."

I furrowed my eyebrows, confused. "But Hayden, you—"

"Either way, you can't fight him," Blake interrupted me. "Wait. Do you plan to?"

"I don't know, man. I wish I could cop out of it because that asshole fights dirty."

"And he can pack a punch," Masen said, scratching his jaw.

"Please Hayden, you can't fight." I used the exact words that made him furious with me that morning, but this time, I said them calmly, hoping I wouldn't get the same reaction from him. I wanted to talk to him about fighting and try to explain my perspective, but I had to wait for him to recover first.

"Yeah. They're finally convinced I'm useless, so I'm off the hook for now," he said, and no anger or annoyance laced his voice.

I exhaled the breath I'd been holding, surprised he wasn't provoked by my words this time. They switched topics, but I wasn't paying attention to their guy talk; I was thinking about the changes in Hayden.

This morning, he was able to talk much more than the last three days. He seemed more focused on the conversation, and he didn't look confused. His face looked healthier, having lost its previous peaked appearance. My eyes followed his hand as he gestured, happiness nestling inside of me because he was able to use it. He wasn't snappy or nervous. In fact, this was the first since he woke up that he didn't display any negativity.

"Sarah?" Masen called me, jarring me out of my thoughts. He and Blake were at the door, already leaving. "We said bye."

Hayden smirked. "She's occasionally slow. That's nothing new."

I glared at him. "I'm not slow! I just wasn't paying attention to your conversation, so stop that."

My reply only seemed to amuse him because he was now shaking with silent laughter. "Yeah, baby, we know you're not stupid. It was just a joke."

Ugh. I folded my arms across my chest and said goodbye to Masen and Blake, staring at one spot with pursed lips as they chuckled. I was relieved when they left the room, finally leaving me alone with Hayden.

I looked at him and blushed when I met his fixed gaze. He flashed me one of his rare radiant smiles, which melted all my annoyance away.

"You're so funny when you're like this," he said.

I was too glad to see him act like his old self to think of a comeback. "How are you feeling?"

"You ask me that every single time you see me. And every five minutes during your visits." Yeah, he was definitely his old self.

"I'm glad to see your ability to use sarcasm remained intact."

"Of course. It's my main asset." He gave me a lopsided grin. "After my dick, that is."

I stared at him open-mouthed, but then for some reason, I broke into uncontrollable fits of laughter, feeling hysterical. I hadn't been able to laugh like this since the day of his accident, and now that the dam was opened, I wasn't able to stop laughing. I buried my face into my lap and laughed, all my stress and worry pouring out of me, and it was cathartic.

I didn't know how long this continued, until I felt his hand on the top of my head, and as quickly as it came, my laughter died. A single tear slid down my cheek, and I shuddered. I was shocked by my abnormal reaction.

"I'm a mess," I said to myself and started wiping off the tears, unable to suppress them. *Where are all these tears coming from?*

"Baby." His voice was so gentle, affecting me on a deep level.

I sniffed, my head still in my lap. "I'm okay. Don't worry. It's nothing." I inhaled deeply. I should stop making things difficult when Hayden was the one who needed help the most, but the pain in my chest was too intense for me to get over it that easily.

"Baby," Hayden repeated. "Look at me. Please."

I raised my head and felt a twinge in my chest at the concern in his eyes. They penetrated into me, showing me just how much he cared about me. "Come here." He motioned with his hand for me to sit next to him.

"Are you sure—"

"*Come here*," he repeated. "You won't hurt me, if that's what your overanalytical mind is thinking. Relax."

"Okay."

I jumped up and sat next to him. He raised his hand and ran it through my hair, studying it with a smile, and my breath caught in my throat. I went to a hairdresser after Hayden's accident who styled my hair into a pixie cut and swept my long bangs to the side, managing to fix the damage Christine had made. It looked nice, but Hayden hadn't commented on it so far, and I was nervous as I waited for him to say something.

"It suits you," he finally said, and my heartbeat accelerated. "Your new haircut. It looks cute on you."

Blush covered my cheeks, and I looked away, growing warm under his fervid gaze. "Thank you." He chuckled, and I had to look at him. "What?"

"You change colors like a traffic light."

I pouted. "Do you have a problem with that?"

He grinned. "Why would I have a problem with that? It gives me material to tease you."

"Oh so, it's a fuel for your torture?"

"Yeah, it's a sweet torture, and I'm loving it." He tucked a strand of my hair behind my ear lovingly and caressed my cheek with the back of his hand. "Now come here."

He motioned to me to lean into his embrace, and I didn't waste a second. I rested my cheek against his shoulder as he kept me as close to him as possible. His warmth enveloped me, and his closeness imbued me with bliss. I needed this—to feel we were one, touching, giving, receiving...

"I'm so happy you're feeling better. This is huge progress compared to just yesterday. It's unbelievable."

"Doc is surprised, too. He said I was recovering faster than they expected."

I closed my eyes, enjoying the way his hand traveled up and down my spine. It was soothing and exciting at the same time.

"I still don't feel like myself, and it's difficult for me to say what I want to say."

"How so?"

"It's like I can't fully reach the words I need. I have a sentence in my head, but I just can't get it out. It's weird."

"I'm sure it'll be better soon."

"It better be because it's frustrating, and I feel like a moron."

I moved to look at his face and cupped his cheek. "No, don't say that. You're not a moron. It's completely normal considering what you're going through. Don't be so hard on yourself."

He frowned. "Why don't you follow your own advice? I already told you to trust in me to always be strong for you, but you still try to suppress your emotions in front of me. Don't do that."

"But you're not well—"

"Don't do that, Sarah. Fuck. We're a team now, don't you get it? It doesn't matter if I'm sick, healthy, blind, disabled, or whatever. I want to help you whenever you need help. I always want to be there for you." He took my hand into his and pressed a kiss onto my palm, not breaking our eye contact. "I need you to be yourself, so don't pretend you're okay when you're not. I feel more hurt when you're pretending than when you're showing me your pain."

I nodded, speechless and touched by his words. Our eyes communicated with each other as we drew closer, and I got lost in the moment. In a whirlwind of love and need, I sought his lips with mine and pressed myself against him, savoring the feel of him. Heat spread through me when our tongues touched and the kiss deepened, and I just couldn't get enough of it.

I was in serious need of air when we separated minutes later. "It feels like ages since we kissed like this," I told him and pulled away, crumpling a paper next to me. Only now, I remembered Hayden had a few of my drawings on his lap, and I was crushing one of them with my thigh.

"Great. I hate when I mess up my drawings." I tried to fix the creased paper, but I knew it was useless. "It's happened so many times."

Hayden snorted. "Yeah, but you have at least ten more of these, so it's not a big deal." He picked one and looked as if he were ruminating on something. "What's more important now, I think, is to determine if you're sane or not." He pressed his lips together, suppressing the smile that threatened to break the surface, and I was clueless as to what the joke was this time.

"Please, do tell. Why do you doubt my sanity?"

He wasn't able to stay serious and cracked a smile. "Because staring at me and creating a dozen of these drawings while I was in a coma is freaky. I mean, who does that?" He made the cuckoo sign.

I didn't miss a beat. "A girl who loves you and would give everything to see you open your eyes and live. A girl whose every waking thought is about you and who wants nothing more than to make you happy. So if drawing the love of my life so I can forget the pain and fear of you dying makes me crazy, so be it."

He didn't even move, let alone reply, staring at me with eyes so soft that my chest constricted.

"Do you know how much I love you?" he said in an unusually hoarse voice and framed my face with his hands. "You're fucking precious to me. How lucky am I to have you?"

He didn't give me a chance to respond, fusing his lips with mine. His kiss was hot and explosive, and it messed with my mind and heart. He moved his hand down my shoulder and arm, creating goosebumps everywhere he touched.

"I need you, Sarah. I need you to stay with me no matter what. You will, right?"

A broad smile came to my face. "Yes, I will. Just as I told you that morning before your accident, I'm not going anywhere. I'm here to stay with you through everything."

His face turned taut. His body followed suit, and a pang hit my stomach. He didn't say anything as he looked at one spot on the floor with a dark expression.

"Hayden?"

He grabbed his head. "Fuck."

Everything in me went on high alert. "What's happening, Hayden?"

"There's something I didn't tell you." He didn't look at me immediately, but when he did, his despondent eyes twisted everything in me. "I don't remember the day of my accident."

Chapter 6

I GAPED AT HIM, MY heartbeat thudding in my ears. His doctor had mentioned the memory loss was one of possibilities, but the impact of his words was powerful nevertheless.

"Your doctor didn't tell us anything about this. Does he know?"

His face contorted in pain. "That's because I told him not to tell you."

"Why?"

"Because you suffered enough because of me, and I didn't want to worry you more. I saw just how much you were hurt, so I asked him to keep it a secret for a couple of days."

"Hayden, I don't need you to protect me. You told me before you weren't fragile, and the same goes for me. We're supposed to share everything. I want you to rely on me, just like you want me to rely on you."

He rested his head against the headboard and closed his eyes. "I'm sorry. You're right. It's just that I thought you would be upset and... Yeah, I didn't want to worry you. Now you know."

I trailed his raw knuckles with my fingers, fighting against fear. I had to be composed and accept things as they were. There was a possibility he would regain the memory of that day, so I had to be optimistic.

"Could your doctor determine if it's temporary or not?"

"He said he couldn't know. Only time will tell."

I sighed. Just as I'd suspected. "You said you didn't remember that day. Does that mean you forgot it completely?"

"It's hard to explain. Kind of."

He groaned, creasing his forehead. He looked like he was straining to gather his thoughts as his unfocused eyes darted around the room. He was quickly getting more anxious, and I ran my hand down his arm to calm him.

"I remember a red car right in front of me. Then a white flash... And... Nothing. I can't remember anything else." He tried to curl his hand into a fist, but it seemed it still didn't move the way he wanted. He glanced up at me. "Were you with me? Where was I? How it happened?"

I sucked in a sharp breath.

He didn't remember our fight.

He didn't remember he'd given me his diary.

He rubbed his temple. "Is everything all right?" I asked him, worried that this might overexert him.

"I'm starting to get a headache."

"Should I call someone?"

"No. I don't want drugs anymore. They make me more confused." He shook his head. "So? How did it happen?"

I stared at my lap, at a loss for words. How should I tell him? How?

"I was there. With you." I clasped my hands together and glued my eyes to them, unable to look him in the eyes. "I was discharged from the hospital." My heart beat wildly. The weight of what he forgot was heavy, but I had to explain it to him. "You were with me, and we were supposed to spend the day together... Then you received a call."

"A call?"

"Yes. I don't know who the person was, but you talked about some match T insisted on." He tensed, and my body responded equally.

"You know about T?"

"No. I just heard you mention him over the phone. I don't know him. You... You didn't get to tell me about him." I still stared at my hands, which now trembled hard.

"Sarah?"

"Hm?"

"Can you please look at me?" I licked my lips and returned his bewildered stare. "What's wrong?"

"We had a fight, Hayden."

He frowned. "We did? When?"

"Right after that phone call. You started arguing with the person on the phone, and you got so mad. I... I didn't want you to fight." I looked back at my hands, but he tipped my chin up and made me look him in the eyes.

"Sarah, just say it and get over with it."

Fine.

"You agreed to that match, but I told you I didn't want you to fight. I was just worried for your safety because you were still injured, and underground fighting is beyond dangerous. But you thought I was trying to control you, and then you got so furious with me, and you told me some ugly things..."

"What did I tell you?" I winced, surprised by his sharp tone.

"You complained that I stopped you from making Christine and her friends pay for setting my hair on fire. You said I didn't accept you and... And that I was lying when I said I loved you. I tried to calm you down, but that only made things worse. In the end, you told me to get out of your sight..."

This was more difficult than I'd thought. I was reliving those moments, and it was killing me.

"Then you left me in front of the hospital, but you didn't pay attention to the red light, and you started crossing the street without looking." A dull pain spread through my chest, more acute with each step down this agonizing memory lane. "And then... You got hit."

Distress distorted his face, his breathing noticeably fast. His eyes grew darker, looking into mine with such force I wasn't sure if I'd messed everything up or not.

"I'm so sorry, Hayden. I shouldn't have reacted that way. I shouldn't have—"

"Please, stop." He drew his eyebrows together. "Stop." He raised his hand in the air in a stop gesture, and I went stock-still, afraid of getting into the same fight with him again. "Just... Fuck." He pressed his hand over his eyes, breathing heavily through his nose.

"Are you okay?"

"Stop. I need to think." He shook his head. "I don't remember it. I don't remember a word of it, and I can't understand... I couldn't have accepted that fight. I couldn't have said all of that. I..." He hit the mattress with his fist and cried out in pain. "Fuck!"

"Hayden!" I grabbed his wrist. "Please, don't do this. You'll only hurt yourself. Besides, you just regained feeling in your hands so don't—"

"I don't remember anything, and all you're saying now sounds so absurd, but at the same it sounds like the kind of shit I would pull on you, and it scares me that I can't remember it!"

"It's going to be all right. I'm sure you'll remember soon."

"You don't know that. You're just telling me this to calm me down, but I can't calm down when this won't end! I hate this. I hate not remembering. I hate this pain whenever I move. I hate being this confused and thinking like an imbecile. I can't figure out even some simple things, which is infuriating!"

"Hayden, please. It's okay. Doctor McConnor said that was normal. He said you'd be able to think clearly when you recover and—"

"*When* will that happen? I'm sick and tired of this! As if I wasn't weird enough with my fucking disorder, I have to go through this now?! When will all this pain stop?"

"It has to stop sometime. It can't last forever." I touched his hand tentatively, hoping to get him to relax, but he flinched and pulled it away from me. He eyed me warily. He had his guard up, and it hurt.

"Sarah, don't lie to me! Stop treating me like a child and feeding me pointless lies. You've been doing that enough for the past two weeks."

I straightened myself up. "What are you talking about?"

"I'm talking about all those stupid 'You'll be fine' and 'You'll wake up soon' you fed me with for days!"

I recoiled. "You heard me? You were able to hear?"

"Yes. And it was the worst." His eyes were cold, reminding me of the old, dark Hayden. "For ten days I'd been hearing people say I was all right when they knew nothing. I wasn't all right! I was trapped with no way out, and all those nightmares and illusions... They lasted for so long. For *too* long." He started taking deep breaths, shaking.

"Now, after everything, I don't want to hear it's going to be all right when I feel like shit. Look, just go. Right now, I'm pissed off, and it's already more than I can handle. I don't want to hurt you, so please, leave."

I stood up from his bed, feeling cold despite how warm it was in the room. I was so close to bursting into tears, but I sucked it up and picked up my bag with a blank expression on my face. I knew it would be for the best if I left, but it stung that he'd asked me to leave anyway. I didn't want to leave him, but if my presence made things worse, I had to accept that. It was hard, but I had to accept that this was his way of dealing with his issues.

"I'm sorry if I did something wrong. I'll leave now." I stood awkwardly next to his bed, feeling painfully distanced from him, and I waited for... I didn't even know what.

"You didn't do anything wrong, so stop fucking apologizing." He hissed. "Fuck. I'm sorry for this." He inhaled sharply. "I don't want to say something I'll regret, and I'm already doing it, so... Fuck. Go!"

I nodded, growing colder the angrier he got. "I love you, Hayden. Don't forget that. I love you."

Something vulnerable passed through his eyes, but other than that, my words didn't have any effect. He was too overcome with anger to control himself. I scurried out of the room and closed the door behind me, leaning against it for support.

I was breathing raggedly, the first tear already leaving a path down my cheek. I was close to losing it. I drew in a long breath, telling myself this was something I should always be prepared for. These unpredictable ups and downs were a part of his emotional baggage.

Besides, he wasn't taking medicine for his BPD at the moment. Since he suffered from a brain injury, he had yet to see his therapist and see what meds would be safe to use in his condition. He had to continue with therapy and make up for the sessions he'd missed, so it wouldn't be surprising if he relapsed.

Then again, I had to stop taking this personally. I'd read that when people with BPD couldn't control their emotions and were about to explode, it was better for them to leave and calm down before trying to solve the issue. Once they calmed down, they could see things clearly and express their problems in an appropriate way. Ms. Kishimoto herself told me to not try to solve issues during arguments but after we both calmed down. Since Hayden wasn't in a position to leave, it had to be me.

I decided to walk back home, despite the low temperature and heaps of snow that created a monotone landscape. I was near my house when my LG notified me of a new text, which pulled me out of my musing. I halted, remembering only now I'd forgotten to tell him about his diary.

I took my phone out of my pocket. I wasn't sure how to approach that topic with him. I had no way of knowing if he would get angry to hear I had it. Would he demand that I give it back? Would he feel very vulnerable? Either way, I didn't feel comfortable having it anymore.

I unlocked my phone, and my heart leapt when I saw Hayden's name on the screen.

"I can finally use my phone now that I can move my hand. But my thumb acts all weird, and I keep messing up. Thank fuck for autocorrect."

I giggled, at ease that he'd obviously simmered down. I was about to text him back, when another message arrived.

"I'm sorry for earlier. I messed that up too. I just don't want to hurt you. We both know I did that more times than we can count. And hdsjahifergsda fuck typos."

I laughed hard, wishing I could hug him right this second. I wriggled my toes in boots to bring some warmth back to them before I resumed walking, typing my message.

"Are you feeling better now?"

His text arrived a minute later.

"If better means feeling like shit because I had to chase away my girlfriend to calm down, then yeah. I feel like I'm on top of the world."

My stomach caved in. He always masked his feelings with sarcasm, but I understood how difficult this was for him.

He sent a new text before I could answer him, and I halted when his words sunk in.

"Actually, I need that stupid 'You'll be fine.' Whenever you say it, I feel like you care, and I need that. So don't ever stop, okay? Forget what I said. And forget whatever I said to you before my accident that day."

I choked with love and need for this complex guy. The first snowflakes landed on my cheek, and I looked up at the dark, cloudy sky. There was something stifling in the way darkness spread everywhere as the white particles fell all around, and I wished for a clear, starry sky that could bring me serenity.

I typed a new text, trying to convey how I felt in a relatively small amount of words.

"I'll always stay next to you and make sure you know you're not alone. I'll always tell you I need you and you're the love of my life. Didn't I tell you that before? Yes, you're the love of my life, Hayden. And I don't care if you don't feel your hands, or have memory loss, or have a disorder, or anything else you find wrong with yourself. You're mine and that won't change. Ever."

My pulse raced, anxiety strumming my nerves because I'd shared my most profound feelings with him. I didn't feel cold anymore. I looked at Hayden's house as I passed it, and the absence of lights created a strange loneliness in me. I wanted Hayden out of the hospital and back to a normal life. I wanted to experience so many things with him...

My phone chimed, and I took a deep breath before I opened the message, nervous about his response.

"Those words sound like they came straight out of the trashy romance movies Carmen likes to watch."

I gaped at my screen, color rising to my face.

"That was a joke, so don't make that face you're making now. I'm actually smiling like a fool, and I wish I could kiss the hell out of you. I want you to say those words to me directly next time. Got it?"

His next text arrived shortly after.

"And you're mine, Sarah. Only mine. I even have a tattoo to prove that."

What? A tattoo?

"What do you mean by that?"

I paced up and down my porch as I waited for his answer. I wasn't in a hurry to get inside and face my mother.

"It means you'll find out as soon as you get me naked."

I blushed furiously, and the image of his ripped body popped in my mind. His body and tattoos were a potent combination that awoke an old desire in me, which had only grown more powerful. I wanted him. I wanted him as much as he wanted me.

I typed a message fast, having no idea what made me say the next words.

"You can always send me nudes."

His reply came quickly.

"Baby, I'll send you my nudes gladly. All you have to do is ask."

I entered my house with a grin, the image of our naked bodies entangled together bringing heat to my cheeks and insides.

I was pulled out of my reverie as quickly as it started when I saw Lydia and my mother in our living room. They were watching a rerun of *True Blood*. I didn't want to see Patricia, but it would be impolite of me not to greet Lydia.

"Hi," I told her, barely sparing a glance to my mother. She didn't even pay attention to me; her gaze was fixed on the screen. Her bruises had already faded, and since she hadn't been drinking as much as before, her eyes were unusually clear. Unfortunately, sober Patricia wasn't even close to a decent human. She was still miles away from caring about anyone but herself.

"Hello, sweetie. How was school?"

I smiled bitterly. This woman cared more about my day than my own mother. She was probably baffled that Patricia and I were practically strangers now, but she didn't question it and acted friendly each time she saw me, which I was grateful for.

"School was normal," I replied briefly, impatient to leave. Patricia's presence didn't sit well with me, and I had no energy to put up with her more than necessary.

"I'm glad to hear that. Also, I wanted to ask you about your early action application. You mentioned trying getting into Yale?"

My lips parted. I completely forgot about Yale's Early Action. They were supposed to email me their decision by the middle of December, which meant I most likely already had the answer to what my future had in store for me.

"Yes, but I still don't know if they accepted me." I glanced at mom, expecting her to say I had no chance of going to such a prestigious college.

"If you do get in by some miracle, which isn't likely, don't expect me to pay for it," Patricia spat, her eyes still on the screen. "You're on your own."

Lydia twisted her hands in her lap as she looked between Patricia and me, clearly uncomfortable, but Patricia's insult didn't have any effect on me.

So, I just shrugged and said, "I'm better off on my own anyway."

I turned around and marched out of the living room, wishing Lydia hadn't had to witness that. My pulse sped up when I entered my room and turned on my laptop to check my email. My nerves were doing a wild dance. These last few weeks, everything had faded into the background as I dealt with Hayden's condition and the midterm craziness, and now I could hardly breathe with rising excitement.

I opened the browser and entered my Gmail password twice, my hands shaky. Unless I was deferred or didn't receive financial aid, which I would know about around March, this was it. If I didn't get in, I'd have to change my plans and dreams and settle for some other college. I'd have to forget about Yale's amazing art program and all the possibilities it could offer me in the future.

On the other hand, if I got in, I would be able to learn from the best professors and expand my connections. I'd be able to take a variety of courses that would help me perfect my art. And...

And I would be separated from Hayden.

Oh God. All of a sudden, Hayden was part of the equation that was my life, and I could no longer plan my future without him in it. I'd never thought about what college he would choose. I was always focused on getting out of Enfield and creating the life I wanted, but I couldn't only think about myself anymore now that we were together.

I never asked him about college, so I didn't know where he wanted to apply. Had he ever planned on leaving Enfield? Or going to college? He'd said he didn't know what his dreams were, so there was a possibility he wouldn't attend any.

My Gmail loaded, and there it was. An email from Yale that was sent several days ago.

My anxiety went through the roof. Okay. It would be okay. I just had to click on it, and whatever it said, it would be okay. Yes. I could do this.

I closed my eyes shut and clicked on the email blindly, my breathing heavy. *Take a deep breath in. Take a deep breath out. It's going to be okay.*

I held my breath as I opened my eyes, focusing on the contents of the email... And I saw it.

An offer of admission.

I got into Yale.

I GOT INTO YALE!

"Yes!" I jumped high with my fist in the air, laughing like a maniac.

Finally, after so many days, a huge load was lifted from my shoulders. This was a dream come true. They accepted me. I was good enough to get into Yale. I was able to follow my dreams.

My loud laughter rang through my room, revealing the pure euphoria I felt. I reached my window in spurts of laughter and was about to start dancing when I cast my gaze at Hayden's room.

Unexpectedly, my laughter died, and my stomach hollowed out.

Hayden needed me more than ever. I couldn't disregard his loneliness that was heightened by BPD, and if I told him I was leaving for college...

This was bad.

How was Hayden going to react to this?

Chapter 7

"YOUR WORLD HISTORY teacher should change his profession," Mel said as soon as we were out of the classroom.

This was her first day in East Willow High, yet I was more excited about it than she was. She kept glaring at people, mumbling something about how she should've stayed in bed instead of coming to school.

"You mean *our* world history teacher. And what do you mean?"

"I mean he would be better off working with people with insomnia. He made us all fall asleep as he droned on about the Axis powers!"

I shook my head as chuckles parted my lips, looking at Jess's text on my phone.

"I'm waiting at your locker."

"Jess is waiting for us," I said to Mel.

I noticed the way other students looked at her. She was new, and following East Willow High's "laws," she had to experience a lot of staring, finger-pointing, and hushed conversations about her. I had to give her credit, since she didn't even flinch under their inquisitive stares, walking confidently with her head held high.

"I never thought the day would come when I'd admit some other school is worse than Rawenwood High. The students there are awful, but look at all these insects. They're just buzzing around and gawking, and the only thing they're good at is getting on your nerves. They're worse than flies."

I broke out in laughter. I enjoyed her interpretation of East Willow High's students a little too much. She was a breath of fresh air we needed.

She rolled her eyes. "It's not funny. I've already heard a few girls say my punk style was an eyesore."

I skimmed over her black Dr. Martens with a gray skull print, black ripped jeans, and Green Day long sleeve shirt. It was hard to imagine her wearing any other kind of clothes. These were perfect for her.

"What did you tell them?"

"To choke on their high heels and drink bleach."

I halted. "You really said that? And how did they react?"

67

"What do you think? They didn't quite worship me and decide to make me their queen bee." She heaved a long sigh. "Seriously, Sar, I've only been here for a couple of hours, and I can already see this place is falling apart. It's a mess. That principal, Anders? Someone needs to kick him out. He told me not to make any problems at his school. *Me!* Just because I, and I quote, 'look the way I look.'"

I led the way to my locker, frowning. "And what would be 'the way you look?'"

"Like Rambo with a ton of makeup."

I let out a spurt of laughter. "*What?*"

"He means I look too violent. He was surprised my school record at Somers was more or less 'clean.'"

"Don't take it personally, Mel. He's that way with everyone. He's a horrible, corrupt man who only cares about himself and the image of *his* school."

"The image of *his* school is already as awful as it can get, so I don't know who he's fooling with all that talk about the 'reputable' East Willow High."

Jessica grinned when she spotted us. "Hey, girls." She opened her arms wide and pulled me into a hug. "Congratulations, Sar! Yale, huh? That's amazing!"

Mel patted my shoulder. "That's our geek. Destined for big things." I turned to look at her and smiled back at her. "I knew you'd make it."

"Thank you." I caught her extended hand, feeling proud of myself for a change. My confidence and spirits were boosted now that I knew I'd made it. "I almost had a heart attack when I saw it."

"We have to celebrate," Melissa said as we headed to the cafeteria. "We should go out and have some drinks—"

"We're underage, Mel," Jess told her.

"There's surely some place that will let us drink! It's not like I haven't done it before. Come on, loosen up!"

"I'd like to celebrate with you, but I can't until Hayden gets better. To be honest, I'm not in the mood for celebrating when he's in the hospital."

Mel nodded. "You're right."

"Is Hayden feeling better?" Jess asked me.

"Yes and no." I exhaled a long sigh. "Overall, he's getting better, but there's something else. He has some memory loss."

Mel's mouth dropped open. "Are you serious?"

"Yeah. But it's not what you might think. He can't remember the day of his accident, that's all. I just hope it won't be permanent."

"I'm so sorry, Sar," Jess said, her brows pulled into a small frown. "How are you holding up?"

"I'm trying to stay strong and positive. It's hard, but we've been through a lot already and we came out of it, so we can't give up now, can we?"

Mel nodded. "That's the spirit. There's no point in being pessimistic. He survived the worst, and I'm sure that even if he doesn't recover the memory, you two will be able to cope with it."

"Thanks, Mel. That helps a lot."

"How are your classes so far?" Jess asked Mel.

"If I hadn't attended them, I never would've known the meaning of true happiness. Not because I'm able to attend those horrible classes, no. But because I learned that happiness is being away from this, what do you call it, Sar? Hellhole?" I nodded, laughing. "Yes. Being away from this hellhole. That's true happiness."

Jess and I were still laughing when we entered the cafeteria. Melissa was funny when she was grumpy, especially with the way she looked at everyone—like they were bugs she'd like to squash—but I hoped she would cheer up.

She acted tough, but her parents' divorce affected her more than she wanted to admit, and I wished there were a way for Jess and me to help her. We tried talking with her about it a few times, but she always dismissed it, acting like it wasn't a big deal, but I already knew her well enough to know she was putting up a front.

We reached the end of the lunch line when Melissa stopped, her eyes zeroing in on something on the other side of the room. I followed her gaze to Blake, Masen, Steven, and a few of their football teammates at Hayden's table.

"Oh look. It's Poo, an Even Bigger Poo, my brother the idiot, and their friends." Mel shook her head. "So he decided to show up in the end. While I had to listen to mom complaining about him spending the night away and not answering her calls." Pain twisted her features, but it was quickly replaced by anger when she grimaced. "That irresponsible idiot. Look at him, all chill with his brainless friends and not even bothering to turn on his damn phone. I'm so going to strangle him." She strode over to them, leaving us to gape at her.

"What is she doing?" Jess asked.

"She probably wants to talk with Steven. Come on." I motioned to her to follow me. "We can't let her face them all alone. I'm sure Blake, Masen, and the others won't be civilized."

"But I'm sure they won't dare harass her in front of her brother."

I understood why she didn't want to go anywhere near their table, but we couldn't be sure with Masen, Blake, and the other douchebags on their team. I wouldn't be surprised if they made fun of Mel, despite Steven.

"Come on. We're her friends. She's clearly pissed off, and I don't want her to do something reckless."

We were halfway there when her loud voice reached us. "Why do you even have a phone when you don't use it?" she hissed at Steven who sat reclined in the chair with his hands behind his head, his face blank.

"This is getting old. I'm seriously thinking of changing my number," he said. "You and mom wouldn't know it, of course."

I was more than aware of the curious glances Jess and I received from Hayden's teammates when we stopped next to Mel, and I shifted on my feet. We looked stupid just standing like this, like we were her bodyguards. I didn't regret coming over, though, because Mel was too angry, and Mel and anger weren't a good combination.

"And I'm thinking of changing your face. I don't know what you were doing last night, but you should've at least called mom—"

"Stop being a control freak, sis. You always do that. Mom is more than enough when it comes to the controlling department. I came to school, and isn't that what you wanted? So relax and go somewhere with your friends. Or better yet"—he looked at Jessica and me and flashed us a suggestive smile—"How about you join us?" He winked at me, and my cheeks responded with an intense blush. I almost sneered at his attempt to charm us.

"How about not?" Blake said, glaring between him and Jessica.

One of Hayden's teammates gave Steven an incredulous look and chuckled. "Are you *loco*? That's Hayden's girl. You seriously have the balls to flirt with her?"

"Hey, I'm allowed to look at her, right?" Steven replied with a shrug of his shoulders. "And Jess is cute, too."

I clenched my jaw, burning with shame. I was about to nudge Melissa and tell her to leave it be when Masen added, "I agree with Blake. How about not?" He looked coolly at Mel. "With the way she's fuming right now, you'll end up with a broken nose, bro."

Melissa smiled at him sweetly. "I'm glad you recognize my abilities, you wimp."

"Being an ogre is nothing to be proud of, Satan." Blake, Steven, and the others burst into laughter.

"She does look like an ogre," another one of Hayden's teammate said. "A pretty one, but still an ogre."

Mel bared her teeth. "Shut your mouth, or I'll shut it for you." She fisted her hand, the veins on her temples bulging out.

"You won't shut shit," Masen said in a bored voice. "We aren't playing Mortal Kombat here. It takes much more than a controller to kick someone's ass."

She raised one eyebrow. "I thought we already established that I was capable of inflicting serious pain? Do you want me to remind you, Barbie?"

Their teammates met this with hoots of laughter. I glanced at Steven, partly expecting him to defend Mel, but he looked like he couldn't care less about Mel or Masen, leaning against his hand as he played idly with his fries. His dilated ocean blue eyes were unfocused as they moved between Melissa and the others, the dark circles under them a testament of a sleepless night. He didn't look quite well, and I suspected he was either wasted or still had the remains of some drug in his system.

"And do I have to remind you that just because I don't hit girls, it doesn't mean I'll allow you to do whatever you want?"

She snorted. "'Allow.' You're not my dad to allow me to do something or not. Now stop talking because you're really getting on my nerves."

She turned her attention to Steven, opening her mouth to say something, but Masen beat her to it. "Either you like me and can't ignore me, or you got a stick up your ass."

I gasped. I glanced at Jessica to check her reaction, but she barely paid attention to them, her cheeks crimson red as she looked fixedly at her feet.

I caught Blake staring at her, finding a strange intensity in his eyes that reminded me so much of the way Hayden looked at me.

Mel's laugh broke through my flow of thoughts, holding no humor. "You would love that. You would love if I gave some attention to your little STD magnet, but it's too bad I don't give a damn about you."

Masen snarled at her. "Oh I see. For someone who doesn't give a damn about me, you are really obsessed with my dick." He smirked and winked at her. "Admit it, I make you wet." My jaw dropped.

"Mel, come on. Let's go—" I started, but she didn't look at me, her face twisted in disgust as she returned his gaze.

She didn't say anything at first, but then she half-smiled. "No, Barbie, that's where you're wrong." She grabbed Masen's open bottle of Coke from his tray. "*I* make *you* wet." To everyone's shock, she poured all the remaining Coke directly onto his crotch. "For real."

"Bitch!" Masen jumped up and lunged at Melissa, but Steven finally decided to resume the role of her brother and step between them. They had the attention of the whole cafeteria now, and my stomach coiled, reacting to unwanted exposure.

Steven glanced over his shoulder at Mel. "Enough! For Christ's sake, Melissa, go away and leave us alone. I can't deal with your temper at the moment." He directed his stern gaze at Masen. "You better go and clean yourself up before she decides to go full crazy on you."

"She's mental," he spat, looking at Mel like he wanted to crush her. His body exuded tension, and I thought he would retaliate, but he listened to Steven and walked away, muttering something under his breath.

"Serves him right," Melissa said with her hands on her hips, her chin tipped high.

"What the fuck is your problem?" Blake asked her, standing up. "It's like it's not enough to see Fats' ugly face, but you also have to butt in where you're not wanted. If you want a fight, you're going to get it." Jess took a step back, her eyes instantly teary.

"Don't speak like that about Jessica," I told him off.

"Yes. Don't speak like that about her," Mel said. "And what's with that stupid nickname—Fats? You better—"

"Forget it, Mel," Jessica let out. "Some things will never change." She squared her shoulders and looked right at Blake. "Maybe I'm fat and ugly, but you have a horrible personality. And you know what? I can change my appearance, but you'll always be a horrible, disgusting jerk, whom no one would ever love." Blake's nostrils flared, his face darkened by fury and disbelief. "Even if some girl would fall for you, I'd call her crazy and—"

"Shut up," he roared, a curtain of hurt shading his eyes briefly. He eliminated the distance between them, but Mel and I stepped in front of Jess, shielding her from him.

"Don't come near her," I warned him.

"Make one more step, asshole, and I'll kick your dick so hard you won't be able to have children," Mel barked.

"Let's go." I pulled Jess and Mel with me, already emotionally tired of their back-and-forth fighting.

No one stopped us, thankfully, but the hatred in Blake's gaze was enough to give me chills as it followed Jessica.

"I'll destroy you, Fats," he shouted. "You're going to regret this!"

Melissa rolled her eyes. "So dramatic. Where does he get those idiotic sentences?"

We took our food and went to our table, followed by hundreds of curious eyes. I could never hide from the unwelcome attention, which chased me endlessly.

I wasn't hungry anymore, and the rice and vegetables on my plate were suddenly unappealing to me. Jessica looked equally unenthusiastic about her food, upset by her exchange with Blake, but she managed to hold her tears at bay.

"Jess?"

"Yes?"

"What's going on between Blake and you?"

She tensed, and her gaze darted over to Hayden's table. Redness poured into her cheeks.

"That's a great question," Mel said. "What on earth is happening between you two?"

Jess's face got redder. "Absolutely nothing."

"I wouldn't call what just happened nothing."

"He hates me and bullies me. Why is that so difficult to understand?"

Melissa shook her head and pointed her fork at Jess. "Nope. I don't buy it. There has to be something you're not telling us—"

"Are you serious?!" Jess exploded. "What do you want to know? That he threatens me every single day and bullies me until he has me in tears? That he calls me names and makes me feel awful? That I feel sick every time I see him? Do you want all the horrible details, Mel?"

She raised her hands defensively. "Sorry. It's just weird. That's all."

"Weird? You're telling me about weird? Then what do you call this thing between Masen and you?"

Mel's brows knit together. "Hey! Don't turn this back on me. And there's nothing between Masen and me. I would do the same to Blake or anyone else because I despise all of them." She burst into chuckles. "Although, that face he made when I poured Coke on him... Priceless. Okay, I admit, showing Masen his place does bring me extra satisfaction."

She didn't stop chuckling, and I sighed. "Whatever floats your boat," I told her and looked at Jessica. "I'm just glad that you stood up to Blake, Jess. That was awesome."

She bit at the cuticle of her thumb, trying to cover her flushed face with as much hair as possible. "I don't know what made me do it. I was terrified, and I hated it. He's going to make me pay for that."

"We aren't going to let that happen, Jess."

Mel curled her hand into a fist. "Yeah. I'll break his nose first. I'm tired of seeing these imbeciles. I dealt with them in my school, and I sure as hell am going to deal with them here too."

I smiled, admiring her once again. She was assertive as always and didn't let her fears chain her, always pushing forward despite everything and everyone. I wondered why I'd never been able to break out of the old fears that kept me restrained.

Each time I wanted to fight back, I couldn't. I was so afraid of the consequences. My mind always created the worst outcomes for my actions, the consequence of all those times I tried to defend myself only to make things worse. My fears prevented me from taking a stand against bullies.

Mel looked like she didn't care about tomorrow or possible retaliations. She looked like she could deal with everything that was thrown her way, and I respected her immensely for that.

"What's the problem with Steven now?" I asked her. "Why did you get so angry with him?"

She ran her hand through her hair before she took a piece of cucumber. "He's more problematic than ever. He's never home these days. The situation is pretty tense because we'll have to stay at my grandparents' place for a while, and they completely disapprove of Steven's behavior. They pressure him to change and stop ruining his life, but as expected, Steven doesn't like that. Add our parents' divorce to this, and it gets real messy. His phone is off most of the time, and I barely have a chance to talk with him."

"Is he using more often?" Jess asked her.

"More often? He's stoned every single day, and not from any light drugs, no." She looked at Steven, concern shadowing her face for a quick moment. "I'm so scared for him. He has no clue that his 'lifestyle' is a one-way ticket to destruction. I'm afraid one day I'll just hear he has—" She stopped, like she was about to say something she didn't want to share.

"He has what?" Jess encouraged her.

Mel's smile was so dazzling in its obvious insincerity it was painful to watch. "Nothing. Don't mind silly me."

I wanted to tell her not to bottle up her true feelings and rely on us to be there for her, but that would be hypocritical of me. I had to believe she would do that in time on her own.

My phone vibrated, so I took it out of my pocket, smiling because I knew it was Hayden.

But that smile got wiped off when I opened his message and read the words that broke my heart.

"I'm so sorry. I deserve to die because of how I treated you that morning. I'm sorry. I'm so sorry for everything."

Chapter 8

THE TRIP TO THE HOSPITAL passed in a blur; the pressure in my head tightened with each passing minute. I'd run out of the cafeteria before I could explain Hayden's message to Jessica and Melissa, too worried about Hayden's state of mind to waste a second. I'd texted him saying I'd come right away, but he didn't reply. He didn't respond to my calls either.

My heartbeat reached a sickening speed by the time I made it to his floor. I dreaded entering his room, imagining him devastated, and I barely got any comfort from the fact that he'd obviously remembered our argument from that morning.

I didn't bother to knock. I shoved his door wide open only to screech to a halt. He was *crying*, his bloodshot eyes prominent on his extremely pale face. "Hayden!"

He flinched when he saw me and sank into his bed like he wanted to put a distance between us. I closed the door and dashed to him.

He covered his eyes with his forearm, as if he was trying to hide himself from me. "What are you doing here?" His voice was raspy, shattering me to pieces. "Please go away. Don't look at me like this. Go away!"

I wrapped my fingers around his wrist to pry his arm off his face, but it was futile. "Please let me see you. I'm not going anywhere. I'm here."

Sobbing, he turned his head further away, and it was tearing at my heart. I gave in to my emotions and pulled him into an embrace, holding his head against my shoulder as he convulsed forcefully. He slid his hand to my back and grabbed my jacket, burying his head into my neck before he let out a long sob. I held him close as he shed tears, succumbing to my own.

"I'm sorry, Sarah. I'm so sorry. I'm so sorry." I didn't recognize his pain-stricken voice. "I remembered some things I said... I'm sorry for everything. I'm the most horrible person—"

"No, don't say that. It's okay. It doesn't matter—" I began in a soothing tone, but it didn't make any difference.

"It matters!" His hand clutched my jacket harder, bringing me flush against his body. "It fucking matters! You've done everything for me! Everything! And how have I treated you?" His voice broke, and I shuddered, tears soaking my face. "All those words I've said..."

I moved as close I could get to him without hurting him and laced my fingers through his slightly longer hair. "I understand, Hayden. That wasn't you. You couldn't control it. I understand you didn't mean it."

He shook his head against the crook of my neck. "I was supposed to learn to control it. That fucking therapy was supposed to help me with control!"

"It takes time. Sometimes it takes years to accomplish that, so don't blame yourself. I understand."

"I don't deserve your understanding! I don't deserve you. I don't deserve anything."

I drew away and grabbed his face, making him look at me. His red eyes twisted the knife of pain deep into me. "You deserve *everything*. You're my most precious person, and I love you. Your soul is so pure, and you don't even see it. You're an angel."

He shook his head adamantly. He searched for something in my eyes, clinging desperately to my jacket, and it was almost unbearable witnessing his low moment.

"I'm not an angel. I'm unworthy of your love. You saved me twice and accepted me after everything. You make me feel loved and happy, and you're always so full of understanding. You've spent the last two weeks here, always taking care of me, and it rips me apart knowing I'm hurting you so much."

His tears cascaded down his cheeks, searing through my chest. I wiped one tear off his face with my thumb. Then another. And another. One by one, I removed them all and slid my thumb to his lower lip, brushing it slowly. Our gazes locked.

"That's why I'm fighting for this," I told him. "I'm fighting for you, me, *us*. I know who you are, and I don't want to let these obstacles separate us. I'll be with you all the way."

He didn't say anything, but his eyes told me everything. They turned soft and incredibly warm as we looked at each other in long, charged silence. With each breath he took, he seemed calmer, never letting go of my gaze, and I could slowly relax too.

He offered me a small smile and cupped my face. "I don't know how, but something changed in me after the coma. For ten days, I had extreme illusions and nightmares, and it was one of the most terrifying periods of my life. I thought I was going to break any moment. I thought I was going to lose it and there would be no going back." His fingers ran along the edge of my jaw, sending tingles over my skin. "I was so scared. I could hear everything, but not all of it made sense. I felt hopeless and all alone in the unknown with no way of getting out. For. Ten. Fucking. Days." He shut his eyes.

"And then I woke up, and you were there, right in the midst of all my confusion and fear. You were the only light on my dark road. You're always there, whether you're far away or close, whether we hate each other or not... Just knowing you exist makes this world better. I feel better. And all the things you do for me..."

His fingers trailed to my neck, conjuring warmth that cocooned my flesh. His eyes found mine, imparting so much through his heated gaze.

"I've changed. Now I know I can do this. I can get out of this circle of struggles and drawbacks. You and I can, no, we *will* be better. Life is too short to doubt everything. I was too close to dying, closer than ever, and I don't want to waste any more time on the same shit. I have to be better than this.

"So no matter how down I get, no matter how strong the pain is, no matter how long it takes, I'll always keep fighting to be a better guy. For me. For you. For us."

Flutters of joy filled my belly. His words were something I'd always hoped for; they were a path to a brighter future.

Our lips met, fulfilling my deep yearning for him. A burst of pleasure spread through me when his tongue connected with mine and his fingers skimmed down my neck. He grazed my lower lip with his teeth before he tugged it sensually into his mouth, and I couldn't think properly. I was quickly becoming light-headed.

I pressed my forehead against his, needing a few moments to catch my breath and collect my thoughts.

"I'm so happy you feel this way. So, so happy." My voice didn't sound like mine; it was too hoarse. I moved back to look at him. "I want us to work it out. To change for the better and fully accept each other."

His lips curled into a half-smile. "Yes, Captain Sarah. As you command."

I laughed, shaking my head. "We have to talk about our differences and work on them one by one. We have to meet each other in the middle, but before that, we need some healthy boundaries. What you did yesterday was right." I took his hand. "Instead of getting into a huge fight, I should wait for you to cool off and think more clearly."

"That's what I thought, too. So from now on, whenever I get uncontrollably angry, I'll leave until I can pull myself together." He wrapped his fingers around my hand and gave it a hard squeeze. "What's fucked up is that most often I can't even figure out why I'm angry, which just upsets me more. I can't read my own thoughts or moods well, but I don't want you to be my punching bag when that happens. I need you to be away from me so I can't hurt you."

I looked at our connected hands that fit against each other perfectly, like they were designed for it. He was willing to work on himself and change, and it meant so much. We both needed to work on our flaws, but everything was easier when we had each other's support.

"There's something I wanted to tell you," I said. "This accident has changed me, too. It reminded me of how short life is, and I don't want to spend it thinking negatively every day. I feel that compared to losing the person you love, holding grudges for the past is petty and brings me resentment and other bad feelings I'd rather exclude from my life. I trust you, and I know you can do much better. I don't want to hold something you regret against you so... I've forgiven you, Hayden. I've forgiven you for everything."

He didn't say a word. He didn't even move, holding my gaze in a way that sent my heartbeat into a frenzy. And then he burst out laughing, despite the pain from his broken ribs. His laugh contained a note of joy and bliss I'd never heard before, and I stared, mesmerized, at him. It was like a sunray in a room shrouded in darkness. A ray of hope and pure happiness. So beautiful.

His laughter dwindled into a soft smile. "You've forgiven me? For real?"

I matched his smile. "Yes. For real."

"*Thank you.*" He smashed his lips on mine for the briefest moment before he peppered my face with kisses. "Thank you. Thank you. Thank you." He returned to my lips and deepened the kiss as he unzipped my jacket and pushed his hand inside. "Thank you..." I couldn't respond, relishing in the feel of his hand roaming across my waist to my neck. "I love you," he whispered into my hair and pressed me against his chest. "Once more, you colored my darkness."

A trail of warmth blossomed in my chest. "I love you too. So much."

He slid his hand down my spine, reaching my lower back. Each of my cells was set alight under his slow caresses.

"What you said that morning about fighting was right," he said. "I didn't mean those words. I didn't mean that you want to control me. It all comes from the stupid part of my mind that simply won't shut up and always makes me doubt."

"I understood. I understood even then that you didn't mean it."

"I can't tell you how sorry I am. So sorry. I know I'm not fair. I always blamed everyone else, even though I know too well how wrong I can be. It's not fair, and I need to change that." His hand halted on my hip, infusing me with burning awareness. "Fighting has been an important part of my life, and it became as natural as breathing to me. It helps me cope with pain and other things, but it's also something that keeps me away from you, and I'm torn. I'm torn between doing what keeps me sane and what's right."

I reached for his hand and intertwined my fingers with his. "I just want what's best for you. I accepted you as you are, but I can't be okay with you getting hurt and risking your life every time you go there. I want you to be safe. Just like you want me safe."

"I know, but it's so hard. I don't know any other way to deal with myself, and I feel lost." He clenched his jaw and diverted his gaze away. "Sarah, I'm scared," he said this so quietly I didn't understand it at first. I was floored that he was so honest, trusting me with his deepest feelings.

I palmed the back of his head and willed him to look at me. "I'm here. I'll always be here, and I'll help you. We're going to find new answers together."

I felt we'd just crossed an important part of our journey. We managed to find a common language, and we weren't going to give up or give in to our demons, which helped me reinforce my trust in us.

He reached for the letter on the top of the stack placed next to his hygiene kit. "I read your letters." Melancholy shaded his face as he scanned its contents. "Everything you wrote, said, or did... It means so much to me. I'm ashamed of all those times I distrusted you or thought you were the worst. You didn't deserve it. You didn't deserve any of that shit, and as the days go by, you show me more and more just how much of a treasure you are. You're my treasure, and I'll always love you and fight for you. *Always*."

I was unable to get a word out, but there was no need, since his lips met mine, and the world stopped to exist. Our tongues danced slowly, giving rise to bursts of pleasure, and I grew warm at his nearness. I couldn't resist moving my hands down his chest and over his stomach, reaching his hips. He moaned and drew his hand up, right under my breast, almost covering it...

"We seriously need to stop," I mouthed breathlessly and stopped his hand. "You're hurt, and we're in a hospital."

"Do you think I care?" he muttered, nuzzling my neck. I was seriously losing my mind. I let out a raspy breath when he placed a wet kiss right below my ear, almost tempted to let him do more.

With regret, I pulled away and sat on the chair. "I want this, but not here and not like this."

He smirked. "So you admit you want me?"

I blushed, looking sideways. "I think we've already confirmed that."

"It doesn't hurt to confirm it again. And again... And again."

My face turned a deeper shade of red, and a laugh barreled out of his mouth. His eyes went down and raked all over my body, making me feel naked, even with all the thick clothes I wore.

"So. Do you remember the whole morning?" I asked him.

"Don't change the subject now."

I dug my teeth into my lip and took his diary out of my bag. His eyes grew round. "The reason I ask is this. You gave me your diary that morning. Do you remember it?"

His amused expression fell. "I don't remember it, but I know I wanted to give it to you. Did you read everything?"

"Not everything. Here." I handed it to him, but he seemed reluctant to take it. "What are you thinking about?"

"I'm thinking how I feel too vulnerable right now, and I hate it."

"I get why you feel this way, but you honestly have no reason to. I'm not judging you, Hayden. Everything I read just helps me get more connected to you. It doesn't repulse me or make me love you any less."

"Does it, now? Are you sure there was nothing I wrote that made you regret being with me?"

"I'm one hundred percent sure. That's who you are, and I love you with all your flaws. I want to be with you during all your highs and lows. That's what love is."

He arched his eyebrows. "Since when did you become a philosopher?"

"I've learned from the best." I pointed my finger at him with a grin. He grabbed it and pulled my hand to his mouth, leaving a soft kiss on my palm.

"I can teach you something else too." His smirk was naughty, which invited heat to my cheeks. "Something more pleasurable that will make you squirm and—"

"Like playing Super Mario? I often squirmed with excitement when I played," I babbled to avert us from his suggestive words.

His mocking expression didn't falter as he studied me. "I don't play video games, Sarah. Only real games." He winked at me. "Here. Take it." He gave me the diary back. "You can return it after you read everything."

"Are you sure?"

"I'm sixty nine percent sure." His smile was wicked, and as if obeying a command, my cheeks reddened all over again.

"Hayden! How do you manage to turn everything into something sexual?" His smile turned into chuckles, and the sound warmed my whole being. He'd smiled more than usual today.

"It's your dirty mind, baby. I'm not doing anything. But..." He motioned me to come to him.

"What?" I asked, refusing to play that game.

"Come here."

Rolling my eyes, I stood up and leaned to him. He caught the back of my head and pulled me closer until his lips touched my earlobe. I shivered.

"But I'll be glad to do *everything* to you," he whispered and placed a tiny kiss below my ear. "Just say the word."

An intense sensation flooded my stomach, and need rushed through my veins. I wondered how he managed to sound and look so sexy when he was stuck in a hospital bed, wearing a patient gown and a cast. Only he could pull that off.

"I can see there's nothing wrong with you. You've completely recovered," I replied sarcastically. I wore an annoyed look on my face, but what I felt was far from it. He made huge progress today, especially compared to the previous days, which brought me immense relief.

He was going to be all right. Whether it took several days or several months, we were going to get through it all, and I was ready for it.

Chapter 9

WITH CHRISTINE GONE, Spanish was bully-free, and I could finally enjoy it and fully focus on the lecture. After their expulsion for setting my hair on fire, Christine, Maya, and their friends had been sent to schools out of Enfield, so I didn't have to worry about seeing them around. Small mercies.

Kevin was in this class too, which surprised me because he looked younger. He hadn't noticed me when he arrived a minute before our teacher, moving to his desk with his eyes glued to the ground to avoid curious onlookers.

I went to him after class, a little anxious about striking up a conversation. "Hi," I said as I stopped next to his desk.

He raised his eyes and just stared at me like he couldn't understand why I would talk to him, but then his gaze lit with recognition. "Right! Sarah, isn't it?"

"Yeah."

He gave me a sheepish smile, and the dimples in his cheeks made an appearance. "Right. *Hola*, S-Sarah." His cheeks and ears grew red. "It's nice to know we have S-S-Spanish together. *Cómo estás?*"

"*Muy bien, y tú?*"

"*Yo también.*"

Our cheeks were now equally red, but despite how awkward we were, I was glad I'd approached him. He looked like he needed friends.

"I see you have new glasses." I motioned at his brown frames.

"Yeah. It was t-time for a change," he joked, but I noticed a trace of dejection in his voice. "The last ones had a b-b-boring color anyway."

My heart sank. I hated Masen for what he'd done to Kevin's glasses. "I didn't see you at school last week."

His expression went from innocent to sour, and he remained silent as we walked out of the classroom. I already regretted my words, fearing they had been too intrusive. Kevin seemed like a good kid, yet he'd had to experience that horrendous humiliation last week, and I had a hunch he'd been hiding or playing hooky.

He pushed his glasses up the bridge of his nose and cleared his throat. "I s-s-skipped some classes," he mumbled with his eyes downcast. We walked through the crowds of students, but he didn't look at anyone, trying to be as invisible as possible. "I was eating in the restroom."

His revelation hit me hard. I stopped and looked at him with a lump in my throat. "I'm so sorry, Kevin. You should've come to Jessica or me. Remember what Jess told you? She said you could hang out with us, and the offer still stands."

He blushed at the mention of her. "Jessica? How is she?" he asked quite shyly, confirming my suspicions.

He likes her.

My smile was gigantic. "She's great. She mentioned just the other day that it would be great if you joined us for lunch."

It was sweet how soft his eyes became at this. "She did?"

"Yes. So let's eat together, okay?"

He nodded quickly, his smile matching mine. "Okay."

Jessica and Kevin were both cute, innocent souls, and they would look perfect together. I was all excited about it as we reached the cafeteria, waving at Jess and Mel who waited next to the doors.

"Hey!" I greeted them.

"Someone's happy," Mel said with an amused twist of her lips and cocked her head at Kevin. "And who are you?"

"Kevin! Hey!" Jessica beamed at him.

"Hey," he replied with dazed eyes as he looked at her. How cute was that? Melissa cleared her throat, picking up on their vibes. Kevin blushed. "Right, s-sorry. I'm Kevin."

Mel's smile outmatched mine. "You mean, you're cute." She winked at him and broke into chuckles when his cheeks turned redder. "Kidding, kiddo. I'm Melissa." She wrapped her arm around Jessica's shoulders and pulled her against her side. "And you're just like our lovely Jessica, all shy and cute. So sweet."

I gaped at her, watching her transform into a matchmaker in a second. Jess and Kevin's gazes didn't move from the ground.

"Mel," I warned her through gritted teeth. "Don't do this now. Let's eat."

Her face was a picture of innocence as she shrugged. "Sure. We don't want to miss the tastiest school food there is, note the sarcasm. Come, children." She motioned to Jess and Kevin to follow her. I met Jess's exasperated gaze with a shake of my head.

"That's Mel for you," I told Kevin apologetically.

"She's nice," he said, and my lips curved up. I was glad we could all get along from the start.

My smile vanished the moment I saw Masen, Blake, and Steven in the lunch line. They stood with their backs to us, so they didn't see us yet. If only it could stay that way.

"What are you going to take?" Kevin asked Jessica, studying the food choices.

"Macaroni with meatballs. One of my favorites."

"Really? Mine too!"

Mel met my gaze with a knowing smile and leaned to me. "OTP," she whispered into my ear. "They're almost as cute as babies. So innocent."

"You act like you're their mother," I whispered back at her.

"More like godmother to their future children. I can already imagine how sweet they will be."

I raised my brow. "Are you nuts? They barely know each other and you're already imagining their children?"

She pressed her hand against her heart and looked into the distance. "But they will know each other, and their love will blossom, and they will be a golden couple, and it will be so perfect, and I'll spoil their children and..." She continued babbling, reminding me of the excessively dramatic actors on the stage when their characters professed their profound love.

"That's too many 'ands' in just one extremely long sentence," I interrupted her monologue when she stopped to take some much-needed air. Luckily, Jess and Kevin were so deep in their conversation about their favorite foods they hadn't heard her. "Besides, we still don't know if Jess likes him too."

"Nonsense. She will for sure, if not already."

I sighed at her stubbornness, but then I met Masen's gaze and tensed. He moved in our direction with Blake and Steven, and my gaze flickered to Blake. He was glaring at Kevin, his jaw set in a hard, unforgiving line.

Jess laughed at something Kevin had said, unaware of Blake. Blake stopped behind them in a wide-legged stance and observed their interaction, the air growing thick with impending conflict.

My stomach gave a nervous jolt. Not this again.

"What are you now? A statue?" Mel scoffed at Blake. "Stop standing there and move already."

Blake ignored her, sneering at Jess when she turned around. She froze when she spotted him. "You fit each other, losers." He indicated Kevin with a jerk of his head and shifted his cold stare to him. "I feel second-hand embarrassment just watching you two."

My blood boiled. I was tired of this. I was tired of watching the same antics over and over again.

"Do you want me to poison your food?" Mel said, pointing at Blake's tray. "There's something seriously wrong with you that you can't stop lashing out. You're walking PMS." *Stop this.*

"The pot calling the kettle black," Masen replied. "I'm expecting you to pull out your voodoo dolls and perform some nasty rituals on us any moment now, Satan." I was going to explode any second. *Enough.*

"Do you even hear yourself? No, of course not. After all, your IQ isn't even average." *Stop!*

"While your IQ, which stands for Irritating Queef, exceeds the highest score ever measured," Masen bit back.

Blake and Steven laughed out loud. "Now that's a burn, sis," Steven said with a lazy smirk, enjoying this drama a little too much. "Seriously, though. Who's this wuss here?" He pointed at Kevin and grimaced. "Look at him. He'll start crying any second—"

"Will you all stop it?!" I erupted, completely losing it.

Everyone grew silent, gaping at me. Blood surged into my cheeks, but for the first time, I didn't care about the maddening tempo of my heart or everyone's unwanted attention. For the first time, I reached my limit and was finally able to speak my mind.

"Every single day! Absolutely every single day you do this, and it's sickening," I glared at Blake and Masen. "Are you jealous?" I directed this at Blake. "You've been obsessed with Jessica, and now you want to ruin her friendship with Kevin? Kevin has never done anything to you, yet you bullied him.

That's completely unfair, and I'm revolted by it. And you"—I pointed my finger at Masen—"Why can't you leave Melissa alone? Stop getting riled by every single thing she says. I just want to have a normal lunch without all of you arguing, bullying, and competing who will throw the best insult! Grow up!"

My adrenaline ebbed away by the end of my rant, which left me breathing heavily as I watched their shocked faces. I garnered the attention of all the students around us, and only now the reality of what I'd done hit me. My old, reclusive shell opened to pull me back into its depths.

Avoiding everyone's gazes, I dashed out of the cafeteria. I needed to escape this place and all these people. I rushed into the nearest restroom and supported myself against the sink, quite disturbed by my reflection in the mirror. My reaction eliminated any pride I might've felt, leaving only desolation in its wake. Would Blake bully Jess more because of me? Would Blake and Masen bully me again? Would the other students ridicule me?

The door opened, and Mel came inside, a small smile curling her lips. Instead of making a witty or sarcastic comment, she just reached me and pulled me into a tight hug.

"I'm proud of you, Sar. That was amazing." Her unexpected words brought about a fuzzy, warm feeling in my chest. She was *proud* of me.

"That was horrible." I closed my eyes shut, feeling like crying. I didn't know where my earlier courage came from, but there was none of it now, only the fear of consequences.

"No, it wasn't. You were fighting back, and it was one of the best things I've ever seen. Honestly, it was way overdue."

"You don't think I exaggerated?"

"Exaggerated? Are you serious? I would've beat them, all the while throwing trash on them, but I like your *tame* version." Humor bubbled in her voice. "It was civil and courteous like you, but at least you put them in their places. You finally managed to conquer your fears and fight back, which is more than awesome, girl."

We separated, and I glanced back at the mirror, studying my confused face. It had a healthy color, unlike it had when Hayden was in a coma, but the dark circles beneath my chestnut brown eyes remained, like a neon sign that said "I hadn't slept in ages." Overall, I didn't look like a badass. I looked like a scared little girl.

I wished Hayden was here so I could get lost in his hug and warmth. Maybe I worried excessively because Hayden wouldn't let them do anything to me, but I didn't want to drag him into this. I didn't want to be that girl who needed saving. I wanted to deal with this on my own.

"Sar, don't overthink it. You're going to be fine." She looked at me in the mirror with an encouraging smile. "Savor what you just did and consider it your small victory because you're much stronger than before, and I'm sure you're going to get even stronger." She flexed her arm and patted her bicep. "Like me or Chuck Norris."

I snorted. I felt slightly better after her pep talk. "Where are Jess and Kevin?"

"They're in the cafeteria. Don't worry, those douchebags left them alone. I threatened Steven that I'd reveal his biggest secret to his friends if he didn't send their asses away." She snickered. "Of course he had to listen to me, so that was settled." Her phone vibrated, and she pulled it out of the pocket.

I was all smiles. "What's his biggest secret?"

Her laugh rang out loud, echoing through the empty restroom. "He'll kill me if he ever finds out I told you, but it's totally worth it." She leaned to my ear and whispered, "He crapped himself in his sleep. A few times, actually."

"What?!" I whipped my head to look at her. I couldn't stop laughing, clutching my stomach when the waves of laughter grew stronger. "How? How is that possible?"

"Don't ask me. He's a true gem, that stupid brother of mine. And it's not something that happened a long time ago, no." Chuckling, she unlocked her phone. "Oh look, it's Mateo."

My smile dropped. A tense silence crashed on us, likely to reveal the sudden pounding of my heart. "You two... You message each other?"

She gave me a sideways glance. "Yes. Is something wrong with that?"

I frowned, unsure of what to say to her. We hadn't mentioned Mateo even once, seeing that my days revolved around Hayden's recovery and Melissa's around her move to Enfield and the divorce. I knew they occasionally texted each other while I was with Mateo, but it never crossed my mind that they might still be in contact.

"No, it's just... I didn't expect that. You two weren't close before I met him, so... I don't know."

"So it's weird we're now friends?" she asked, cutting to the chase.

I shrugged. "It's unexpected."

"Well, we are. He's a good guy, and it's not like I can't hang out with him just because you two don't have a good history."

I didn't like her sharp tone, but I chose to ignore it. She had the right to do whatever she wanted, and I didn't have anything against their friendship. The truth was that the last time I saw him I did something that created the gnawing guilt I still felt whenever I inadvertently thought about him. I wished I could explain my reasoning to him, but I knew I would be the bad guy either way, and I was apprehensive about seeing him again.

"How is he?"

Her thumbs worked fast as she wrote a message. "He's okay." She didn't look away from her screen.

"Is he?" She stopped writing and looked at me. "I just hope he's happy."

She sighed and hit send, maintaining our eye contact as she pocketed her phone and crossed her arms over her chest. "What do you want me to tell you? That he moved on? He didn't move on. He doesn't want to talk about this, but I can see it eats him up on the inside. You and I didn't discuss this, but what you did that day in the hospital was outrageous. He didn't deserve those cruel words."

I turned my back to her and started pacing the room, wishing she could understand my reasoning. "I already told you and Jess about Hayden's disorder and the issues he faces, Mel. As a person with BPD, he has extreme trust issues and insecurities. The thread between his trust and total distrust is so thin even a small thing could break it. I can't even compare his jealousy to a regular guy's jealousy. In that moment, I had to choose between keeping Hayden and my friendship with Mateo, so I made my choice."

"Still, you could've said something else—"

I glanced over my shoulder at her. "What? What could I have said that would prevent the situation from escalating and make Mateo leave the room? However I phrased it, Mateo would still be hurt and I would be the villain.

And I said the truth. I can't be friends with him before Hayden and I can enforce our relationship and trust. I can't stay in contact with him or be friendly when Hayden can easily interpret that as flirting."

"But it's not flirting!"

"But Mateo still has feelings for me!" This made her clamp her mouth shut. "I don't want to lead him on. Honestly, that friendship would be too painful and uncomfortable because I would always be aware he has feelings for me I can't reciprocate, and imagine how he would feel? It would be selfish of me to keep him as a friend when he would always want more. Being near me would make it harder for him to get over his feelings for me. Is there a point to such friendship?"

I'd already experienced this with Kayden, and it had been painful for both of us, but mostly, it had been painful for him. I'd felt horrible for not being able to return his feelings, making things worse by underestimating them because I felt too uncomfortable. Sometimes, cutting all ties was for the best.

"And as I said, Hayden and I need to work on our trust, which comes gradually. Maybe one day we'll all be able to move on from this mess, but until then..."

She tsked, giving me a look filled with sympathy. "Until then you're going to wear that guilt in you."

"Well, it's not like that's something new to me. After everything, it feels like I've felt guilty my whole life." My smile didn't reach my eyes. "Guilt is my middle name. Ha ha."

"Geez, Sar. Come here." She pulled me into another hug. "I know I can be a bitchy friend sometimes, but you know I just want you happy?" I nodded against her shoulder. "I'm sad Mateo and you feel this way, but I understand that both of you need time. On the bright side, things are going well with Hayden, so you can all resolve your issues sooner rather than later."

I broke our embrace, glad that we avoided getting into yet another tiring argument. "Do you think Jess and Kevin are all right?"

"Of course they are! Besides, they need some time alone so their romance can blossom."

I chuckled as I followed her out of the restroom, intending to use the rest of our lunch break to eat at least something. I just hoped one day everything would be okay between Mateo and me and, more importantly, he would be happy. He didn't deserve any less.

Chapter 10

THE SILENCE IN MRS. Black's car on the way to Hayden's house was tense. It showed me her relationship with Hayden hadn't improved, despite how differently she treated her son. I took Hayden's hand next to me to chase away his bad mood, but it did nothing of the sort. His head was turned away from me, his eyes fixed on the snow-coated buildings and shops we passed.

The holidays had started five days ago, and Hayden was finally discharged from the hospital this evening. According to his doctor, he'd showed an extraordinary progress. He remembered more of the day of his accident, and he was able to fully move his hands. He'd been working with a physical therapist the last few days, who helped him walk around the room and ward since his muscles had somewhat atrophied after all those days lying in bed.

They removed the cast from his left arm yesterday, so he could use both hands now, though he had to do the exercises his therapist showed him to regain mobility and reduce stiffness. His broken ribs were still healing, causing him pain from time to time. This irritated him more often than not, but he managed to deal with anger and tension, relying on me whenever it became hard.

We spent all our time together since there was no school, mostly watching funny YouTube videos and movies on his MacBook, and I was able to learn so much more about him. He loved writing poetry, coding, and working out, and disliked pop and country music, anime, and variety shows. His pet peeves were slow drivers, long lines, and people accidentally stepping on his shoes, and he preferred CDs over digital albums, hence the many CDs always lying around his room.

He was ever so sweet, showering me with kisses, declarations of love, and promises that he would take care of me, respect me, and do his best to be better, and it often felt like I was dreaming. Everything was so perfect I was afraid it would shatter. I knew there would be a lot of bumps on our road, but when would the next bump come?

Was this the idealization phase, where everything I did was met with utmost adoration and approval? Was I a person he'd put on a pedestal until I did something wrong and he kicked me off? I'd experienced Hayden's devaluation, so I couldn't delude myself with naive thinking. Sooner or later, I'd enrage him, but we needed to find our way of dealing with it.

I held onto the words Kayden told me a long time ago: *"Whenever one person becomes his enemy, they're on Hayden's black list for good. However, he keeps coming back only to those he truly, deeply cares about, despite everything."*

"So what would you like for dinner?" Carmen asked us, ending the silence between us.

She took a paid leave so she could stay with Hayden and take care of him during his recovery, which was a huge step forward. She was finally ready to fight for her son and give him love, and I was happy she stopped using her job as her refuge. She learned to accept him and decided to help him on his long journey to recovery.

This didn't mean that Hayden changed the way he treated his mom. Quite the opposite. The more she tried to regain his trust, the more he retracted into himself, refusing to let her come any closer to him.

"Hayden?" I asked him, looking at his profile. He didn't move; his eyes remained on the scenery outside. "What would you like?" *Nothing.* He didn't even blink.

I wished I knew what was going on inside his head. I thought he would be happy that he was going home at last, but he withdrew into himself the moment we exited the hospital and stayed silent, wearing a constant frown on his face.

"How does pizza sound?" she asked, glancing between Hayden and me in the rear-view mirror.

"It sounds great. What do you think, Hayden?" His unresponsive hand was cold beneath mine, and I wondered if he was aware I still held it. His eyes were glazed, like he was in his own world, seeming troubled by something. "Hayden? Are you okay?"

I nudged him, and he finally moved, giving me a disinterested look. "I'm not hungry."

"You have to eat something. You need energy," Carmen told him. "Besides, this will be our first time to eat all together, and I can't wait to—"

"I'm not hungry," he repeated sharply, glaring at her.

"But Hayden—"

"I said, I'm not hungry!" He yanked his hand away from mine and crossed his arms over his chest.

She winced. The corners of her lips dipped down, but she didn't argue with him. "Okay. No dinner then. I'll make something for you, Sarah."

I didn't know how to react so I just nodded. The atmosphere between them was strained, and I didn't feel comfortable being in the middle. I didn't know the reason for Hayden's mood change or if I contributed to it or not.

"I'm also not hungry," I told her, which was true. Since Hayden's accident, my meals consisted of wolfing down food without enjoying it whatsoever, and this regime didn't change. I had zero appetite.

"That's not okay. You must eat. You're already too thin, and I don't want you to get sick."

There it was, the thing adults always said to skinny children. I smiled, touched that she cared enough for me to say it.

Hayden's accident helped me form a stronger connection with her. We spent long hours sitting next to each other in the hospital, shedding tears together and letting our sorrow bring us closer, and it was etched in my memories forever. It reminded me of the moments we shared after Kayden's death, but this time there was no suffocating guilt that held me back from reaching out to her. This time we shared our fears, regrets, and wishes, which helped me understand her better. It also brought me her unconditional support and the motherly warmth I never had.

"Thank you, Mrs. Black."

"I told you already to call me Carmen, sweetie. We're not strangers."

My smile broadened. "Yes, Carmen."

Hayden looked through the window again with a darker expression. Acting on an impulse, I kissed his cheek, and his eyes widened at me.

"What was that for?"

"I just want you to feel good," I whispered into his ear and kissed his earlobe, causing him to shudder. I smiled. It was great to know my kisses affected him the same way his affected me. "What's wrong?"

He held my gaze, and for a moment, I thought he was going to tell me, but then he tightened his jaw and looked away, refusing to open up to me. "Nothing."

"It can't be nothing when you're like this."

"Stop pushing me for answers. You won't get any."

My stomach curled. I leaned away from him, having a hard time accepting that he wasn't able to share his problems with me in moments like this. Would he ever be able to open up to me when he was the most vulnerable? Would he ever let himself rely on me when he needed it the most?

I gazed out of my window, entangled deeper in my rushing thoughts, when I felt his hand on mine. My eyes snapped to his. "Hayden?"

"I'm sorry," he mouthed. "I suck at this. Let's talk about it later, okay?"

"Okay."

I covered his hand with my other hand and let him lean his head against my shoulder, pretending I didn't notice Carmen's curious glances in the rearview mirror. He couldn't share his thoughts with me, but our closeness and silent touches would have to do for now.

Hayden refused to let us help him walk when we arrived to their house, struggling to maintain balance as he trudged through the snow with his duffel bag hung over his shoulder. Carmen and I had cleaned the driveway today, removing the piles of snow that had accumulated on the ground, but there was a thick layer of snow now that slowed him down.

I followed Hayden to his room, while Carmen went to the kitchen to make dinner, giving us some privacy. As we reached Hayden's room, I glanced at Kayden's door, and my heart swelled with the memories of this afternoon.

Earlier today, I gave in and went into his room, spending some time reminiscing about Kayden and all our moments together. Out of all the rooms I cleaned these days, Kayden's room was the only one I hadn't entered because I was scared of drowning in the old, potent emotions that inhabited my being.

However, there was no bitterness or crushing sadness as I sat there in silence and let my gaze wander around his neat room. I was able to smile and think about all those hours we'd spent on his floor playing video games, watching anime and movies on his laptop, or reading mangas. I was able to remember him without regrets and guilt. Finally, after more than two years, I was able to move on and let my broken heart heal piece by piece on this long path of self-acceptance.

I smiled and entered Hayden's room. I was instantly greeted by the remnants of his strong scent that always allured me, and a pleasant shudder rolled down my spine. Hayden plopped down on his computer chair and buried his head into his hands, taking a deep breath as he threw his head back.

"Hayden, what's going on? Talk to me."

I crouched in front of him and palmed his wide open knees, but he didn't move, breathing heavily into his hands. Worry clouded my mind. I pulled his hand slowly to me and intertwined our fingers.

"Don't hide things from me. I want to share your pain and troubles. Just like you once told me, I can't be okay when you're not okay, so let me take the weight off your shoulders."

His eyes flew open, fiery with an emotion I couldn't recognize. They burned into my heart, mind, and world, and I couldn't breathe. I pressed a kiss on his abraded knuckle, holding his stare that grew darker.

I wasn't aware of moving, but suddenly I was kneeling between his legs. I cupped his cheeks as we looked at each other, connected to him in an inexplicable way. Our breaths merged as our gazes roamed across our faces, and all coherent thoughts ceased to exist for a few blissful moments.

"Please stay with me," he whispered and pressed his forehead against mine. "Stay here tonight."

My heart began its wild rhythm. I wanted nothing more than that. "Yes. I'll stay."

He cracked a huge smile and wrapped his arms around my waist, bringing me closer to him. He pressed his thighs into me, his hands moving low on my back in an intimate move, and heat flared through me.

"I'll ask your mom to let me sleep on the couch in the living room."

His smile faltered. "No. Stay in my room," he implored.

His plead touched something deep in me. "I... I'm not sure that's okay. Besides, Carmen is here and it might not be appropriate—" I didn't even finish my sentence when I saw him shut down. He moved his chair back and stood up abruptly, moving over to his window.

"Forget it."

I inhaled an unsteady breath. "Hayden? I—"

"I said, *forget it*. You can go now. I don't want you to waste your time on me here. Go home and get some rest."

I got up to my feet and twisted my hands together, reproaching myself for always letting my insecurities win. "No. I want to be with you. I—"

He gripped the window sill. "Go home. I'm tired, and I don't need you here anymore. Good night." He didn't look away from the window; his posture was rigid as he took quick breaths.

"No." I erased the space between us and hugged him from behind.

Now that I knew how he functioned, the meaning of his words was more than clear to me. I hurt him so he tried to push me away, but letting him push me away would convince him I didn't care. In reality, he wanted me to stay and fight for him, but his mind twisted it into this.

"I'm not going anywhere. I didn't say that because I don't want to be with you or because you're a burden to me. I said that because I'm embarrassed, okay? This would be my first time to spend a night in my boyfriend's room, and I didn't want your mom to think I'm an easy girl, but then again, I don't really care if she thinks that. I want to stay here. That's what I've wanted for so long, so as you'd say, screw my insecurities. I'll stay." I finished blabbing on a deep inhale, hoping I didn't say anything that could unsettle him and push him further away.

I rested my head against his shoulder. "I love you, Hayden. I'm sorry for always being so insecure about insignificant things. That's something I'm trying to change, and I don't want you caught up in the middle of it."

"Then why can't you relax for once and be impulsive? Why do you have to overthink everything?" His sharp voice cut deeply through me, but I didn't let it submerge me in pain.

"Because I've been overthinking my whole life, and now I don't know how to loosen up. I have yet to learn how to shut off all these negative thoughts and enjoy the moment." I kissed his shoulder, worried because he had yet to move. "Just know I'll always love you, and I'll stay here because I want to. I'll always stay."

Neither of us said a word for a long while. His breathing evened, but he was still motionless, and I just hoped he would believe me. I hoped he would be able to see this from a different angle.

"Hayden?" I curled my fingers into his shirt, tightening my grip around him. "Please, say something."

He didn't, not until he took my hand on his chest and kept it firmly there. "Why didn't you put up new blinds?" I glanced at my bare window across from us, surprised by this sudden topic. "That's something I thought about a lot. Was it because you were afraid of what I could do to you if you defied me?"

His question awoke new questions I had no answer to. I never thought much about it, giving in to him all too easily. Why didn't I put new blinds?

I stepped back, mourning the loss of the heat his body radiated. He didn't face me, keeping his gaze on my window. "I honestly don't know. I mean, I was afraid of you, yes, but..." My chest tightened when the realization slowly formed out of the dark recesses of my mind. "But I also..."

"What?"

"I felt connected to you that way." I reached for my chest, startled by the truth.

All that time... All that time I thought I hated him, fearing and despising everything he did, yet some part of me had yearned for his attention. I never craved the things he did to me; I craved his eyes on me. I craved to be in his mind and occupy his thoughts like he'd occupied mine. I was so sure I wanted him out of my life, blind to the attraction that drew me to him. He was the opposite pole of the aberrant magnet that never failed to pull me in.

I didn't notice him move, my lips parting when he stopped inches from me and tipped my chin up. His eyes were warm and affectionate, and my breath caught.

"You and I both went through a lot before we accepted our feelings. I was attracted to you no matter how hard I fought it. I tried to get you out of my mind, but you were always there. I did such sick shit to you without even realizing I needed you if I wanted to stay sane."

He backed me to the wall and caged me in with his arms. I grew hot, aware of his body that was almost flush against mine...

"I hate myself for always being a dick. I'm trying my hardest to keep control over my emotions." His lips caressed my earlobe as he whispered into my ear, and it became difficult for me to focus on his words. He moved to kiss me, but three knocks rapped at the door.

"Sarah?" Carmen said through the door. "Dinner is ready."

Hayden's lips brushed against my ear, tantalizing my sensitive skin. "Go," he whispered. "Unless you want me to devour you right here and now."

I had to clear my throat two times so I could speak. "I'll be right there!"

Hayden's seductive smile only added to my muddled thoughts. I seriously needed some distance away from him so I would remember how to breathe and act normally.

I pulled away. "I'll tell her I'll stay here."

"Great. In the meantime, I'm going to take a shower."

Images of naked Hayden filled my mind, and I groaned involuntarily. *Relax, Sarah. He's just going to take a shower. No need to get too excited about it.*

Hayden didn't miss my reaction. His lips formed a full smile as he watched me put up a fight against my not so innocent thoughts. "It's just a shower, baby. No need to make a big deal out of it. *But* if you want to join me—"

"Um, I think I hear your mom calling me again. See you!"

I bolted out and closed the door behind me like I was being chased by a serial killer. I blushed harder when his laughter followed me as I went downstairs to join Mrs. Black, all the while hoping my face didn't show what exactly was on my mind.

• • • •

"HOW DO YOU LIKE MY pasta?" Carmen asked when I swiped the last piece off my plate. She'd just shared some funny stories from her work, and I'd been having a great time.

I stopped for a second to study her face that looked more relaxed than just a couple of days ago. She'd been stoic all that time, but it had taken a toll on her. Her blue-green eyes had lost their usual light, surrounded by more wrinkles than ever, and her face had never looked more aged.

"It's delicious. Your cooking is amazing as always."

"Thank you. I don't have time for cooking anymore, but I miss it. Since I'm not working now, I'll make more meals for Hayden and you."

I blushed, surprised she'd mentioned me. "Me?"

Her smile was soft, reaching a deep part of me that needed her care more than I'd ever admit. "Yes, honey. You. I want to help with anything you need. I'll be there for you, too."

Emotions clogged my throat, and I put my fork down on my plate. "Thank you. I... I appreciate that."

My reticence reared its head and forced me away from any form of closeness. I felt so much, but I couldn't let those feelings burgeon, because if I did, I'd be crushed if she turned her back on me like everyone else one day. So, I just gave her a tight-lipped smile, hoping she would drop the subject.

She didn't. "Since you don't have a good relationship with your mother, I want you to know you can always rely on me. I'd been a bad mother myself, and I had my own fair share of mistakes, but Hayden's accident helped me remember what I never should've forgotten."

She reached across the table and cupped my hand, and I stiffened at the unexpected touch. I didn't know what to say. I didn't know how to act. So I waited for her to continue.

"Life can be cruel. I could've lost my both sons that night, and now this, and the implications of it are tremendous. Hayden is my only family left, and if I'd lost him too... If he died this time..." She shook her head. "I'm ashamed, so ashamed. I'm ashamed to admit that after seventeen long years, I've finally accepted Hayden. I've finally accepted him for who he is."

Her first tear connected with the wooden table, a tiny, a glimmering drop marking the start of many more to come as she held my hand and cried quietly.

And I let my shield crumble, tired of trying to stay emotionally detached. I stood up and came behind her, hugging her in a way I'd never hugged my own mother. I placed my head on her shoulder and closed my eyes. My tears fell on her blouse.

I'd never felt closer to her than now. Her hands held me and didn't let me move, and I snuggled up to her without conscious thought.

"You're a wonderful girl, Sarah. I always liked you." She tugged me to sit on the chair next to her, her eyes conveying a slew of emotions that stole more and more of me. "I'll be honest with you. I wanted you to be with Kayden. I expected him to tell me one day that you two got together, and I wanted nothing more than that, but we can't control our hearts. You always only had eyes for Hayden." She ran her hand through my hair, and a smile pulled at the corner of her lips. "And I'm so happy Hayden managed to win your heart. That boy deserves it. He deserves it more than anyone, and I'm glad the girl he fell for is you. I look at both of you as my children, and I'll support you through everything."

My heart was sent into a tailspin. "I..." My voice was foreign to me, and I cleared my throat.

I wanted to tell her so much, but nothing came to my mind as new tears trickled down my flushed cheeks. I felt something important changing in me, which gave me life and hope despite all my darkness and doubts, and I wanted this to be so much more than a fragile, precious thing that could break any moment.

"So you can talk to me about anything," she went on. "I'll always be here to listen to you and help you. I'll be a mom to you too. You can always rely on me."

She pulled me into her embrace, unlocking more locks I'd put around my heart, and for the first time ever, I felt like this house could be my home. One day, I could feel like I belonged here.

"Thank you for everything. I appreciate this so much."

She caressed my cheek with the back of her hand, giving me so much with such a seemingly small gesture. "Don't thank me, sweetie. I'm the one who should thank you. Hayden and I are so lucky to have you. You're special. Don't ever forget that."

Chapter 11

EMOTIONS BUBBLED IN my chest as I climbed the stairs. In some unfathomable way, Carmen and I had bonded, and I was beside myself with joy. My cheeks were beet red when I told her I was going to spend night in Hayden's room, but she only cast me a knowing smile before she gave me the green light.

I knocked on Hayden's door. "Come in."

I entered and closed the door behind me as I raised my gaze, only to come to an abrupt stop. He wore only his gray Adidas sweatpants, which put his ripped chest and stomach on full display. My eyes roamed over the tattoos on his chest, shoulders, and upper arms, trying to take in every design and word that decorated his taut skin. He was covered with many words, just like the walls of his room.

"I... I never knew you had so many tattoos." *I never knew you were so ripped and gorgeous...*

Get a hold of yourself, Sarah!

His amused face told me he knew exactly what I was thinking. He claimed the space between us and stopped right in front of me. Being this close to him, it was next to impossible for me not to stare at his tattoos, but I managed to tear my gaze away and meet his transfixing eyes.

"Come on. Look at them. I know you want to." He tipped my chin and grazed my lips with his, sending my heart into overdrive. "Try to find yours," he whispered and stepped away to give me space.

My tattoo! I remembered his text with a jolt to my chest. I was finally able to see it.

Enticed, I began exploring, admiring the talent of the person who had created these realistic tattoos. I caught sight of several single words dotting his body randomly.

Tainted
Shattered
Jaded
Defeated

Hated
Forgotten
Broken
Pained
Damaged

And much more.

The pressure built quickly in my head and chest, rising with each grief-striking word on his skin. My eyes stopped on a punching line on his bicep.

"Save me from the pain that comes from you."

Then another.

"All those lies. All those lies they feed me. There's no peace within."

And another...

"Wake me up from the nightmare that I am."

I looked at his other bicep.

"Darkness is what I seek
Forgiveness is what I need
Refusal is what I get
Loneliness is what I have"

I breathed out a raspy sigh. "Hayden..."

He glanced at that spot. "That kind of sums up how I've felt my whole life."

I trailed my fingers over it, saddened by the amount of pain that breathed life into these words. "I'm so sorry. How I wish you never went through anything like this. I'm sorry."

He just shrugged. With a quiet sigh, I shifted my gaze to a large tattoo of a river that started from the upper left side of his chest and spread across his left shoulder. The surface of the water was shimmering, reminding me of the Connecticut River we visited that night more than a month ago, and its poignant meaning struck me.

He'd told me he loved rivers and that watching their shimmering surface calmed him. It was moving that he'd decided to tattoo this.

"It's beautiful," I whispered, fully aware of his eyes that followed my every move.

A glance to the left revealed an undefined black shape with smudged edges that occupied his right shoulder and skin above the right side of his chest. It reminded me of a cloud. The profound blackness twisted something in my gut.

"What does this represent?" I brushed my fingertips against it, and goosebumps appeared on his skin. I met his eyes that held a breathtaking mix of emotions.

"It represents my emptiness."

"Your emptiness."

I caressed the area this tattoo covered, and he took a sharp breath as our eyes clashed. He liked when I touched him like this. I moved my fingers slowly over his skin.

"Can you tell me what it feels like? That emptiness?"

He let his gaze wander around the room as he contemplated the answer. "It starts from not knowing who you are. Not knowing what to do with your life. You have no purpose, and you feel worthless and lost. So you just keep wandering around, asking yourself what's the point. You feel like the gaping hole that sucks all your happiness out of you will never disappear."

I looked at the tattoo, feeling his pain coursing through me. How hard his days must've been with all those negative thoughts and doubts. It saddened me that he had to experience things no one ever should.

"I felt lonely for so long," he continued. "And it always felt endless. I have a void that feels like it's never going to be filled, and the worst part is that I don't even know what can fill it. There are so many things I need: happiness, security, self-trust, love, *you*, but everything always seems out of reach. It seems unreal. So I go around in circles every single day and hope I'll survive tomorrow, which is most likely going to be another shitty day."

"I'm here." I cupped his cheek. "I'm real, and I'll always love you and make you happy. I want to help you with everything you need. Remember that. Tomorrow may be difficult, but we'll get through it together."

He covered my hand on his face and leaned into it, closing his eyes. "Thank you, Sarah. Everything feels easier when you're with me. Somehow, you ease the pain and bring light into my life."

"I'm a lighthouse, and you're a lost sailor on the sea?" I cracked a half-baked joke to erase the remains of dejection from his gaze.

He raised his eyebrow. "You really need to work on your jokes, baby. I'll forget what it means to laugh if you keep your cringe-worthy humor."

I tsked. "Touché."

My eyes snagged on the familiar words underneath the tattoo of emptiness.

"I'M PAINED, LOSING MY SOUL,
UNTIL DARKNESS SWALLOWS ME WHOLE."

These words were in the middle of a smeared circular shape that emphasized them. The question I'd always wanted to ask arose again, and I met his burning gaze.

"Why do you think you're losing your soul? Is it because of your emptiness?"

He didn't respond immediately, devouring me with his eyes. Standing next to him like this felt more intimate than anything we'd experienced together so far, and I basked in all the feelings that surfaced and pushed me further into his world. He was opening up to me more than ever before, letting me see all of him.

"I've known my darkness for so long." His raspy voice brimmed with emotions. "It destroyed me piece by piece until there was nothing. Until I lost all hope and forgot there was ever anything good to begin with. Until I completely gave in to that inner monster, which grew stronger with each disappointment, hurt, and betrayal. I got so used to being rejected and neglected that this became my reality—a fucked up world with no goodness or love."

Our fingers intertwined. "I felt like you for a long time, which is why I understand what it means to see the world as completely black," I said. "So many vile, selfish people, who care about nothing else but themselves. But then there are moments like this that show me this world has a lot more shades than we think. It shows me that true happiness is possible."

"That's why I don't ever want to lose you, Sarah. You brought everything good in my life. You helped me realize there's so much I can give to the world. You remind me that it's worth fighting against my messed up mind."

I placed my hand over his heart and his pulse quickened. I smiled. "Well, that's because, just like you once said, your heart belongs to me." I winked and lowered my gaze to my hand.

My next words died on my lips when I noticed a tattoo of tiny stars. Did they represent Kayden and his love for stars?

"The stars? Why..." My voice faded when I read the small lines under them right across his heart. At first I didn't understand them, but I read them again, and my heart stopped.

They didn't represent Kayden.

No, they represented something entirely else, and I recalled the memory I'd buried in my mind a long time ago.

It was Kayden and Hayden's fifteenth birthday party. It was overly crowded, so I had to elbow my way to the table with tequila shots in the corner of the living room.

I hadn't been sure about coming here, because this was also Hayden's party. He didn't hide his annoyance when he heard Kay had invited me, and he even told me I'd regret it if I came. I would've listened to him if only Kay hadn't pleaded with me to come.

I did my best to blend in and steer clear of him. Thankfully, he was too occupied with enough alcohol and girls to pay attention to me, but then again, jealousy stirred deep in my belly. Whenever I looked for him in the crowd, he was kissing with a different girl, and I wished I could eradicate these images from my mind.

So I drank. I'd never gotten drunk before, but right now I hoped alcohol would drown my anxiety and help me forget Hayden's dark eyes filled with animosity that haunted me even in my dreams. Once more, I wished he could see something more in me than a perfect target to torture. I'd tried so many times to quench my feelings for him, but it was useless. I couldn't prevent my mind from creating all those fantasies in which he would grow to love me.

I snatched another glass of tequila and emptied it in one gulp, not bothering to take a lemon or salt. My vision was somewhat blurry, and I struggled with balance as I put the empty glass on the table.

I felt unusually carefree. I had so much energy in me, I needed to dance it out. I wanted to dance like there was no one else in the room and be wild.

My eyes searched for Kay and found him dancing with Natalie across the room. He was dressed the same as Hayden, in a black crew neck shirt and dark jeans that fit their well-defined bodies all too well. Kayden wanted to spend time with me, but I told him not to be silly and stay with his girlfriend. Besides, that girl already disliked me enough. I didn't need to give her more reasons to sneer at me whenever she saw me or create nasty rumors behind my back. She was a top class bitch, but there was no doubt she was madly in love with him. Also, Kay claimed he knew her better than anyone else, so maybe there was some good in her. Maybe.

I looked past a few teenagers swaying to the beat to Hayden sitting on a couch with a girl on his lap, who was busy kissing his neck. My jealousy flared up, but then I met Hayden's stare, and every other feeling but anticipation faded. It was short lived, though, because his eyes held only contempt for me, which put another dent in my stupid hope. I would never see anything in his eyes but hate.

I reached for another tequila shot. I was about to pick it up when someone's hand stopped me before I could reach the glass.

"Don't you think you've had enough?" Kayden asked me. His eyes were glazed, showing he'd drunk more than enough alcohol himself, but he was handling it way better than me.

"Kayden!" I squealed. "Always so caring!" I actually giggled, acting like all those girls who flirted with Kayden in the school hallways. I chided myself internally.

He sighed. "Okay. Now I know you've had enough."

"Nooo, not quite. Where is Natalie?"

"She's somewhere with Christine and the others."

"She'll be jeaaalous." More giggles escaped my lips.

He raised one eyebrow and half-smiled. "It doesn't matter. She knows you're my best friend, so she has to get over it. Come on." He grabbed my arms when I stumbled, and I let out yet another giggle. He pulled me after him.

"Wait. Where are you taking me?"

"To the kitchen. You're drunk, and I want to get you some water."

I dug my heels into the floor and tugged on his hand to stop him. "Don't be a party pooper, Kay! Let's dance!"

He was surprised by my behavior, but he didn't complain as I led him to where people were dancing. The music changed to an upbeat pop song, and everyone turned into dancing maniacs who didn't care if they looked embarrassing or not. Just like me. I did a few silly dance moves I wouldn't dare try in public otherwise, and Kayden grinned, watching me shake my hips with my arms raised in the air.

He put his hands on my waist and matched my movements, giving in. His eyes glimmered happily as he looked at me. "You're so crazy."

"Crazy is my middle name, yeah."

"Are you enjoying the party?"

"My friend tequila is great company."

He laughed and removed a strand of my hair from my sweaty face. "No more tequila for you. If I knew you would try to get yourself drunk, I never would've let you out of my sight."

"Oh come on, Kay. Don't be so overprotective. I'm fine."

I was far from fine, which showed very quickly. The tempo of the song went faster, and it became more difficult for me to maintain my balance as we sped up. I constantly tripped over my own feet, growing queasier, so when Kayden twirled me around, I felt like I was going to puke.

I clamped my hand over my mouth and bent, hoping I wouldn't embarrass myself right in front of all these people. They were from our school, so if I threw up, I'd be bullied more than ever.

Kayden grasped my shoulders and leveled his face with mine. "Can you hold it in until we reach the bathroom?"

"I think so."

"Come on. I'll help you."

We moved through the walls of people who pushed into each other, slowing us down, but luckily, the worst of nausea had passed, and I was able to keep it together.

"Take deep breaths," Kayden instructed as he guided me. "Keep your head up."

I raised my head to look at him, more than grateful that he was doing this for me. My vision was too blurry, and I felt dizzy, but I managed to focus on his face. "You're an angel, Kay."

"And you're drunk. Don't stop. Just a little bit more."

The bathroom downstairs wasn't available, so he took me to his room. A couple of people were making out in the dark hallway, but Kay didn't pay any attention to them. I grew sleepy by the time we entered his room, so I sank into Kayden's soft bed and rolled over to my back with my legs and arms flung widely apart.

I yawned. I no longer felt queasy. Kay didn't bother to flip a switch, so it was dark, and the bright glow of the moon was the only source of light.

He stopped above me with a frown. "Aren't you going to puke?"

"I'm fine now. Don't jinx it!" I closed my heavy lids, smiling from ear to ear.

His long sigh told me just how much he didn't believe me, but I was too sleepy to care about it. The music was just a dull throb in the distance, and my ears buzzed in the quiet of his room.

It seemed like I closed my eyes for just a few seconds, but when I opened them, I was alone in the room. I squinted at the glowing stars on the ceiling, trying to see them clearly, but there were so many of them, and I was too drunk. I smiled when I remembered Kay telling me he was going to take them off because they were childish, but I thought they were cute. They suited his sweet personality.

Someone opened the door, and I tilted my head back to see who it was through blurriness. I was barely able to discern Kayden's tall form as he closed the door and approached me. I returned my gaze to the stars above me.

"Kayden, you didn't have to check up on me. I told you I was fine."

He didn't say anything. He sat next to me on the bed, and out of the corner of my eye, I saw him look at the stars too.

"I honestly don't know what you see in stars. Don't get me wrong, they're beautiful. It's just that I really, reeaally tried to find some deeper meaning to them, but for me they're just countless tiny spots that confuse me instead of giving me any answers."

He didn't reply, and I wondered if I offended him. I'd never admitted to Kay how I felt about space and all those things that fascinated him because I didn't want to hurt his feelings, but something spurred me on to be completely honest with him now.

"I'm sorry if this offends you. That wasn't my intention. I mean, I admire your passion, but whenever I think about all that unlimited space, I feel overwhelmed. It's scary, you know? The more we learn about it, the more we see that we know nothing, and it's scary how tiny, so tiny, we are compared to it."

Kayden seemed kind of different, and I felt completely at ease. Inexplicably, he gave off something that made me feel like I could tell him my deepest thoughts, which I'd never truly done before. Or maybe that was just because of alcohol and it had nothing to do with him.

I looked from one star to another aimlessly, aware of the heat of Kayden's body. He'd shifted so that he was closer to me, and his hand, which lay next to mine on the bed, was almost touching me. For a reason I couldn't understand, I wanted that hand to cover mine, but just the thought confused me.

"Now I'm blabbering, and I'm probably boring you, but thank you for listening to me." I glanced at him, but he didn't move his gaze from the stars, so I couldn't see his face.

"Happy birthday," I whispered and closed my eyes, suddenly emotional. "Thank you for everything. You made me the happiest I've ever been, and I'll always treasure the moments with you."

Remaining silent, he took my hand. The feel of his skin on my skin was pleasant, giving momentum to my pulse.

"Your hand is so warm." I giggled. I was a bit confounded that his touch felt this nice. "And I'm drunk."

Not missing a beat, he moved his hand up and caressed my wrist with his thumb in a circular motion, which felt intimate. My blood pumped faster. I'd never felt this way with Kayden, and the more we stayed like this, the more unusual I felt, conflicted about the emotion that grew more potent with each stroke of his thumb. I couldn't understand why he was doing this.

I sat up and faced him, meeting his gaze. "What—" His eyes and unsmiling expression gave him away.

Hayden.

I froze, almost sobered up. I racked my brain to remember every single word I'd said since he came in.

His eyes were so dark, verging on black, but there was no usual coldness in them. Instead, they were filled with warmth I'd never seen before, and I couldn't *begin to understand it. His fixed stare created a concoction of feelings that had always brewed under the surface and waited for him to bring them out.*

Just earlier this evening, I hoped for this, and now that I was seeing it... Was this another one of his games? My heart battered against my ribs, hungry for this small sign of affection from him, clinging to the naïve hope that this might mean something for him.

My gaze fell on his hand that still held mine, and fire skimmed along my nerves. I couldn't believe he was holding me like this.

No, he must be playing me. I snatched my hand away and stood up, growing dizzy again as I glared at him. I expected him to turn this into a cruel joke any second. "Hayden? What are you doing?"

He took in my hostile reaction and almost instantly, his eyes lost all their warmth, mockery replacing a brief confusion on his face. "I'm listening to your bullshit and asking myself how much more stupid you can get."

A fresh wave of nausea crashed over me, and I didn't know if it had all to do with my drunken state or his horrible words. I was furious, mostly angry with myself for not looking at his face sooner.

"Stop calling me stupid and stop playing with me! I'm not stupid, and I'm not your plaything! Don't ever pretend you're Kayden again."

"Or what? Stop shitting me. Besides, I didn't pretend. You assumed I was Kayden. I just played along."

Why? Why did he come here and touch me like that? He'd never showed me anything but hate, and I wished I could know what had been going through his head.

I didn't voice my questions. I headed for the door, but he blocked my way.

"Let me pass, Hayden."

He took a step closer. "And if I don't?"

I bolted past him, but he grabbed me and pressed me against the wall. He seized my hands and brought them above my head, and my body warmed with his sudden nearness. He positioned his other hand low on my hip and brought his lips too close to mine, taunting me, but what shocked me the most was how much I enjoyed this. I was afraid and excited, studying his fierce eyes that burned into me.

"You're nothing, Sarah, and you'll always be nothing. I don't know why Kayden wastes his time on scum like you, but let me make this clear: as long as

I'm here, I'll make sure you suffer. And when you think it can't be worse, I'll hurt you so much you'll wish you never entered our lives."

I shuddered with fear and disgust. I fought to set myself free, but his hold on my hands was too strong, and the more I struggled, the stronger his grip was. Now that we were this close, I could smell his fragrance that affected me more than I wanted to admit, making me susceptible to him, and the juxtaposition of my feelings sent my mind spiraling.

"You're sick," I bit out boldly thanks to all those tequila shots. I'd never dared talk back to him, but now that I saw his face twist into a grimace of surprise and rage, I felt like I'd been missing out on it because I enjoyed it too much.

"I'm sick—of you. So sick. You're going down. Kayden is an idiot for thinking you're something special, but I'll never make that mistake."

He pushed away from me abruptly and walked out. My stupid body actually longed for him, thriving on the encounter that wasn't romantic in the slightest but interpreting it as such.

He would never be mine, but I blurted out the words the sober me wouldn't ever say, "Never say never."

Chapter 12

I BLINKED RAPIDLY AS the memory of their fifteenth birthday dissolved, and a horde of butterflies settled in the pit of my stomach. I focused on the lines across his heart again and reread them.

> *"Countless tiny spots that confuse me instead of giving me any answers*
> *Whenever I think about all that unlimited space, I feel overwhelmed*
> *The more we learn about it, the more we see that we know nothing*
> *It's scary how tiny, so tiny, we are compared to it'*
>
> *Just the way I feel about you."*

These were the exact words I told him on his fifteenth birthday, combined with the last sentence that reflected his deepest feelings.

I slowly met his gaze. I'd completely suppressed the memory of that night in Kay's room. Hayden was so different then, amplifying my feelings for him, which only made everything hurt so much more when he subjected me to more bullying.

"You... You tattooed my words?" *Right across his heart.*

He nodded. "Yeah. That's your tattoo."

"But why did you do that? Why these words?"

There was so much love and need in his eyes, and my chest throbbed hard. "Because that's exactly when I started liking you. I even wrote down these words on the paper back then and left it in my drawer."

My heart beat fast, fueled by his nearness and words. I'd thought I didn't interpret his actions correctly. I'd been so sure that was a game for him. But I couldn't have been more wrong.

"I came to Kayden's room to intimidate you, but in the end, it was you who intimidated me."

Oh. "How?"

His finger trailed my jaw on its way to my neck, and it was tantalizing. "I saw you lying on Kayden's bed, and I completely forgot about my plan. I was only able to feel. Before I knew what I was doing, I sat next to you, and it was something I never experienced before. I looked at those stupid stars on the ceiling, but I didn't see them. Instead, I saw your face, and all I was able to think about were your words. I related to the way you felt about the universe. I related to your feelings of confusion and fear because that was exactly how I felt about you the more I saw you."

I shuddered when he caressed my earlobe with his thumb. "I thought it was all just a game. I was sure you were playing with me."

"Everything would've been easier for me if that were the case, but it wasn't. For a moment, I was able to forget we were enemies, but then you saw it was me and not Kayden. I was terrified of what I felt in that moment, so I tried to push you away."

"When did you tattoo this?

Sorrow flickered across his face. "I went through a hard period after you rejected me at the hospital." He swallowed and looked away. "I hated you, Sarah. I really did. But then, I didn't. I couldn't. Even when I thought you were the worst, I kept coming back to you, and one day I was drunk and so high on thoughts of you I just wanted to have that moment on me. So I tattooed that most important moment over my heart."

Tears collected in my eyes. "Did you ever regret tattooing it?"

"No. It's twisted, right? But no, I never regretted it."

"So you tattooed the words that symbolize the moment it all began for you. That's..."

He shifted his weight, tilting his head to the side. "That's too much?"

"No, not at all." He'd listened to me and memorized my words, and now they were forever imprinted on his skin. The first tears spilled out, and I squeezed my eyes shut.

"Hey." He brought me closer to him. I shook as I shed silent tears. "Hey. Don't cry. Why are you crying?"

"I'm just so happy. Thank you for getting this tattoo." When I opened my eyes, I saw him smiling at me with affection in his gaze.

"How about you?"

"What do you mean?"

"When did you start liking me?"

My heart fluttered against my ribs. I brushed my tears away and sniffed. "It happened more than a month after I moved to Enfield. Kay and I were watching a movie in his room, and I had to use the bathroom. Since the one in his room didn't work, I went downstairs and..." I stopped, unsure of how he would react when he heard I'd been eavesdropping.

"And?"

"And I..." I bit into my lip.

"What's the matter?"

"Okay, so don't get mad at me or anything, but I saw you and Blake in your living room together." His smile dropped. "You were hugging him as he cried and—"

"What did you hear?" He looked so serious, and I didn't know how to interpret it.

"Not much. I forgot most of it. I just know Blake said something was his fault and he mentioned a girl's name, but I don't remember it." He looked at me with no reaction. "I'm sorry. I shouldn't have listened to you two, but I didn't tell anyone about it. Not even Kayden."

His gaze was reflective as it dropped down. I couldn't get a read on him.

"I'm sorry," I repeated. "I stayed listening mostly because I was shocked by you."

"Me?"

"Yes. You were completely different. Up until that moment, I thought you were heartless and evil because you treated me so horribly. You never expressed even a sliver of positive feelings, but then I saw how you wanted to help him and be there for him. I saw that you *cared*. And I don't know how, but something changed in me. I saw there was good in you, and that's how it started."

"You recognized good in me?" He looked for something in my eyes.

"Yes. I understood there was more to you than what you showed to the world. You were alone, misunderstood, and in pain, just like me. I guess those things made me relate to you. They helped me feel closer to you."

He watched me for a prolonged moment, and I noticed a slight trembling of his lips. "Even then you had a big heart," he mouthed. "You were capable of caring for me despite everything I did to you."

I took his hands into mine. "It doesn't matter now. You changed. It's the only thing that matters."

"I know." He stared at our hands. "Still, there's one thing I don't get."

"What?"

"Why did you kiss Kayden?"

Shame claimed me, and I lowered my gaze, pulling away my hands from his. I used Kayden that night. Kay wanted it to happen, but that didn't make me feel any less guilty.

"I... Please, don't judge me."

"Why would I judge you?"

"Because it was a mistake." I twisted my hands together. "It happened the last time he and I visited the Nepaug state forest."

His forehead creased. "That time when Kayden was hurt and told me I won?"

"Yes."

"But why did he feel that way when he got what he wanted? He liked you and got to kiss you. He should've been happy about it."

"Because as I told you before, I couldn't return his feelings. And he knew I liked you." The shame in me doubled. "He told me I could kiss him and pretend he was you." I looked away.

"What?"

"Yes. So I did exactly that. I kissed him pretending it was you. I basically used him, and I feel horrible because I hurt him and he didn't deserve that—"

"You pretended it was me?" he said in a raspy voice, and I turned my head to look at him. He was *smiling*.

"Y-Yes—"

He grabbed my head and crashed his lips to mine. I was surprised at first, but then I kissed him back, breathless and trembling under the searing intensity of his kiss. His hands slid down my neck and over my shoulders until they stopped on my waist, emanating the rising heat of his body. I loved the sweetest pleasure his kiss evoked, yearning for more before he pulled away.

"If you only knew how many times I drove myself crazy thinking about your first kiss. I was dying to kiss you, to finally claim your lips..." He skimmed the seam of my lips with his finger. "I wanted so badly to be the one who kissed you first."

"In a way you did. It was your image in my mind when I kissed him. I was kissing you." I sighed. "But I feel like a terrible, twisted person for doing that."

"Don't. I don't want you to feel that way. Fuck." He smiled. "I can't lie. I'm so happy about it. I'm not happy about Kayden, but I'm happy you were mine even then. Not even Kayden could change that." His smile grew bigger, reminding me of a small boy who got his favorite toy, and the next thing I knew, I was pressed against his bed with his body right on top of mine.

"Hayden!"

"Ah fuck!" He grimaced as he supported himself with both arms that now caged me, relying mostly on his healthy arm. "I forgot about my elbow and ribs." He remained where he was as he searched for something in my eyes, and my heartbeat quickened. "I can't believe you actually kissed him thinking about me."

"That makes two of us." My gaze was irreversibly drawn to his naked chest and abs.

"You can touch me, Sarah, you know," he said. "I need you to touch me."

My stomach did a flip. I grew restless, craving to feel his skin and let myself do what I wanted for so long. I ran my hands down his chest and stomach, relishing in his strong, flexing muscles. His eyes grew darker as I explored his body, his face twisted in pleasure my touch brought him.

"I love touching you," I whispered.

"Fuck, Sarah."

He groaned and slammed his lips on mine. His kiss was rough—*all consuming*. His tongue was fervent against mine, creating a heat in me that grew stronger. He broke the kiss only to plant open-mouthed kisses along my jaw and neck, sucking and nibbling. It felt too good. I threaded my fingers through his silky hair and pulled him much closer to me.

Hayden moved in between my legs, and the proof of his arousal pressed against my stomach as his hand neared my breast. His kisses brought pleasure that clouded my mind, and I couldn't resist pressing myself against him—

He hissed and rolled off me, landing on his back. He fisted his hands on his sides, breathing heavily.

"Hayden?" I brought myself up to one elbow and peered into his face. "What's wrong?"

"Fucking ribs. They hurt so much." He wore a grimace of pain, and a bead of sweat rolled down his temple.

"I'm so sorry. I forgot to pay attention."

He chuckled but stopped a moment later when he winced in pain. "Yeah? Me too. Come here." He beckoned me to lie down next to him. Wasting no time, I put my head on his shoulder, and his arms wrapped around me to bring me closer to him.

"Am I crushing you?" I was careful not to crush his ribs as I settled against him, the remnants of pleasure coursing through me.

He tipped my chin to look at him. "Relax. I don't care about that. What I care about is you and how awesome you make me feel." His finger traced my lips, nose, cheeks, and chin before it went lower, over my neck and collarbone... Everywhere he touched, it burned. "I want you, Sarah."

Blood rushed to my cheeks. "I want you too."

He kissed the top of my head and embraced me. "I'll show you how good it can be. Soon."

I squirmed with need. Just his words did wonders to me, and I grew more restless as I thought about being with him in the most intimate way. I was ready. I wanted to do it with him, and I was already yearning for more touches and kisses... But this wasn't the time.

"You're messing with my mind when you're naked like this. So put a shirt on," I told him.

"I like messing with your mind. Especially when I'm naked."

I blushed again and glanced away from his amused eyes. "Hayden! Have some decency!"

"Where's the fun in that, grandma?"

"Stop calling me grandma!"

"Why, grandma?"

"Stop it!"

Rolling his eyes, he got up and put a black Linkin Park shirt on before he tossed me another shirt.

"What's this for?" I asked. It was a black Breaking Benjamin shirt that was so big it would reach my mid-thighs.

"You don't plan to sleep in your sweater and jeans?"

"I can just go to my house and get my pajamas."

He shook his head. "I want to see you in my shirt. Come on. Wear it."

I grew hot. I would be only in my underwear and his shirt, and we would sleep next to each other... *Okay. Don't overthink it, Sarah. There's nothing you should be nervous about. Absolutely nothing.*

He smirked, reading me like an open book. "Nothing is going to happen, Sarah. But if you insist..." His voice trailed off, and the impact of his words got me all flustered. I jumped from his bed and darted to his bathroom, hoping he didn't see how red I'd become.

"I'll change in your bathroom."

"There's a spare toothbrush in the cabinet," he said through his laughter. Avoiding looking at him, I went into his bathroom and locked the door.

My heart thudded fiercely as I took off my clothes and put on his shirt. I brushed my teeth and double checked my legs, more than glad I'd shaved them yesterday. I was getting self-conscious fast. My hair was messy, my face was pale, I had a few pimples on my forehead and cheeks, and I wasn't sure if I smelled sweaty...

Stop it, Sarah! You're overthinking again! You look good. Besides, he already saw you naked.

Riiight. That memory wasn't helping. My anxiety only increased.

I washed my face and tried fixing my hair with trembling fingers. I repeated to myself what he'd told me once. It didn't matter how I looked, because I was the most beautiful girl to him. I shouldn't pay much attention to details.

Taking a deep breath, I opened the door and stepped into his room. It was dark, save for the street lights that provided a faint light. Hayden lay in his bed, seemingly already asleep. I exhaled slowly and tip-toed to his bed, extremely nervous about walking around him almost naked. I didn't take my eyes off of him as I moved the covers aside and slipped into bed, watching his chest rise and fall evenly.

Suddenly, he yanked me toward him, and I barely had time to support myself so I wouldn't end up crashing onto his chest.

"Hayden!"

"What took you so long?" he muttered and opened his eyes to look at me.

"I... I was getting ready. I thought you were asleep."

"That's not so unlikely since you took forever in there." He smirked. "And what were you getting ready for? We're just going to sleep together, *literally*."

I was glad that he couldn't see me blush in the darkness. "One can never know with you, Hayden. I wouldn't be surprised if I woke up in the middle of the night with you doing *something* to me."

He burst into laughter, and flutters congregated in my belly. I managed to make him laugh. *Amazing.*

"My girl finally learned how to roast me," he said sarcastically, but all I could think about was that he said *my girl.* "Now, don't give me any ideas, because I would love nothing more than to wake you up like that."

Okay, I was way out of my league. The more I played his game, the more ensnared in it I was, and I was inexperienced compared to him. He wasn't a virgin, and he didn't have inhibitions when it came to sex, or so I'd heard in school hallways from gossiping girls.

I lay down next to him and placed my head on his shoulder, trying to calm down my raging heart. I was too aware of his nearness, his perfect scent, his hard muscles underneath my head that felt better than any pillow because they provided me a sense of security. I wanted him, but what if I did something wrong?

"What are you thinking about?" he asked me, stroking my hair slowly.

I decided to be honest. "How I can't keep up with you when it comes to sex. I'm inexperienced, and I'm afraid I'm going to disappoint you."

"Don't. It doesn't matter. I'll like whatever you do."

"You're just saying that to make me feel better."

"It's the truth. Don't you get it? I love you, so anything you do will be the best fucking thing ever."

His words created a smoldering heat that grew when he slid his hand down my neck and shoulder, coming dangerously close to my breast. My cheeks flared up. I was more conscious of my small breasts than ever.

"Besides, you can always practice." He lowered his hand to my breast. "And practice." He completely covered it. "And practice."

Breathe, Sarah. Breathe.

"I love you, Sarah. So don't be ashamed in front of me. Okay? Remember, we're a team now."

And with that, he kissed me, showing me just how true his words were.

Chapter 13

I MOVED THROUGH A POORLY lit room filled with blood, sweat, and shady-looking people. I was thankful Kayden was by my side because this place gave me the creeps. Most of the crowd had gathered in the center of the room, and loud cheering and shouting reverberated through my mind.

"Kill! Kill! Kill!"

"Finish him!"

"Black! Black! Black!"

"Come on, Axel! Finish him!"

My heart rate doubled, and I felt sick. I clamped my hand over my mouth.

"You all right?" Kay asked me.

"I'm fine, but Hayden isn't. We have to save him!"

"Kill! Kill! Kill!"

The chanting became louder, sharpening my fear, dragging me to the edge of panic. I had to help Hayden!

I darted through the crowd, pushing people aside on my way to him. He was fighting against Axel in the middle of a clear patch of ground, and from the sounds of it, he was losing. His whole face was bruised, and the blood from his cuts dripped down his face to the floor. It looked gruesome, just like the rest of the wounds on his body. He was barely standing on his feet, and I couldn't bear to see him like this.

"Hayden," I screamed, but it didn't come out of my throat.

Kay wrapped his arms around me to prevent me from getting any closer to Hayden. Axel's body was huge and packed with heavy muscles, but he didn't have a face, only blurred nothingness in its place. I remembered Hayden say that Axel played dirty, which was confirmed the moment he took a knife out of nowhere and lunged at Hayden.

"Hayden," I screamed again, but once more, it was silent, and I started thrashing against Kayden in a desperate attempt to set myself free. "Let me go! Why aren't you helping him?! He needs help!"

"We can't help him, Sarah," his voice was as calm as ever. "Only he can help himself," he said the exact words he told me a long time ago, and I grew still.

"What did you say?"

"I'm saying that fighting is his way of dealing with pain. It's twisted because it helps him stop the pain, and it gives him pain, which he needs."

"What are you saying? He needs pain?"

"Yes. He needs it. He yearns for it. It's horrible, right? How you need to get rid of that pain, but at the same time, you need it? You're addicted. Pain is who you are and without it... You lose yourself."

Hayden dodged Axel's knife, and my surroundings turned into a blur as Kayden's words ricocheted through my mind.

If this was his way out, if this helped him find himself, how on earth would he ever stop fighting?

Hayden's scream ripped through the room, and I looked up to see him fall to the ground with Axel's knife sticking out of his chest.

No.

No, no, no!

Everything played out in slow motion—Kayden fading away from me, Hayden bleeding out on the ground, Axel high-fiving someone before an older man, who I assumed was the mysterious T, appeared...

"Hayden! No! Kayden, come back!" Not this! No!

I looked at Hayden's pale face, experiencing the strongest pain ever, and it was like my whole world was crumbling. The memory of Kayden's glassy eyes haunted me as I fell to my knees and went to Hayden with the last particle of strength in me. I was surrounded by eerie silence and motionless people who kept following me with their prying eyes.

By the time I reached Hayden, he was already dead, lying in the pool of his blood, and everything stopped to exist. My reality turned black, and fears and sorrows wrapped me tightly until there was nothing left but a gaping void, desolate and soul-destroying.

Before I could let out a scream, I was pulled away from the dark room—

I snapped my eyes open, and terror washed over me. My heart thumped furiously against my chest. I was ready to burst into tears, but then I remembered I wasn't in my room.

I turned to look at Hayden, expecting to see him sleeping, but he was very much awake. He stared at the ceiling, and even in the darkness I could discern his tormented expression. Something that troubled him, something that didn't let him sleep. Had he slept at all?

All my fears and pain temporarily forgotten, I caught his upper arm and nudged him.

"Hayden? Hayden, are you okay?"

He returned my gaze with a vacant look in his eyes, and my stomach twisted. No, he wasn't all right.

"Please, tell me what's going on." He just stared at me, looking more lost than ever, and I felt helpless.

I was about to reach for him, when he suddenly moved on top of me and kissed me, which put a halt to all my rushing thoughts. I responded immediately, relishing in the warmth deep inside of me, until I felt his pain seeping into me. He communicated it through his lips that moved desperately across my neck, giving me a bittersweet pleasure that made my heart ache.

His hand found its searing way beneath my shirt and up my waist and stopped on my breast. Already breathless, I grasped his head that hung low above my breasts, but then I stilled when something wet hit my shirt above my left breast. Another droplet quickly followed, falling next to the first one, and terrible pain dug its claws into my chest.

"Hayden?"

He didn't move, his hand frozen on my breast. His tears kept falling, and I realized too late he'd been trembling all this time.

"Hayden, look at me." I tried to make him look at me, but he didn't budge. "I'm here. Look at me."

He finally raised his head, and I barely managed to suppress a whimper. His features were distorted with devastating pain, and his tears silently slid down his cheeks, leaving heartbreaking evidence of his deep-seated agony.

"You're going to be okay. I'm here," I whispered to him and turned on the lamp on his nightstand.

Remaining silent, he lay back down and looked fixedly at the ceiling, his breaths coming fast. My eyes never left his as my mind worked to come up with a way to help him.

"Tell me what is bothering you. You'll feel better if you share it with me." His breathing got faster. "Hey." I leaned over him and cupped his cheeks to draw his attention back to me. "Breathe slowly."

He frowned. He remained quiet, but his eyes said more than enough. His hand was so cold when I took it in mine.

"I'm here with you. I'll listen to you. Breathe slowly."

I repeated this a couple more times until his breathing reached a normal rate, which reminded me of the time when he helped me with my panic attack. He was still far from okay, but the worst had passed, so I sat against the headboard and pulled his head into my lap.

"Talk to me," I encouraged him once more and caressed his hair.

"I can't sleep," he finally said in a gravelly voice. "Whenever I close my eyes, I see terrifying images."

I waited for him to continue, but he didn't. He was very vulnerable, so it would be difficult for him to open up to me, but I hoped he would. "Do you want to talk about it?"

His face was a landscape of his silent battle when he closed his eyes and clenched his jaw. I didn't push for the answer, stroking his hair slowly.

"I see so many things. I see Kayden. I see you. I see myself failing over and over again. And much more."

Kayden. Painful questions resurfaced, and I stilled my hand. My eyes went to his scar. "What about Kayden?"

"I see that accident. I see it too often, and it's too much."

The familiar guilt slowly peered its head out, but I didn't dwell on it. I refused to let my old mindset destroy the progress I'd made. "What do you see?"

"The moment we get hit... It's ridiculously unreal and horrifying. One moment we were walking, and the next... Pain. Confusion." He touched his scar and curled his hand into a fist. "He was lying on that pavement with all that blood around him and..." He sucked in a sharp breath. "And that face. The same face that would never smile again. That night is always on repeat."

Sharp pain tore through me, and I squeezed my eyes shut. I'd forgiven myself for my mistake, but that didn't make me feel any less sorry about it. "I'm so sorry, Hayden. I wish you didn't have to go through this."

"I don't know what to do to make it stop. Then there's you. The moment when Josh stabbed you keeps haunting me. You were lifeless, and there was so much blood, again. Too much." He fisted his hands on his sides. "Or when Brad aimed that rifle right at your head in the woods. It feels like I'm already in that dark reality where you're dead."

A tremor rocked me. His words were painful, and I couldn't imagine how terrible he must feel each time he replayed these moments in his head.

I ran my fingers down his cheek. "I'm completely okay. Don't worry about me. That's in the past."

"It doesn't feel that way. It feels like it will keep messing with me. Everything you went through, all those fucked up things I did to you... And I can't *ever* erase them."

I ran my fingers down his cheek. "Hayden, don't worry about it. It's okay. You're not the same person anymore."

"I know, but still. It's not okay. I keep thinking about your letters and all those days you spent next to me in the hospital. You don't know what it was like to hear you and not be able to talk to you or hug you. I wanted to tell you so much, but I couldn't. You were so close to me, and I couldn't lift even a finger."

He entwined our hands and left a kiss on the back of my hand. I moved my finger over his scar, thinking how hard it was to build something, but destroying it could take only a second. We were surrounded with pain, walking on a big chunk of ice that was life, and even a small misstep could lead to our downfall. No one should experience something so horrible, yet Hayden had experienced it for so long, and my heart crumbled. I wished I could erase his sorrow from those days and replace it with happiness.

"I constantly saw all those things when I was in a coma. They were on a fucking repeat. I hated being alone in that room because my mind would wander off and create nightmarish illusions that seemed like they would never end. I thought I was going crazy."

I called to mind what he'd said about us telling him he was all right those days. "When I was by your side, did any of my words help?"

He turned his head to look at me. "Yes." He wasn't smiling, but there was softness to his eyes. "They were the only things that kept me sane all that time. They gave me hope."

I slid my finger over his cheek and jaw aimlessly. "Do you often have trouble sleeping?"

He looked away. "Too often. Sometimes I'm not able to sleep for days."

My brows pinched together. "Does your therapist know about your insomnia?"

"Yeah."

"Did she tell you how to deal with it?"

"She mentioned some relaxation techniques and suggested cognitive behavioral therapy. She also suggested some meds."

"Do the meds help?"

He rubbed his forehead tiredly. "I don't know. I take so many different drugs that I'm sick and tired of them. Every single day."

"I get that it can be too much, but I'm sure they do you more good than you know."

"If you say so."

I smiled at him. "I believe so. You know, I mentioned in one of the letters that I was going to see your therapist, Ms. Kishimoto. I talked with her the day you woke up."

He met my gaze. He was much calmer now, and his eyes had lost the tormented expression. "How was it?"

I recounted what she told me about things that could help our relationship work. "She advised couples counseling. I think we should give it a try. It can help us solve our problems more easily. What do you think?

"I thought about it too. I also think you should start therapy."

My pulse sped up. "Me?"

He pulled himself up and sat next to me. "You also have issues, and I don't want you to hurt. You can't deal with it on your own, because you'll burn out eventually. At least talk to me. What was that nightmare about? You had a nightmare, right? That's why you woke up."

I glanced away. The scene from that dream replayed in front of my eyes, bringing back the pain. "Um, yes. I had a nightmare."

His arms wrapped around me and pulled me against his chest.

"You're safe now. I won't let anything happen to you."

His scent—a mixture of soap and something that was purely male and his—enticed me, and I got more addicted to him. It felt good to be next to him like this and forget about everything but our nearness, skin against skin.

"Talk to me, baby. What was your nightmare about?"

I drew circles on his shoulder as he stroked my hair. I wasn't quite willing to reminisce about it, but I wanted him to hear it.

"You were fighting at that shady place." He tensed, and his hand stilled on my head, but then he let a long sigh out. He didn't say a word, waiting for me to continue. "Kayden was there too. We watched you fight Axel."

He grasped my shoulders and made me look at him. "You know Axel?"

I shook my head, frowning at his look of apprehension. "No, I never saw him. He didn't have a face in my dream. Why are you worried about him so much?"

He leaned against the headboard and pulled me back into his embrace. "He's a sick bastard. I don't want you to ever meet him. He enjoys making others suffer, and the more they bleed, the better."

"But you fought him and won?"

"Barely."

"I'm so afraid. You can get hurt. Can you cancel the fight?" He didn't reply, and my heart contracted painfully. What was he thinking? "Hayden? Please, say something."

"It's not like I have a choice," he gritted out, which doled out a fresh wave of fear.

"Why not?"

He took a sharp intake of breath and fisted his hand on his lap, clear signs that he was controlling himself not to say something. I hoped I hadn't ticked him off. After a couple of seconds, he relaxed his hand.

"Let's not talk about it now. Okay?" he replied gruffly. "So who won in your dream?"

I shuddered. The moment Hayden got stabbed seemed so real. "He killed you, Hayden. He stabbed you, and you were dead on the spot."

"You know most stab wounds won't make you die on the spot?" he half-mocked me.

"Dreams don't have to be realistic," I muttered. "Anyway, Kayden disappeared just then and you... You were lying in your blood. It was so horrible." Pain suffused my chest.

"Shhh." His arms kept me close to him, roaming over my back in slow circles. "It's just a dream. I'm here."

"Just be careful, okay? I can't lose you too. I don't know what I would do without you."

"Don't say that." He tipped my chin up so he could look me in the eyes. "I won't die, but either way, you'll stay strong. Do you understand? You won't fall apart. You're stronger than anything, Sarah. Do you know that? You're so strong."

So many emotions rushed through me as his empowering words echoed in my mind. He believed in me. His words gave me the boost I'd always needed to defeat the demons that fed me with doubts and self-loathing.

"I'm stronger with you," I told him. "I want to be a better person for me and you. I want to conquer my demons and be someone you'll always be proud of."

"I'm already proud of you."

My lips curled into a big smile. "Then I want you to be proud even more."

He kissed my head and held me more tightly. His warm fingers moved over my neck in a way that was bordering on sensual.

"Do you often have nightmares?" he asked me.

"Every single day since your accident."

"How about before that?"

"Yes. I had nightmares, which usually involved Kayden, Josh, Brad... Or you tormenting me." His hand stopped moving on my neck. "But that was before. I don't dream about that anymore."

"Just... *Fuck*." He remained silent for a while; his heart underneath my palm beat faster. "Have you experienced anything else?"

"What do you mean?"

"Do you have any other symptoms of trauma?"

I closed my eyes on a shuddering breath. I'd never given this much thought, but his question only confirmed I had to face the facts. I wasn't okay. I was going through a hard period, experiencing things that amplified my stress, which weakened my already fragile state of mind.

"Sometimes I can't sleep without my lamp on. And I have panic attacks. They aren't that serious, but sometimes they happen more often. And I... I look over my shoulder from time to time to see if there's someone behind me on the streets or even in my house."

His arms wrapped so firmly around me it could become painful if he used any more strength. He stayed quiet, letting me pour out all my deepest thoughts, and I felt vulnerable and at ease at the same time.

"Do you think I'm crazy?"

"Crazy? Are you serious? What's crazy is that you've been dealing with this all by yourself all this time, and it kills me. I want you safe and happy." He kissed the top of my head. "I'm always here for you. And those assholes won't get out of prison anytime soon."

"Josh's and Natalie's trials are scheduled for the end of January, but what if they get out after that?"

"They won't. Josh's father won't let that happen."

"It's ironic because he was the one who always pulled Josh out of tricky situations."

"Yeah, but he won't do that with all that talk about the Supreme Court. He isn't the man who puts his family first. As for Natalie, her parents are poor and non-influential, so she can't count on getting out of this. You can bet Brad won't get out of prison for his good behavior any time this century." He took my hands in his. "You have me, but I think you should go to therapist too."

"I don't have money, Hayden—"

"Money isn't a problem."

"No. I don't want you to pay for me."

"Sarah, enough. I'm tired of the same shit. I know you're not comfortable with it, but this is me we're talking about. We're one, and I want to help you any way I can. I don't care about money, and I'll pay a fortune for your therapy if that means you'll get better."

His words brought tears to my eyes. I felt extremely emotional because he cared deeply and was ready to go above and beyond to make me feel well.

"Thank you, but it's not only about the money. I feel anxious just thinking about sharing my problems with a complete stranger."

"You can't always run from it. It's hard, fuck, I know that best, but it's for your own good. If you want to be better, you have to take that first step and start therapy. Just think about it, okay?"

Now that he put it that way... He was right. If I wanted to be better—if I wanted us to be better—I had to stop refusing help just because it was hard. If I wasn't strong enough to go through this, how could I hope to get any better for Hayden? Besides, he was already trying his hardest to get better, so it was unfair of me to refuse to do the same. I couldn't drag us down with my problems. I had to follow his example and conquer my fears.

"Okay. I promise I'll think about it."

"Great. Now, do you think you can sleep?"

"I hope so." I took Hayden's iPhone from the nightstand and looked at the time. It was 3 am.

"Here." He pulled us down and spooned me, wrapping his arm around my waist. "I want to hold you like this." I closed my eyes and let out a pleased sigh. It felt incredibly good being next to him like this. "I want you to forget everything bad."

"This feels nice." I cupped his hand on my waist and wiggled closer to him. I felt safe and loved in his arms. "I love when you hold me like this."

"I love when I hold you like this too, but stop squirming."

"Oh." I stilled. Blush colored my cheeks when I felt something hard poke my backside. *Oh.* "S-Sorry."

He chuckled. "I mean, keep doing it if you want this to turn into something else—"

"I'll stop." My whole body was hot as the tempting images of us doing various things unfurled behind my closed lids.

His chuckle turned into laughter, cementing my embarrassment. "Sleep tight, beautiful."

Beautiful. "Thank you. You too."

"And if you dream about me again, it better be a wet dream."

"You wish."

His hoarse chuckle was the last thing I heard before I drifted off.

Chapter 14

I FLUTTERED MY EYES open and squinted against the glare of the sun permeating through Hayden's window. I didn't dream anything for a change, which was a relief. I felt relaxed and energized, and even more so with the sunrays bathing the room. They were a reinvigorating sight I missed during these last few weeks of gloomy weather. I stretched with a smile and turned to look at Hayden...

Only, Hayden wasn't here. My smile fell, and I sat up to find a note on his pillow.

"Good morning, baby.

I'm in the gym downstairs. I was going crazy doing nothing, so I had to work out but don't worry. I'll follow doc's advice to take it slow.

I love you."

My stomach did a little flip, and my smile returned to my face in full force. "I love you too," I whispered and reread his note a couple more times, soaking up every single word.

Deciding to save it, I folded it in half and reached for my backpack leaning against his computer chair. I put it into one of the pockets and took Hayden's diary. I needed another "quick Hayden fix."

I flipped through several pages, until I reached an entry I hadn't read.

"Date: Does it matter? Why the fuck it matters when all days are the same?

My therapist asked me how I would describe myself today.

The first thing that comes to my mind is damaged.

And then selfish.

And then crazy.

And then insecure.

And then I don't know the fuck what because it's all fucked up and I'm sick and tired of this shit."

Just like the most of his entries, this was tainted with darkness, and the negative side of his mind showed more often than not. He was full of joyless thoughts that enforced the wall he kept around himself for so long, which made him unable him to see the sunny side of the world. It made him unable to find the path that would lead him away from his self-destructive thoughts. I needed to show him there were so many things that could put a smile on his face. There were so many reasons to be happy and keep moving forward.

A smile found its way to my face. I felt so different compared to the old me. Now, I was able to find that small ray of sunshine in the midst of a downpour of negativity and believe it would produce the most beautiful rainbow of happiness, hope, and love.

I continued to the next entry.

"I don't want to be abandoned. I want to be loved and understood. I want to be significant. I want to be someone's special person, but I'm afraid I'll stay alone forever.

I'm tired of the same old fears.

Fear of rejection.

Fear of not being good enough.

Fear of driving everyone away.

Fear of betrayal.

Fear of waking up to another shitty day.

Fear of not finding the reason to get up the next day.

Fear of that explosive anger that makes me do some fucked up shit.

I understand. I really do. No one can pull me out of it. No one can "save" me. I have to do it on my own. I have to regulate my emotions, take and give equally, fight against myself, and so much more, and I have to do all of that on my own.

But it's so difficult. Everything is so chaotic. It's like that line in a line chart that goes up and down, but mine spikes and dips so drastically that it's impossible for me to deal with it every single day. I'm walking on ice, and I'm making too many missteps. I keep falling.

I want to stop falling.

Sometimes I feel like I want to scream my lungs out. Everything becomes too much and I'm swarmed with so many rushing thoughts that I can't stand them.

I just want one day where all I would feel is peace. No doubts, no fears, no pain, no emptiness...

Just peace.

It has to get better than this shit but until then..."

"Until then, I'll be with you every step of that rocky way," I said with a small smile.

I put his diary back into my backpack and took out my phone to check the time. I had a message from Mel. My eyes bulged out when I saw it was way past nine, and I internally slapped myself for oversleeping.

I checked Mel's text as I rushed to get my clothes.

"Fine. I'll go to that stupid party. Jess told me she and Kevin are going too."

I grinned excitedly. One of Hayden's friends was throwing a New Year's Eve party at his house, and I'd invited Jess, Mel, and Kevin—a new addition to our small circle—to come with us.

I swapped Hayden's shirt for my clothes and cast a wistful look at it. I already missed it on me.

"That's great! We're going to have a lot of fun."

I texted her back and rushed to Hayden's bathroom to wash my face and brush my teeth.

It was a long shot, I had to admit, since Mel didn't like Hayden and Steven's friends, and Jess and Kevin didn't get along with Blake and Masen, but I wanted to use this opportunity to bury the hatchet between us and try to get along.

I was worried Hayden would get jealous or angry when I told him about Kevin and the "welcome party," so I made sure he knew Kevin was just a friend who apparently liked Jess. Thankfully, he agreed to meet him at the party and try to be friendly.

Melissa's answer arrived just as I came out of the bathroom.

"If you think the World War III is great and fun, then yeah, we'll have the time of our lives! I'll beat those assholes into a bloody mush if they even breathe in our direction."

I tsked and shook my head.

"Violent so early? I think it's going to be fun. Besides, aren't you the one for parties? It's going to be fine."

"I'm sad you can't see me rolling my eyes and puking here."

I left my phone in my backpack and headed downstairs to Hayden's gym, passing by Hayden's dad's atelier on my way. That place embodied loss and tragedy, always invoking heavy feelings. His paintings were covered with dust sheets, hiding the windows to his inner place of anguish from the rest of the world. I'd cleaned it twice since I started helping Carmen with house cleaning, and each time I thought how hard it must have been for a five-year old Hayden to find his dad right there after he took his own life.

Did Hayden ever think about his dad, about that exact moment that engulfed his world with darkness from such an early age?

I was so lost in my thoughts I almost crashed into Hayden when he came out of his gym, and I had to press my hands against his chest to keep my balance.

"Oops." My eyes locked with his as a gorgeous smile spread across his slightly sweaty face. I felt instantly high on him. Even with a thin sheet of sweat on his face he was plain gorgeous, especially in his black tank top and black sweatpants that made him look sexier.

"Sleeping beauty has finally decided to grace us with her presence." His smile turned into a smirk when he noticed I was gawking at him. "You want to eat me for breakfast?"

I tore my eyes from his lips to meet his stare, completely flushed. "Since when did you turn into Masen with his sex jokes?"

"Since when did you become obsessed with my body?"

He cornered me against the wall, and his arms caged me as he leaned in to kiss me, not giving me the opportunity to answer. His warm lips played with mine before his tongue slipped inside and deepened our contact. All my conscious thoughts drifted away. I gripped his shirt as his hands slid down my waist delicately and pulled me closer to him until no inches separated us, tempting me to do much more to him... Until someone cleared their throat.

Could the floor swallow me and make me forget this absolute humiliation?

"Good morning, Sarah," Carmen said with a smile on her face and not a hint of reproach in her expression. "Breakfast is ready, kids." She left before I could answer her, and I felt myself blushing hard.

"If you get any redder than this, you'll set a Guinness World Record."

I put my hands on my waist and glared at him. "How can you be so calm about this?"

He rolled his eyes—his trademark. "There's no reason to be ashamed. We were just kissing, grandma."

"Ugh! Stop calling me grandma, you... You, rock!"

He arched his brows. "*Rock?* Why did you call me a rock?"

"B-Because you're stupid! Ha!"

He rolled his eyes. *Again.* "That doesn't make any sense."

"It does for me."

"Then I think your IQ is something to worry about."

I pouted and crossed my arms over my chest. "Thanks a lot."

He guffawed and tapped my nose playfully. "You're making it so easy for me to pick on you. It will never get old."

He kept laughing as he went to his room to change into something warmer, and I couldn't even be annoyed with him. I'd never get enough of his laughter. Carmen was seated at the table when I entered the kitchen, already waiting for us, and my cheeks grew red again.

"Good morning, Mrs. B—I mean, Carmen."

Her smile grew wide. "I made pancakes with bacon and maple syrup and scrambled eggs with bacon, so you can choose." She motioned at them for me to take.

"Thank you." I put two pancakes on my plate and sat across from her. "I'm sorry you had to see that."

"See what?"

"Umm, Hayden and me kissing." I looked away as an intense blush stained my face. I wished Hayden would come in so I wouldn't have to sit alone with her.

"What are you saying? I don't mind that! After all, it's only natural." She leaned her head against her hand and looked at one spot behind me. Her eyes glazed over as she mused on something. "Jason and I were the same, to tell you the truth. He was always so passionate and intense."

Okay. This had taken a weird turn. I wanted to be anywhere but here.

She continued talking about Jason's loving nature, which was similar to Hayden, when a question popped into my mind. "Carmen?"

"Yes?"

"Do you have any photos of Jason?"

She pressed her lips together as she looked at the table, and her brows dipped low. "No."

"Why not?"

Hayden entered the kitchen. "Because I destroyed every single one of them," he replied.

My heart lurched in my chest. He took scrambled eggs with bacon and plopped down in the chair next to me, frowning.

I briefly met Carmen's gaze. The worry I felt reflected on her face. "Why?" I asked him. I had a feeling why, but I wanted to hear it from him.

"Because they were fucking painful to look at. End of story." He didn't look at me as he stuffed eggs into his mouth, moving his fork briskly in increasing anger.

He wasn't aware I knew he found his dad after he took his life, but I wanted to talk about it when we were alone. I understood why he destroyed them. I had done the same with Kayden's photos after his death. I couldn't bear looking at them, so it was the only way to deal with them.

Carmen formed a warm smile to lighten the atmosphere, but it didn't have any effect. "It's great to have you here, Sarah. We're finally able to have breakfast like a family. It sure brings back memories."

In my periphery, I noticed Hayden grow still. "It's nice," I said carefully, watching for his reaction.

Maybe this breakfast wasn't a good idea. She was trying to improve her relationship with Hayden, but for some reason, it didn't sit well with him.

"Is the food okay, Hayden?" Carmen asked.

"It's the same as always," he mumbled. He didn't spare her a glance.

She hid the pain quickly, but I saw right through her. I took a bite of my pancake, wondering what had caused his bad mood this time.

"I just want you to enjoy your breakfast," she told him. "I made the eggs the way you like."

His fork clattered on his plate when he dropped it, and my pulse quickened. He picked up the orange juice and poured it into his glass. "What a devoted mother you are."

Carmen winced. "Hayden," I started, hoping to reason with him, but Carmen interrupted me, "I care about you, whether you like it or not."

Both Hayden and I stopped moving, equally surprised by her words, and I held my breath as I waited for his answer. I didn't like the way his jaw ticked when he finally met her eyes.

"*Care* for me? Is this a joke?"

"It's not a joke," she replied softly.

He fisted his hands on the table. "Don't you think you're too late? Like *seventeen fucking years* late?"

She didn't even blink, enduring his glare. "I know how wrong I've been all these years, and I'm so sorry. That doesn't take away from the fact that I love you. I want to make things right this time."

"You can shove your love up your ass."

"Hayden!" I breathed out.

"I'm not going anywhere." She remained calm, never taking her eyes off of him. "I'll do whatever it takes to improve our relationship."

He hit the table with both fists, breathing through his bared teeth. "Stop acting! Nobody cares about you, bitch! You think that just because you decided to stick around the house and play mother, I'll run into your arms? You made breakfast, and now we're supposed to act like a loving family? Are you dumb?! You make me sick!"

I clamped my hand over my mouth. His words were vile.

"Don't speak to me like that. I admit I was wrong, but I want to right my wrongs. I hope we can start fresh. I hope you'll give me an opportunity—"

Hayden jumped to his feet, and his chair fell backward, creating a crash that sounded twice as loud in the tense room. "Opportunity?! That same opportunity you never gave me?! From the beginning, everything revolved around your precious Kayden! If we were sick, you took care of him first. If we were sad, he was the one you comforted! If he did something good, you had the biggest fucking smile on your face, while I received *nothing*, no matter how much I tried to be good for you."

I stood up to my shaky feet, blinking away sudden tears.

"I'm sorry," she said.

"NO!" He grabbed the glass with his juice and smashed it against the floor. Shards of glass and juice scattered around in a ghastly mess, which reminded me of the old Hayden who became explosive when rage breached all his limits.

"Please—" I began, but he didn't even pay attention to me.

"One sorry won't change shit! And if that lifetime of bullshit wasn't enough, you tried to separate Sarah and me!"

She paled and glanced between us. "I did that to protect you both. I wanted to save you from heartbreak—"

"Who gave you the fucking right to decide if it's going to leave us heartbroken or not?! You never even mentioned it to me! You did that behind my back!"

I wiped away the tears that sneaked out and took a deep breath, but new tears kept coming. "Hayden, I told you she had good intentions. That was just her way of protecting us both from the potential pain—"

His eyes sliced me. "She never even trusted me. She thought I'd hurt you from the start and never gave me a chance!"

"That's not right," she told him. "I wanted Sarah to know how difficult a relationship can be with someone who has borderline personality disorder. I wanted her to know it isn't something that can be solved overnight."

"You told her she wasn't strong enough for me," Hayden replied gruffly, all his resentment packed in these words. "You never trusted me, and you never trusted Sarah. You don't even know us, but you were damn quick to judge us. So you can play your little mother games all you want, but I'll never forgive you."

I'd never seen Mrs. Black so defeated as she was right now. She rubbed her forehead tiredly. "I already apologized to Sarah for my mistake, and now I'm apologizing to you. And I'm not playing any games. I could've lost you too, and it would've killed me. You're my son, and I'll always love you. So I'll keep trying until you accept me."

I hoped these words would reach Hayden and help him see she only wanted the best for him, but his face twisted in unfettered fury, and everything in me turned to ice.

"So you're doing all of this because you're scared of ending up alone?! I needed to be on the brink of death for you to remember you have another son? FUCK YOU!"

He threw his plate of eggs at the wall and rushed out of the kitchen. I couldn't even begin to understand what just happened, but I went after him, my quick steps matching the rhythm of my heart.

"Hayden!" He didn't turn to look at me. He slipped into his jacket and snatched his car keys from the small table in the hallway. "What are you doing? Where are you going?"

"I'm out of here. I can't stand to be here with that lying bitch."

"Please calm down. Let's talk. Let's try to solve this."

He put on his boots furiously. He still didn't look at me. "There's nothing to solve. I'm done with her."

"But you can't drive. Remember what the doctor told you. You have a brain injury—"

"I don't care."

Without a second thought, I grabbed my jacket, slipped on my shoes, and rushed after him into the cold, snowy morning. He wrenched the driver's door open, and I placed my hand on his shoulder.

"At least let me drive." I gave him an imploring look. "Please think about your current condition. I'll take you wherever you want."

His eyes searched for something in mine as he fought an internal battle, and I took a step closer to him. I cupped his cheek. "Let me help you. I don't want you to be alone," I whispered. I was scared that he would drive off and end up in an accident. He still hadn't recovered, and his reflexes were slower than usual, so I couldn't let him wander off somewhere alone.

Just when I thought he would refuse me, he finally nodded and went around his car to the passenger's door. Grateful that he was letting me do this, I got in, unlocked his door, and turned on the heater, happily embracing the heat. There was less snow today, so it hadn't accumulated much during night. However, it was slushy—my least favorite—and navigating the streets could be a challenge.

I adjusted the driver's seat and put my seat belt on. "Did you change to winter tires?"

He stared ahead of him with a tight jaw. "No. So be careful."

"Where do you want to go?"

"River."

"Okay."

I pulled onto the street. He hadn't put his seat belt on because of his ribs, so I had to drive even more carefully. Now that I thought about it...

"Why is there no seat belt warning?" There wasn't a warning the night I drove him after his fight, either.

"I disabled it."

"Why?"

He didn't look at me, his face tense. "Because sometimes I like to race without my seat belt on."

My anxiety spiked, and I swallowed with difficulty. "Why do you like to race without your seat belt on?"

"Because it gives me a rush, obviously."

I was scared to imagine the danger he put himself into each time he did that. I knew he needed danger in his life. He *craved* it, and it was his version of a fix. I couldn't understand it, but I accepted it.

"Does it help you forget the pain?"

"Are you acting like my therapist again?" he snapped, and a heaviness filled my chest. "I don't want to talk about it, so can you stop asking me so many fucking questions?"

I nodded, too upset to say a word. I clenched the steering wheel and forced myself to take slow breaths.

"Fuck, Sarah. I'm not in a good mood right now, so can we just stop talking for a while?"

I nodded once more and bit into my lip. This was a part of him, and I had to learn to deal with it better. If his emotions were too much for him, he would lash out, but I had to be patient and wait for him to calm down until he learned to control it better.

We didn't say a word for the rest of the drive, both of us in our own worlds until we reached the river, and I just hoped this place would bring Hayden a much-needed reprieve.

Chapter 15

HE GOT OUT OF THE CAR the moment I turned off the engine and headed to the same spot we visited before. I zipped up my jacket as I followed him, silently cursing the low temperature. The dark gray sky sparked uneasiness deep inside of me.

I stopped next to him and studied his tall form, which exuded aloofness. It was strangely emphasized by our snowy white surroundings that contrasted him. He didn't move as he looked at the river with uneven breaths, and I gave in to my impulses. I hugged him from behind and buried my cheek into his wide back.

"Sarah?" he breathed out.

"I just want to hold you like this. Please, let me hold you." He didn't reply, but he also didn't try to separate me from him, so I read that as a good sign and got as close to him as possible.

A cold breeze enveloped us in a long silence, apart from the babble of the river. I was shaking, so I pressed myself against him, paying attention to his ribs. The branches of the naked trees swayed graciously in the wind, capturing my gaze as I thought about Mrs. Black.

I felt bad for her because she obviously wanted to make things work with Hayden. I understood why Hayden wasn't willing to forgive her, but did that mean he would never let her make amends for everything she hadn't done?

She hadn't been a good mother to him, but if she was ready to change and give him the attention he deserved, maybe it would be the right thing to give her a chance.

"How can she be so calm about it?" Hayden suddenly asked and cupped my freezing hands on his stomach with his. He brought my right hand to his mouth and huffed warm air over it. "How can she look me in the eyes and speak like that when she sees how much it hurts me?"

"She just wants to solve things as calmly as possible, I guess. She wants to get through to you but doesn't know how."

"You can't solve seventeen years of neglect with a few calm words."

The truth in his words cut to the quick, all the more because I experienced the same feelings of inadequacy and loneliness with my mother.

"Do you believe she's changed?"

"No." He took my other hand and blew warm air on it too. "Did you even see how tired she looked? She was already tired of talking with me. How can I be sure that tomorrow I won't receive the same old treatment?"

"You've got a point. But what if there is a chance that she's really changing? Just like you or me."

He stared into the distance as he mulled over my words, never letting go of my hands. "It doesn't make any difference. I can't forgive her. It's too late for that."

A gush of icy wind sent a strong shiver down my back, and I snuggled closer to him. My cheeks and nose burned. "Then what do you plan to do? Do you want to avoid her for the rest of your life?"

"That's the plan, yeah."

I moved in front of him to face him. I was saddened by bitterness I found in his eyes. "Will that make you happy?"

"I know what won't make me happy, and that's being a fool who trusts her after everything."

I glanced away. Solitude wasn't a solution to his problems, but I didn't know what to say. I thought about his future and if he would go to college, which only brought to mind a more pressing matter.

I met his gaze with trepidation in my chest. "Have you thought about going to college?"

He gave me a wary look. He inclined his head to the side, studying me intently. "Why do you ask?"

I shifted on my feet and focused on my entwined hands. I'd been psyching myself up for days to tell him about Yale, but now that the moment had come, it didn't feel any easier. "I... I wanted to tell you... I applied to Yale and I... I got accepted."

I tore my gaze from my hands to look at him, expecting him to become angry, shout, walk away, *anything*, except what he actually did.

"You did?! FUCK YES!" He fist bumped the air and pulled me into the tightest embrace possible. "I knew it! That's my girl! I'm so proud of you, Sarah. I'm so proud." He left tiny kisses all over my cheeks, nose, lips, and jaw, and I just stood with my mouth agape.

Was... Was this really happening? My heartbeat sped up as I tried to make sense of his reaction. He was proud of me? He wasn't angry?

I couldn't push any words out of my mouth, so I cleared my throat twice. "You... You aren't angry?" My gravelly voice was barely audible through the strong current of emotions.

He leaned away to look at me and wrapped his hands around my upper arms. "Why would I be angry?"

Moisture pooled in my eyes. "Because it feels like I'm leaving you?" I clung onto his jacket. "I'm not leaving you, Hayden. I want us to work this out. I want us to find a solution."

He scrunched his brows together. "I know, Sarah. Look, I always knew this was going to happen."

I straightened. "What do you mean? Me going away to college?"

"You going away to Yale. I knew you wanted to go there. You're a great artist, with a good GPA and extracurriculars to match, so I was sure you were going to get accepted."

My lips parted in silent surprise. My mind reeled with many questions now that I knew he'd been aware of Yale. I was touched that he believed in me, although I couldn't miss the irony—most of my determination to succeed had stemmed from my fervent desire to escape him.

"You really think that?"

His face was dead serious. "No. This is a hidden camera show and you've just been pranked."

Hayden and his other trademark—sarcasm. "How did you know I wanted to go to Yale?"

"I heard you talking about it with Kayden once. You mentioned to him that your dream had always been to go to Yale, so I knew that you would definitely apply for it."

He heard me telling that to Kayden? He'd always known? My eyes roamed over the dormant trees while I thought about what he'd just said. It never occurred to me that he'd known all along about my dream to go to Yale. Had he ever planned to go there too?

"But how about you? Have you applied to Yale too?"

He shook his head. "No. I never wanted to go there, and even if I wanted to, I don't have enough extracurriculars or a particularly good GPA and SAT scores. So there goes that."

My heart dropped at his words. It was followed by an ache in my chest when I considered all the unwanted possibilities. We would be separated, and I didn't want that. His expression told me he felt the same.

"I'm so sorry. I thought you were going to get angry and... I'm sorry for expecting that. I'm so conflicted because going to Yale has always been my dream, but I don't want to lose you."

"I know, baby. And you won't lose me. I don't want you to change your plans or ruin your future because of me. I want you happy. I want you to fulfill your dreams."

Oh my God. He was selfless and considerate and... He was *perfect*.

"But how? How can we work this out? I want to go to Yale, but I don't want us to separate." I sniffed. "Then again, getting accepted doesn't mean anything if I don't get financial aid. So maybe I won't go to Yale after all."

I felt conflicted about this, and I didn't know what to do. I wanted to go to Yale, but I wanted Hayden too. I wanted to follow my dreams and make something out of myself, but did that mean losing Hayden? This was beyond complicated.

"You'll get that financial aid, and even if you don't, I'll help you with it."

"No. I don't want that—"

"Sarah, we aren't discussing this." He palmed my cheek. "I've made your life hell for years, which I can never give back to you. I did so many things to hurt you, and I destroyed you on so many levels. So I want to spend the rest of my life making it up to you."

His fingers moved over my trembling lips before he took my hands into his and blew warm air on them again. "Money means nothing to me. I've always had loads of it. What I really need is your happiness."

"You don't need to buy your redemption, Hayden. As long as you trust me, love me, and treat me with respect, I don't need anything else."

"But I need to make you happy. You've forgiven me, but that doesn't change the fact that I treated you in the worst way possible. So now I want to make things right. Don't refuse me that. Your happiness is my happiness, and if going to Yale is going to make you happy, I'm going to do everything to make that happen."

I had no way of explaining to him how much I appreciated him. He was all I ever wanted in a guy and so much more, and knowing we would have to separate soon was tearing me up little by little.

"But if I go to Yale, what will you do? Do you want to go to college?"

His face turning dismal, he embraced me and cradled my head against his shoulder. "I never had dreams or plans for my future. I never even knew whether I'd go to college or not. But now I know. I want to be close to you. I've thought about this a lot, and I decided to pick a college close to Yale, and we'll rent some place and live together—"

"Whoa. Wait." I pulled away from him so I could look him in the eyes. I'd never even thought about that option, and now that he suggested it... "You want us to *live together*?"

"That's it. I'm taking you to a doctor tomorrow. You're definitely deaf." My smile grew bigger, along with my excitement. "That's what I said, Sarah. We'll rent a place that's near our colleges, and the problem is solved."

Hayden and I would be living together? This day just got so much better.

"Hayden, you're amazing!" I jumped at him and hugged him, sending him a few steps back because he wasn't expecting it.

"Hey, easy! My ribs!" he complained, but then he burst into chuckles. His fingers threaded through my hair affectionately as his other arm wound around my waist to hold me against him.

We had a way to be together. We didn't have to be separated. I was ecstatic!

"You're the best! I love you, Hayden! I adore you!"

I grabbed his face and pulled his lower lip into my mouth greedily. He angled my head and explored my lips before his tongue flicked against mine, which warmed my body from the inside out. Our hands were restless, roaming over our bodies as we tried to get as close as possible to each other.

Without warning, he pushed me down, and I rolled over the snowy ground. He covered me with his body before I could move, his laughter becoming louder when I shot him a glare.

"Are you crazy? It's freezing! And I hate snow! I—" He dumped a snowball directly on my face, which sent some of the snow into my mouth. I coughed, bowled over. "Hayden! You!"

I reached for the snow, rushing to give him a taste of his own medicine, but he grabbed my hand and pressed it against the ground above my head.

"I don't think so," he said with a smirk and smeared a handful of snow on my face with his free hand.

I thrashed against him. "Hayden!" My heart threatened to burst in my chest as I fought for dominance.

His laughter rang through the air, drowning out my grunts and complaints, before he sent us rolling across the ground, completely coating us with snow. I fell on top of him, straddling him with his hands on my hips, and supported myself against his chest that was now rapidly rising and falling.

"Now you're right where I wanted you," he murmured seductively.

I was more than aware of how perfectly our bodies molded together, and I forgot about the snow or the cold. His glimmering dark brown eyes bore into mine, and his laughter diminished. His hands slid down my hips and over the front of my thighs.

"You're devious," I told him, growing hotter under his touches. His hand cupped my butt, pressing me against him, and the motion sent a pang of pleasure through me.

"You're beautiful," he replied.

My already red cheeks burned at his words. "Thank you."

His stunning smile took my breath away. He was truly a work of art. "No, thank *you*. You helped me more than you can imagine. It's thanks to you that I was able to calm down and feel like this."

I ran my finger across his lips and cheeks, stopping on his scar. I caressed it softly. "Feel like what?"

"Happy."

I flicked my gaze back and forth between his eyes and soft lips, mesmerized by him. I smiled back at him. *My Hayden.* "I'm so happy when you're happy. I'll always help you whenever you need me."

"I always need you."

He pulled me in for a kiss, and we ended making out for a couple of intense minutes that had me restless and hot. I felt the happiest ever, exhilarated at the prospect of my future with Hayden as we got closer to each other every day.

We were both damaged—both imperfect—but despite all our issues and setbacks, we were perfect together. I felt like I found my home, and despite the darkness in ourselves and the world, we found our peace, and it was something that was going to help us continue on the right way. And I didn't need anything else.

Chapter 16

"IT'S GOING TO BE ALL right, Sar. Don't let one argument ruin the whole night for you," Mel told me as she applied a dark gray eyeshadow on my eyelids. "And it's not any night. It's *the* night, so don't you dare get all depressed. This party is definitely not my idea of fun with Steven's stupid friends there, but if I can get excited about it, you can too."

"Mel is right," Jess said. She put her eyeliner on next to me. "I'm sure Hayden will calm down and everything will be all right, so don't worry much about it."

I wasn't quite sure about that. I hadn't heard from him since our fight this morning.

Hayden and I had a huge fight because he found out I helped Carmen with housekeeping to earn money. It all started when he noticed that my car was missing from my driveway. I told him about my current money issues and that I didn't want to accept Carmen's money without earning it.

He got so mad at Carmen anyway, and I barely stopped him from picking another quarrel with her.

"I didn't even know about this shit," he'd told me. "You should've told me you had serious money issues. I never would've let you work as a fucking cleaner at my house."

"And what's wrong with working as a cleaner? That's an honorable job."

"It's wrong that you have to work so much when I can easily help you."

"I don't want you to help me that way. I want to be independent, and I can't accept others paying for me when I can do it by myself."

"But working at my house? Do you seriously think I can be okay with that? My girlfriend cleaning my room? No. I don't want you to keep doing it."

I blew my top at that, exasperated because he was leaving me with no choices, even though I was supposed to stay calm. "Then what do you want me to do?! I need money, and I won't accept yours! What other job will leave me with enough time for school and my job at the retirement home?"

"Use your brain, Sarah! You're an artist! You can do a lot with your skills. You can earn money on the Internet. There are so many websites where you can showcase your work and get commissions from clients. Do something that will help your art career."

"But I'm still a minor. I doubt many people would hire me if they found out I'm a high school student."

"Then use your art accounts, for fuck's sake! You have enough people following you, and I'm sure there's someone who would love to have your drawings. You can also set up an account for donations."

"Yes, I can do that, but those things take time. I wouldn't earn much money in the beginning."

Our wrangle continued until he told me he couldn't calm down when I was with him and asked me to leave him alone. I'd sent him a couple of texts during the day and even called him to check up on him, but he didn't respond, and I didn't know what to do. I couldn't be fired up about tonight's party anymore now that we were on bad terms.

"He was right about the websites, though," I told them. "It never even crossed my mind to earn money that way. Besides, I have enough followers on my Instagram and YouTube to start doing commissions."

"So he isn't only good-looking, he has brains too!" Mel said, her voice laced with sarcasm. I rolled my eyes and pinched her shoulder. "Hey! No need to pinch me, ya know?"

I pinched her once more. "No need to talk about him that way."

"Why are you so serious? It's just good old sarcasm. I don't actually think he's stupid, geez."

"So you admit he's good-looking?" Jess asked with a grin on her face, interrupting our bickering.

"I never said he was ugly. I said he was a jerk—"

"Mel," I warned her.

She sighed. "Past tense. I'm not saying it now, okay? I'm changing my tune about him. Now stop moving if you don't want me to turn you into a panda."

"Pandas are cute," Jess said.

"This one will be ugly," Mel muttered as she put on my mascara.

We were at Mel's grandparents' house. Steven was our designated driver, and we'd agreed to pick up Kevin on our way to the party. Chris, the guy throwing the party, didn't go to our school, but I suspected he was from the gang since Steven knew him too. I didn't know how to feel about this.

Hayden was supposed to wait for me in Chris's driveway, and I was anxious about seeing him since I didn't know if he was going to be angry. Just as Mel finished my makeup, my phone beeped, and I snatched it from Mel's bed.

"I say sorry more times than I can count. I'm sorry. I just needed to sleep the day away because I couldn't handle it any other way. I can't wait to see you tonight."

My throat constricted, and I took a deep breath. The heavy weight in my stomach instantly dissolved. He was just sleeping. He wasn't angry with me anymore.

I typed a text quickly.

"I'm sorry for getting that mad. I shouldn't have yelled at you. I can't wait to see you too."

"So?" Mel asked me. "Is everything okay now?"

"I think so. He says he's sorry and can't wait to see me tonight."

She started applying her foundation with a sigh. "So what did you decide? Will you quit cleaning his house?"

"I haven't decided yet. I mean, it *is* an awkward situation."

Mel met my gaze. "But you need money."

"I looked for one of the art websites he mentioned, and I found something interesting. I think I'll be able to start earning enough money soon."

"I'm surprised he didn't offer you money," Jessica said and put red lipstick on her ample lips.

I used a moment to take her in, noticing how gorgeous she looked. Her long straight blonde hair was curled now, with a red flower hairpin attached above her left ear. She wore a short, tight red dress that emphasized her curvy hips, lush backside, and breasts, completing her look with black ankle-strap pumps. I didn't doubt she was going to hook up with someone tonight.

"He offered, but I didn't want to accept it."

"That's my girl," Mel said and reached for her black eyeliner. "Independence all the way."

I looked at myself in the full-length mirror as I stood up, letting my gaze slide all over my body. Butterflies swarmed my stomach when I thought about Hayden's reaction.

I was wearing a black A-line dress that reached my mid-thighs. Mel's mom had bought it in an attempt to make her wear something more "feminine" than her usual clothes. Mel, being Mel, refused to wear it and stuffed it on the bottom of her closet with no intention of ever taking it out again.

She suggested that I wear it instead of my jeans and shirt, and I actually liked it. Mel and I had the same shoe size, so she lent me her black four-inch heels that I felt surprisingly comfortable in.

Mel used styling cream on me, which brought the best out of my pixie cut. My makeup was flawless, applied in a way that accentuated my brown eyes and high cheeks, giving me the sexy look I otherwise lacked.

"You have killer legs, Sar," Mel told me and shrugged on her blazer. "I don't know why you're always hiding them. I'm sure Hayden will go crazy for you. More than he already is, anyway." She winked at me and put on her knee-high steampunk boots.

Unlike Jess and me, Mel looked edgier; her black corset mini-dress and makeup brought out her inner fierceness. She had more eyeliner than Jessica and I combined, but it fit her blue eyes nicely, combined with dark brown lipstick on her full lips.

"And I'm sure all guys in that house will go crazy for *you*," I told her. "You look amazing."

She rolled her eyes and ran her brush through her shoulder-length hair. "Not interested," she muttered.

Jessica bumped Mel's hip with hers and gave her a crooked grin. "Why not?"

Jess's question brought some of my own to the surface. Mel had never said anything about dating or crushing on someone. Now that I thought about it, whenever we talked about dating, she always led the conversation in Jess's or my direction, never talking about herself much. I tried asking her about hooking up with someone, but her answer was always the same: she wasn't interested. Why?

"Exactly. Why not, Mel? You look amazing and you can have anyone you want. Is there someone you like?"

Melissa looked at me like the idea of her liking anyone was absurd. "Of course not."

"Why?" Jessica pressed her.

She started brushing her hair aggressively, noticeably irritated by our questions. "Because, as I said, I'm not interested. Guys are just a waste of time."

"Are you sure you aren't a lesbian or bi?" Jess asked, wiggling her brows at her.

Mel sighed. "No. I'm not a lesbian, or bi, or asexual, or however you want to define me. Is it so strange that I just don't want to date anyone?"

There was something fishy here, but I didn't want to corner her with endless questions. There had to be a reason why she didn't want a relationship. Saying she simply wasn't interested wasn't a plausible excuse.

"If you say so," I said and signaled to Jess with my eyes to drop the subject.

My phone beeped, and I opened Hayden's new message.

"I miss you already."

My smile stretched across my whole face.

"I miss you too, Hayden."

"I bet you'll be the sexiest at the party."

I giggled, blushing.

"We'll be there in thirty."

"Waiting."

The door of Mel's room burst open, and Steven barged in. "You've been taking forever to get ready! You know the party is this year?"

Mel put her hands on her hips and glared at him. "Get out, punk! How many times have I told you not to come in here without knocking? Are you that stupid?"

He didn't even pay attention to her; his eyes lasciviously roamed over Jess and me. He wolf-whistled at us. "You two are sexy. Damn, Hayden is a lucky guy."

I blushed furiously as I lowered my head, pretending there was something extremely interesting in my purse. I was sure Jess had the same embarrassed look on her face.

"Get out of here!" Melissa pushed him outside. "Don't give me a reason to make your eye purple before we even get to the party. I prefer to save my punches for later."

"Thanks, sis. Your love warms my poor, tortured heart," he said right before Mel shut the door in his face.

Mel grimaced. "Can I sell him? There has to be someone who looks for dumb assholes like him. Hell, I'd even give him away for free." Jess and I burst into giggles. "Or hire an assassin to take him out. Even better."

Our giggles turned into laughter, and I finally relaxed, starting to look forward to tonight's party.

. . . .

"SO MANY CARS," JESS muttered when we reached Chris's house. "This is one big party."

My eyes switched from the grandiose manor to the massive line of cars that filled both driveways. A sizeable fountain in front of the house was currently turned off, and a few people sat on its edge despite the cold weather, drinking beer. The most of the snow had thawed, leaving wetness all around.

"What is this Chris? A duke?" Mel said from the passenger seat. Jess giggled beside me.

"His parents are the major players in oil industry," Steven replied.

"So why does he fight if he doesn't need money?"

"'Cause he's bored," he answered in a tone that suggested Mel had asked a stupid question.

Melissa blew her gum until it popped. "He's spoiled, let me tell ya that."

"Nobody asked for your opinion, sis."

Steven parked at the end of a long row of cars almost five hundred yards from the front door, and I looked around for any sight of Hayden.

"How do you feel?" Jess asked Kevin, who twiddled his thumbs on his lap beside her.

He looked older and more rugged with his styled hair and no glasses, wearing his contacts instead. I was sure he could find a girl at the party if he managed to relax. He looked pretty anxious.

"A bit nervous," he replied in a slightly higher voice. "I don't usually go to p-p-parties."

"You don't usually go to parties? What are you? A nun?" Steven said before he opened the door and got out. I was pretty sure he added "Loser" before he shut his door.

Mel turned to look at Kevin. "Don't pay attention to that prick. He doesn't know what he's talking about ninety nine percent of the time. He needs a brain transplant."

Kevin smiled sheepishly at her, and even in the semi-darkness, I could discern the redness on his cheeks. "Thanks, Mel."

Mel clapped her hands. "Okay, children. Let's go."

We got outside, and I whimpered when the cold rush of wind enveloped me. I might as well be naked because this dress didn't keep me warm, and my stockings did nothing against the cold that bit at my legs. I wrapped my arms around my waist and glanced around looking for Hayden again.

I found him leaning against Blake's red Dodge Challenger in the distance, right next to Masen, who was kissing some redhead in a leather skirt with his hands all over her. Hayden's eyes locked with mine as I approached him before they slid down my body slowly and lingered on my legs. I halted mid-step, my body flushing hot under his sensual gaze. I was barely aware of Mel, Jess, and Kevin stopping close to us, watching Hayden cross the distance that separated us.

By the time he reached me, his eyes burned with intensity that swallowed me whole. "Sarah, you... You're *gorgeous*."

He grabbed my face and pulled me into a kiss. Our lips clashed together, and warmth soared in me, quelling the cold from the outside. His restless hands roamed all over my back, until they stopped on my bottom and pulled me flush against him. I grew dizzy from his kisses and closeness.

"Horny kids! You have an audience," Mel called at the top of her voice. Hayden and I broke our kiss to look at her. "It's good to see you've recovered and are ready for some action, Hayden."

Her smile was too sweet, and I felt Hayden tense. I sent him a pleading gaze to not pay attention to her goading. Even though Mel was supporting us now, I hadn't expected her to act one hundred percent friendly with him yet.

"Remember what I told you?" I whispered into his ear. "She promised me she wouldn't goad you anymore, especially now that she knows about your disorder. This is just the way she jokes, but she has no intention of hurting you."

Hayden nodded and cast her an emotionless gaze. "Nice to see you, Melissa."

We all gaped at him, astonished by his unexpectedly polite answer despite the monotone voice. I felt immensely grateful that he was trying this hard for me.

Mel looked away and scratched the side of her neck. "Yeah. Nice to see you too," she muttered.

Jess smiled at Hayden. "We were worried about you. It's amazing how quickly you've recovered."

Hayden's lips curled slightly. "It's good to be back. You look nice," he said in approval and snaked his arm around my waist. My smile grew big when Jess blushed and grinned at him.

"Thank you."

"And this is Kevin Burks," I told Hayden, motioning at Kevin. "He's the transfer student I told you about." My smile wavered a little when I remembered how awkward it felt telling him Blake and Masen had bullied Kevin.

Kevin gave Hayden the once-over, red as a radish. "Hello. It's nice to meet you." He stared at the ground as he extended his hand for a hand shake.

Wearing an amused expression, Hayden accepted his hand. "You can look me in the eyes, Burks. I won't bite you." His voice was light, but Kevin blushed even harder and barely glanced at Hayden before he snatched his hand away.

"Are we, we, we going inside now?" Kevin asked Mel, his face pinched.

"Sure. We don't want to catch STDs," she answered with a sneer. Her eyes were on Masen, who was still kissing the redhead without paying any attention to us. "Let's go." She made a beeline for the front door, and Kevin and Jess followed her.

I met Hayden's gaze. There was a mixture of amusement and discomfort on his face. "What?" I asked.

"He was checking me out. It felt weird."

I whipped my head at Kevin. "Are you sure? Kevin? I thought he liked Jess." I focused on the way he looked at Jess and confirmed my suspicions once more. "Yes. I think he likes her."

"Maybe he's playing for both teams?"

That thought never occurred to me, but seeing the way he reacted with Hayden, that could be the case.

"As long as he's not into you, I'm okay with it." He pecked me on the cheek.

"There's no need for you to be jealous. You know that, don't you?" I placed my hands on his shoulders and brushed his lips with mine. "I only have eyes for you. Besides, no guy can compare to you. You're the handsomest, smartest, and greatest guy I've ever met."

"Yes, baby. I'm a Mighty One," he said flatly, with a serious face, but then he rolled his eyes. I burst out chuckling.

"I'm sorry," he said when my chuckles quieted. He ran his hand across my cheek. "I'm so sorry for today. I acted like a jerk. You're right. Since you don't want to take my money, you don't have many choices, and I don't want to take your choice away from you. I don't like you working at my house, but I won't force you to stop. I'll respect your choice."

Once more, I was floored by his progress. He tried his best to understand me, even when he didn't agree with my way of thinking.

"Thank you for this, but I understand it's weird. So I'll look for some other way to earn money. You were right about selling my drawings. I want an art career, so I might as well start it now."

"Yoohoo," Mel shouted to us from the front door. "It's damn freezing out here, so can you do us all a favor and continue your talk when we get inside?!"

Masen groaned and finally separated himself from the redhead. He glared at her. "Will you shut up already?! I can't stand your banshee voice!" He was slurring his words, showing just how drunk he already was.

Mel's sugary smile wasn't pleasant in the least. "And I can't stand your entire existence, but can I do anything about it?!"

Masen flipped her off and smirked at Kevin. "Look who we have here. It's girly four-eyes Burks! Isn't it too late for you to be away from your mommy?"

"Not tonight, man. Drop it," Hayden warned him, and I smiled gratefully. He wasn't going to let them bully Kevin.

Masen raised his arms defensively. "Okay, bro. Let's pretend we're all best buddies tonight."

Melissa looked like she was going to rip his eyeballs out. "I'm going to murder someone, and it will all be in the morning's headlines," she said when Hayden and I joined her, Jess, and Kevin. "I can already imagine it: A Seventeen-Year-Old Kills a Pathetic Asshole on New Year's Eve."

"Come on, Mel," I told her. "Let's go inside before this turns into a battlefield."

Masen and his redhead were right behind us, and we entered the house together, which was filled with blaring music, drunk teenagers, sweat, and lots of smoke. We took off our jackets and left them with countless others in the huge entryway closet that spoke another tale of how rich Chris's family was. I was sure finding my jacket in the sea of others later would be an impossible mission.

Hayden checked me out now that he could see my nice dress, and he took his time. My body buzzed with awareness. He wore a gray long-sleeve shirt and black jeans, looking beyond sexy, which he complemented with black earrings, black leather bracelet, and black boots. I'd already noticed some girls openly stare at his delectable body, and it felt more than amazing knowing he was only mine.

He licked his lips before he met my stare, and his eyes grew even darker than usual.

"Fuck. You're going to drive me crazy tonight," he said into my ear before he bit my earlobe, intoxicating me with his words and touches. I hoped we could get some privacy later on so we could make out.

"I can say the same for you. You're sexy."

He groaned. "Don't provoke me, baby. Come on. Let's join the others before I decide to do something to you right in this closet."

I couldn't stop smiling. His hand found mine, and he led me to an enormous living room. It was decorated with various Christmas ornaments, wreaths, and garlands, and a giant Christmas tree stood in one corner of the room, embellished with lights and white glass balls. I was surprised it was still in one piece with all the drunk people dancing dangerously close to it.

"Blake should be somewhere here," Hayden said as we moved through the dancing crowd.

I glanced over my shoulder at Jess, Mel, and Kevin and gave them a thumbs-up, soaking in the euphoria of the people around us. Everyone's mood boosted my own, and I was pumped up about starting a new year next to Hayden and my friends.

"I hope Blake won't cause a problem because of Jessica and Kevin," I said to Hayden.

"I'll make sure he won't," he replied.

"I don't want to cause problems between you two."

"Don't worry about it. He'll come around."

Blake, Steven, and a few of their friends occupied a couch along the left wall. Steven was seated next to Blake with a blonde on his lap, whom he was busy necking. Blake stood up when he saw us approach, carrying a half-finished cigarette in one hand and a red Solo cup in the other. His gaze moved down my body before his lips formed a smile.

"Looking good, Sarah."

I returned his smile and nodded. I could say the same for him. He was dressed in jeans and a dark shirt that showed off his muscular body, making it obvious why he was a girl-magnet. "Thank you, Blake."

I didn't know how to act next to him since only a couple of days ago I'd laid into him and Masen in the cafeteria. They were nice to me after that, surprisingly, but it didn't feel right. Hayden was the only link that connected us, and while they were civilized for his sake, they didn't reserve the same treatment for Jess, Mel, and Kevin. Hayden promised me he would talk to them and make sure they left my friends alone, but I didn't expect anything but strained relationships. Would Masen and Blake ever accept my friends?

"Keep your eyes on her face," Hayden warned him with a barely visible smirk on his face.

Blake was about to retort when his eyes landed on Jess, who stopped next to me. His face changed expressions swiftly, from disbelief to confusion and something I couldn't pinpoint, and it was bewildering. His lips parted as he assessed her appearance, too fazed to say anything, but then their eyes locked, and he bared his teeth.

"This has just turned into the shittiest party ever," he said loud enough for Jess to hear him. I held my breath when he turned his attention to Kevin, who stood at Jessica's side, waiting for an insult. However, he didn't say a word. He spun around and stomped away, carrying his drink and cigarette with him.

Jess's expression was indecipherable as she watched him. "It's like I'm a disease," she said barely audibly, but I could detect the hurt in her voice. "How much more horrible he can be?"

"Who cares about that asshole?" Mel said and handed her and Kevin cups with beer. "Let him choke on his cigarette before he drowns in his puke. Now let's dance!"

She snatched another cup from the nearby table for herself and pulled Jess and Kevin to the dance floor.

"I'll stay here with Hayden for a bit. I'll join you later," I told her when she glanced at me in question.

"Suit yourself."

Hayden sat between Steven and Masen, who both had girls on their laps now, and pulled me onto his lap. I giggled, thrilled that he held me like this, which turned into more when he kissed me and erased everything from my mind but the feel of his lips and hands on me.

I moaned into his mouth when he slid his hands down my back and gripped my hips to draw me closer to him. I was restless as I explored his chest and shoulders, enjoying the way his muscles flexed under my touch. I was affecting him just like he was affecting me, and both of us were lost in our small bubble.

Hayden broke our kiss a couple of minutes later and reached to take a cigarette from Masen.

I frowned. He shouldn't be smoking because of his brain injury. "Hayden, you know smoking isn't good for you because of your condition. You can make things worse—"

"One cigarette won't kill me."

"Not smoking also won't kill you."

He rolled his eyes and grabbed a lighter from Masen. He looked too eager to light his first cigarette after almost a month. "Right now, I feel like it will." His eyes held mine as he put the cigarette into his mouth. "I promised I wouldn't drink tonight, which is already hard enough, but I need a cigarette. Just one, so stop pushing it."

"Come on, Sar," Masen told me, stroking the redhead's back idly. "Give him a break. One cigarette won't make a difference."

I pursed my lips together. I wasn't convinced, but I didn't want to start an argument when Hayden was so set on doing it. I didn't want to make him angry. At least he wouldn't drink tonight, which had to count for something.

After a few years of constant drinking, Hayden was finally making an effort to give up alcohol, and his brain injury made this decision easier. His condition would take a turn for the worse if he returned to drinking, so he had to refrain from it, at least for some time. I was well aware alcohol was his buffer against his dark emotions, so I appreciated all the more when he tried quitting.

I went to get a beer for me and Coke for him and returned to his lap. At the same time, Steven and his girl stood up and headed out of the room, with his hand plastered on her butt as they walked away.

"So, Decker, is your friend available?" one of Hayden's friends asked. He was sitting on the couch's armrest, pointing at Melissa. "She's hot."

Mel was currently swaying her hips to the rhythm of the music, her eyes closed. She was attractive with curves in all the right places, so it was no wonder she'd caught his attention.

"She doesn't have a boyfriend, but I don't think you stand a chance with her," I told him and took a sip of my beer, thinking about what she told Jess and me just an hour ago.

He gave me a sideways look. "Why not? All chicks dig me. Unless she's a lesbian?"

I snorted and took another sip. Such overconfidence. "She's straight."

"Then why not?"

"The real question is why you're interested in that nut case," Masen countered. "You seriously think she's hot? Look at her. She's like a circus attraction with all that scary makeup. Of all chicks in the room, you had to pick her."

I glared at him. "Don't talk like that about her. Besides, she's your friend's *sister.*"

"Even he knows she's cray cray," he replied nonchalantly.

"He's right," Blake said and took the seat Steven had left next to Hayden and me. He chugged his beer and glanced at me with unfocused eyes. "She's crazy. You sure know how to pick your friends."

"Blake," Hayden hissed, his body growing rigid.

"It's okay, Hayden," I said and looked back at Blake. "It's not a secret that up until recently I was also one of the 'losers.' Isn't that right, Blake?" I needed alcohol if I was going to say what was on my mind, so I downed my beer in one go.

"Don't ruin this evening, Sar," Masen said. "It's New Year's Eve! Come on, we didn't come here for this."

"Then when do you want to talk about it?" I glanced between Masen and Blake. "Like it or not, Melissa and Jessica are my friends, so if you can't treat them nice, at least ignore them. Don't make their lives more difficult." I looked at Blake entreatingly. "Please leave Jess alone. She feels horrible each time you take a dig at her, and it's frustrating. She's my friend, and I don't want her to be treated that way, just like you wouldn't want anyone to treat Hayden that way."

A tiny voice from the corner of my mind whispered at me to me to stop talking, reminding me that he might bully Jess more whenever I interfere, but I hated seeing him do her wrong.

Hayden held my waist more tightly, but he didn't say anything as he waited for Blake's response. Blake wasn't even looking at me but out the window. His jaw was clenched hard, and I could clearly see a vein pulsating along it, telling me I'd overstepped.

I'd never felt this bold before, and I didn't know if that was because of Hayden's presence or I'd become tougher. All I knew was that I couldn't stay silent. Not when my friends' and boyfriend's happiness was on the line.

"Fine. Whatever," Blake spat out at last, and I gave a sigh of utmost relief.

"Thank you," I replied. I truly hoped this was a turning point in the way he treated my friends.

Two cups of beer and two shots of tequila later, I left my purse with Hayden and let Mel drag me to the dance floor, feeling sloshed. I stopped next to an equally drunk Kevin and Jessica and sent them a goofy smile.

"Are you having fun?" I asked Kevin, who danced quite awkwardly but still managed to make it look cute. At least he was trying.

"Yep. It's awesome, but Jess didn't let me s-s-stop even for a s-second."

"Hey! Don't whine!" Jess smacked his shoulder playfully. Her glazed eyes attested to the amount of alcohol she'd consumed. "We should enjoy this night! It's the best time of the year!"

"Exactly!" Mel agreed and shook her hips. "And I don't plan to spend it sitting! No, sir!"

I stuck my tongue out at her and went into a fit of laughter when Jess spun me around. Her happy face was covered with a thin layer of sweat, just like mine. Her bubbly excitement was contagious.

She pulled me closer to her and brought her lips to my ear. "Blake has been watching me all night."

I gaped at her. *What?* I glanced at Blake as subtly as possible, and there he was, reclined on the couch with his legs wide open and eyes set on Jessica. His expression was unreadable, but something told me it wasn't animosity that drove him to watch her this intently.

Feeling bold thanks to the alcohol, I voiced something I'd wondered about for quite some time. "Do you like him, Jess?"

She stilled, which was followed by a brief glimpse of sadness on her face. "I don't know, Sar."

I grasped her hands. I understood how torn she must be feeling. "I think he likes you."

She answered with a laugh that held no trace of humor. "You're kidding me, right?"

"Then how do you explain this? He can't take his eyes off of you. And he looks at you all the time."

"He bullies me all the time."

"Hopefully not anymore."

She frowned. "What do you mean?"

I told her about my conversation with Blake earlier. Her face scrunched up in a grimace of disapproval, but then Kevin bumped his hip against hers as he made a clumsy spin, and her scowl transformed into a smile. Abandoning her worries, she stepped over to dance against him. I grinned as I watched them almost dry hump each other, moving faster when the tempo of the current pop song picked up.

I put my hands around Mel's neck and swayed my hips, matching her movements. We smiled at each other like fools, both doing some sexy moves

I'd never done before, but right now it all seemed so natural. Everything was a blur, and my coordination was poor, but I didn't care. It was New Year's Eve, and it was turning into the best night of my life.

I spun around with Mel's hands on my hips and met Hayden's stare, which took all the air out of my lungs. Even from here I could discern the intensity in his eyes as he watched my every single move, and I longed to feel him against me.

"I wouldn't be surprised if you two slept together tonight," Mel said into my ear.

I glanced over my shoulder at her, chuckling. "Why?"

"Because of the way he looks at you. He clearly wants you. So are you going to do anything about it?"

My breath hitched, and I looked back at Hayden, who was unaware of anyone or anything but me. I felt like he was undressing me with his eyes, but then two girls approached him and Blake, hiding my view of him, and jealousy tore through me. I stopped dancing and fixed my gaze on the short blonde who twirled a strand of her hair around her finger as she spoke to Hayden, while her brunette friend ended up on Blake's lap.

My heart thumped wildly as I waited for Hayden's reaction that never came. He looked disinterested, with his hands pushed into his pockets, but that didn't quench my jealousy. No, it burned stronger the longer she stayed there without getting the message to leave him alone. He shook his head at her and focused his attention elsewhere, but she didn't give up. The moment she placed her hand on the back of the couch and leaned closer to him was the moment my jealousy exploded, leading me closer to them.

Not fully aware of what I was doing, I pulled the blonde away from Hayden and got in her face, taller than her by a few inches that gave me an immense sense of power. "Stay away from him," I hissed with a voice I didn't recognize. "He's not interested in you."

Her sneer altered her beautiful face into something downright ugly. "What did you say, bitch? Nobody cares what you think. Scram!"

She flicked her long hair as she turned back to Hayden, which hit me directly across my face. My anger spiked big time. I didn't know where this courage came from, but I grabbed her shoulder and yanked her around to look at me. "He's my boyfriend, so you're the one leaving. *Scram!*"

The displeasure on her face replaced the initial shock, but she remained silent as she gave me a condescending glare. She marched away, and I grinned, proud at myself for acting this fiercely.

I couldn't believe I'd said those things! It was liberating and fulfilling, and I wished I could be this fearless after I sobered up. It felt amazing!

I finally turned to look at Hayden, and my lips parted when I read the expression on his face. It was a mixture of awe, pride, and something dark that stirred everything in me. Briefly glancing at his friends, I saw they all watched me with either respect or surprise, and I barely stopped a smug smile from breaking out.

Hayden stood up and halted in front of me, never breaking our eye contact. "You're something else when you're drunk, baby."

I sucked in a long inhale. "Do you think what I did was wrong?"

He raised his eyebrows. "Wrong? Fuck, no. Come with me."

He grabbed my wrist and pulled me after him, pushing through the crowd on the way out of the living room.

"Where are you taking me?" I asked him. My breathing quickened as excitement permeated my every pore. I needed this moment with him badly.

"To one of the guest rooms. We'll have some privacy there."

A guest room. My blood hummed with desire. He was opening a part of me that wanted this more than anything, and I remembered what Mel told me.

He wants me. So am I going to do anything about it?

Chapter 17

HAYDEN TOOK ME INSIDE a room on the second floor. The outside lights coming through a large set of windows provided enough light, so we stayed in the dark. I barely had time to take in the king size bed in the center of the room when he locked the door and spun me around, fusing his lips to mine. My purse dropped to the floor.

I moaned into his mouth. The taste of Coke was sweet on his tongue.

He moved his hands down my waist, backing me to the bed. "You're so fucking hot when you're jealous like that."

He covered my mouth with his again and kissed me like he starved for me. He pushed me down on the mattress and covered me with his body, supporting himself with his uninjured hand as he kissed my neck.

"Hayden..."

I wasn't able to think. I wasn't able to form even one coherent sentence as he trapped me with addictive kisses and touches. I threaded my fingers through his hair and pressed his head against my neck. His fervent kisses seared my skin. He rolled us over so that I straddled him with his hands holding my hips, and he captured my lips once more, rocking me against him slowly. I leaned away to look at his face.

He looked different. His features were distorted with desire, making him look even more attractive and irresistible, and his half-lidded eyes burned into me. His swollen lips invited me to nibble them, and I did just that, eliciting a moan from him.

"You're perfect, Sarah."

I could feel his rapid heartbeat getting faster under my hand on his chest. I needed him so much. What was he doing to me?

His hands reached the hem of my dress and started raising it, caressing each inch of my uncovered skin. I grabbed his hands and stopped them.

"I want you, but please not here," I whispered, unsure of where this would lead us.

He didn't move as he studied me, impatience etched into his face. Groaning, he let go off my dress and ran his hands up my sides, tugging me down for another kiss. His tongue slid through my parted lips and stroked mine fiercely, which spurred my need for him even more.

"You're such a tease," he said, his voice completely husky. "You seriously have no idea what I want to do to you."

"I know, but I don't want to do it here. It's my first time, so..." I looked away, embarrassed to talk about this, even drunk.

He pressed my forehead against his before he gave me the softest kiss ever. "I understand. And I don't want your first time to be here either. Besides, I need you to be relaxed and sober." He pecked my forehead. "You know I won't hurt you?"

"I know."

He flipped us around once more so that he was on top of me. "You can trust me. I just want to make you feel good."

We grew silent. Our quick breaths mixed together as we observed each other. "You're beautiful." He cupped my cheek. "Your striking brown eyes, your cute cheeks, your full lips..." His fingers moved across my cheeks and lips ever so gently. "This mole right here..." He touched the spot on my jaw. "Everything. I like every part of you."

I was mesmerized by the way he looked at me and touched me. "Are you sure you're not drunk?" I whispered.

"No, but I feel like it. You're fucking with my mind. I don't need alcohol to drown my thoughts when I have you." His fingers traced my forehead, nose, lips... "How does this feel?"

He slid his hand over my neck and collarbone, and my breathing grew heavy. I closed my eyes. "Good."

"Open your eyes." I met his heated gaze. "Don't hide from me."

He leaned down and planted a kiss on my collarbone that sent a shudder down my back. Holding my waist possessively, he lowered his lips across my skin until he reached the scoop neck of my dress. He looked at me when I stopped him. "What?"

"I..." I glanced away.

"What?" he pressed for an answer.

"I..." I closed my eyes again. I was too ashamed to admit what was on my mind. "I have small breasts. So, they're not so pretty."

He astounded me when he started laughing. It was a hearty, at the top of his lungs laughter, and I blushed to the roots of my hair.

"Why are you laughing?" My voice gave away my mortification. I covered my breasts, but he gently pried my hands away from them. His eyes were incredibly soft as he looked down at me.

"Yeah, I noticed you have small breasts. I have eyes, you know? And it's high time you check your hearing, since I just told you I like *everything* about you. Even your small breasts." Palming them, he kissed one breast over my dress and then the other.

"Hayden..."

I clutched his head when he moved up and sucked on one sensitive spot in the hollow of my neck. It was slightly uncomfortable, but more than that, it evoked pleasure, and I squirmed.

I tugged at his hair. "What are you doing?"

He pulled away and looked at that spot with clouded eyes. "Leaving proof that you're mine."

His hands became restless, touching me everywhere before they stopped on my most intimate part, and it felt too good. I never let go of him as he made me experience something that was carved deep into my mind to be remembered forever. His lips on mine drank my moans before the world stopped to exist in my rapturous haze, and I'd never felt more blissful than right now. I loved him. I loved him so much.

"You're so beautiful. I love you," he said hoarsely and hugged me close to him.

"Hayden, that was... I..." I didn't recognize my own voice. "I love you so much."

Our lips met again, and we continued kissing until someone turned off the music downstairs. Moments later, people started the countdown. It was already midnight.

"The countdown," I told him excitedly.

"Come here." He sat up and pulled me to him. "I finally get to start a new year with you."

"4!"

"3!"

"2!"

"1!"

"HAPPY NEW YEAR!"

Hayden pressed his lips on mine before I could say these exact words to him. He slid his tongue over mine, and I felt like my heart was going to burst from the sudden explosion of emotions. I ran my hands over his strong back, basking in the feel of his muscles underneath my fingertips—basking in *him*. I felt beyond happy to be able to share this moment with him and start a new year in the most special way, memorizing it forever.

"Happy New Year, Hayden. I love you."

"Happy New Year. I want to spend so many more new years with you."

"We will. We'll spend many, many more... That's a promise."

He gave me a quick, soft kiss. "I have a present for you."

I raised my brows. "Another one? You already gave me a Christmas present."

He'd gotten me a book on coloring and lighting for digital paintings, which showed me once more how well he knew me, gifting me something so special.

He pulled something out of his back pocket. "Yeah, but this is something I wanted to give you tonight. To show you how important you are to me."

I studied the envelope he held. "You didn't have to."

"I had to." He handed me the envelope, and I noticed slight embarrassment in his features, which indicated my reaction meant a lot to him.

"I'll like it for sure," I reassured him.

He stared at some spot on the bed, avoiding my gaze. "Just open it."

I opened the envelope and drew out a folded paper. A smile played across my lips when I saw a poem.

"For Sarah.

We're two dysfunctional pieces that will find their way to become a whole again.

Happy New Year

You. Me. Nothing. Everything.

Love. Hate. Success. In vain.
Dark and light every day, and it drives me insane.

But what is the sun without the rain?
Just like happiness without pain?

You gathered the pieces of my broken mind.
You helped me see hues when I was color blind.
You were the one who showed me happiness is real.
You kissed away my darkness and allowed me to heal.

In your kisses and touches I see my light.
Your smile and joy give me the reason to fight.
You're injecting life into me and keeping my pain at bay,
I've been running away, but now I'm here to stay.

Hold onto me and never let me go.
I'll keep you safe through every high and low.
I'll love your sorrow away and keep you near.
Together, we will conquer our darkness, pain, and fear.

You're my next intake of breath, my next heartbeat, my next
reason to be happy.

I'll hold you forever.

I love you.

Hayden"

My hands shook by the time I finished the poem. The warmth in his words enveloped me and filled the old dents in my heart with all-consuming love.

"You said you wanted me to write you poems. So..."

I met his gaze. "This... This is beautiful. Thank you so much!"

My chest constricted with burning adoration that propelled me to clutch his shoulders and kiss him hard. I felt delirious as my hands found their way over his chest and stomach, pouring all my love into the contact of our lips and bodies. He grabbed my hands and moved them under his clothes, letting me feel his abs. The contrast between his soft skin and the hard ridges of his muscles was ravishingly attractive.

I pulled away to look at him, curling my fingers against his waist. "I love you so much. This is the best gift."

I pecked him on the lips a few times, and they curved into a breathtaking smile. I was so in love with him.

"You're as excited as if you won the lottery."

"This is even better than the lottery!"

His smile faded away as he cupped my cheeks and leveled his face with mine, his warm breath fanning my lips. "This is nothing, baby. Besides, your Christmas gift was way better."

I'd given him a small notebook filled with some of my drawings and short love messages that imparted my most profound feelings to him. I shook my head, grinning. "I don't think so. Yours is way, way better."

His grin was even bigger than mine. "No, yours is."

I chuckled. His phone buzzed in his pocket, and he snorted when he took it out and read the message. "It's Masen."

"What does he say?"

"'Happy New Year, dipshit. Will you join the party already, or are you still busy fucking?'"

I burst out laughing. "He can't live without his dirty jokes and be polite for once, can he?"

He winked at me. "Where's the fun in that?" He placed his arm around my shoulder. "Come on. Smile for the camera."

He switched to the front-facing camera and extended his hand, preparing to take our first photo together. I smiled widely with bubbly excitement, ready for this beautiful moment to be saved forever.

"You look like a shark when you smile like that."

I grimaced and snapped my eyes at him. "*What?*"

A sound of shutter broke out just then, and a mortified gasp escaped me, turning into a shriek when I saw the photo of my horrible expression. My eyes were glassy from alcohol, which looked even less attractive. Needless to say, his blank face was ridiculously handsome even without a smile decorating it. Such disparity in our appearances wasn't fair. There went our first photo.

"Hayden! You ruined it! You ruined our first photo ever!"

He raised one eyebrow and looked at me like I'd gone crazy. "I ruined it? You're the one who made that stupid face!"

"Because of you!"

He shrugged. "Nobody asked you to get annoyed. And it's not like you're taking a photo for a magazine, so chill."

I folded my arms over my chest and pouted. "Delete it."

His mouth curled into a lazy grin. "No can do. This one will forever hold a special place in my heart." His tone was nothing short of sarcastic. He enjoyed pushing my buttons too much. "Now let's take one more."

"You better not say something bad." I smiled, wearing my best expression for the camera, but the moments passed, and he still didn't take the picture. "What are you waiting for?" He didn't respond, and I turned my head to look at him. "What are—"

His lips came down hard on mine, and another shutter sound went off. Redness colored my cheeks as we looked at each other. My heart thudded a chaotic beat by the time he broke our kiss, living off the onrush of happiness and love in me.

"There. The best photo ever." His face practically glowed as he looked at our photo with adoration, which showed the moment our lips connected. It was adorable.

"You're so devious," I muttered.

"I have to uphold my reputation." He pecked a kiss on my forehead. "Let's join the others."

I returned the poem to the envelope and put it in my purse. "Let's go."

A goofy smile stubbornly remained on my face when we went downstairs holding hands. We returned to the living room, but we couldn't find anyone. My eyes looked around for any sight of Jess and Mel.

"Where are they?" I asked Hayden.

"Hey, man! Happy New Year!" A blond guy emerged from the crowd and gave Hayden a half-hug, a crooked smile plastered across his face.

Hayden patted him on his back. His posture and expression were a sure sign of how he didn't want this guy in his personal space. "Yeah. Same to you, Chris. Cool party."

"As always." He winked at him before he looked at me. "Who's this?" His leering gaze roamed all over my body.

Hayden stepped right next to me and took me by hand, baring his teeth at him. "My girlfriend," he gritted out.

Chris met his gaze, getting the message. "*Girlfriend*? That's new." He winked once more at Hayden. What was it with him and winking? "It's interesting to hear someone finally managed to get Hayden Black. Congrats." He tapped Hayden on the shoulder and moved past us. "Enjoy the party."

Hayden's stern gaze followed Chris until he got out of the room. His jaw worked. "I hate the way he looked at you."

"Hey, it's okay. You don't have to worry about that. I mean, we can't stop others from looking, but that doesn't mean anything."

He looked at me, unconvinced. "Doesn't it? How can I be sure he won't steal you from me?"

I felt like someone had kicked me in the gut. We were back at this again, and I hated knowing he was so insecure and expecting to get betrayed every time something like this happened.

"He'll never steal me from you because I love you, Hayden." I placed my hand on his shoulder, trying my best to convey the truth with my expression. "You're all I need and want, and I don't care about the others. They will never stand between us."

He still didn't look convinced; his jaw was tightened as he stared off into the distance.

I left a soft kiss on his cheek. "After everything we went through, I would be crazy to even look in someone else's direction, not that I want to. So please don't let someone unimportant affect you."

I put my lips on his and nibbled on his lower lip. He didn't move away, but he also didn't respond to my kiss, and I saw he wasn't fully persuaded. Slowly, he wrapped his arms around my waist and drew me closer to him, separating his lips from mine.

"I hate this. I don't want to lose you." His voice carried sadness and insecurity, and I felt powerless because I couldn't eradicate his negative feelings. I could only help him cope with them and hope that time and his strong will would allow him to win over his insecurity.

"You won't lose me. I love you."

His serious face remained unchanged as he searched for the truth in my eyes. Finally, he nodded. "Let's look for the others in the kitchen."

He took my hand and led me there. I didn't fail to notice he didn't say he loved me too. He was far from okay, which effaced all residues of joy I felt just a few minutes ago.

"There you are!" I barely caught sight of Mel rushing out of the kitchen when she grabbed me and pulled me into a crushing hug. "Happy New Year!" She kissed me on one cheek, then another, and then on the forehead.

"Okay, okay! Enough!" I had to use my strength to unglue myself from her, laughing. "You're drooling all over my face." She looked much drunker than me, which explained this highly affectionate reaction. "Happy New Year to you too."

She wrapped her arms around me again and buried her head into my shoulder. "I haven't seen you since last year! It's been such a long time!"

"Ha ha," I replied sarcastically, unamused. I met Kevin's gaze. "Happy New Year, Kevin," I told him over Mel's shoulder. He stood at a weird angle as he ogled Hayden.

"Happy New Year too, S-S-Sarah. Happy New Year, Hayden." He beamed at Hayden and took a step closer to him, trying something that resembled a hug, and my jaw dropped. I'd never expected Kevin to act this openly with Hayden, all the more so since he'd just met him. Hayden moved away from him before he could touch him.

"Enough with fucking Happy New Years. All of you sound like broken records," he snapped and looked at Melissa, who finally separated herself from me. "Where's your brother?"

"In the kitchen with your dearest friends." She smiled at me and leaned to my ear. "Where have you two been? Did something happen?" She looked pointedly at the hickey on my neck, and I rolled my eyes.

"You'd like to know, wouldn't you?" I glanced around us, but I couldn't spot Jess anywhere. "Where's Jess?"

Mel's face fell, and she pursed her lips together. "Right. Jess. She's in the closet with Blake."

"*What?*" How on earth did this happen? *Why?*

"Did you say Jessica is with *Blake*? In the *closet*?" Hayden asked her, looking shocked himself.

"Go figure," she replied.

I shook my head. "How did this happen?"

"A few people started to play seven minutes in heaven. Stupid, I know. What's even more stupid is that Jess and Blake somehow got paired, so they went into the closet."

I dragged my hand down my face. "Where are they now?"

"Still in the closet, but I think seven minutes is about to end."

I gave Hayden a panicked look. "Blake will do something to her."

"He won't. Relax."

"I can't believe this! Where is that closet?"

Mel pointed at the white door under the staircase, which was across from where we stood. Just then, it burst open, and Jessica rushed out. Even in the dimly lit hallway I could see tears glistening on her face and her disheveled hair, as if someone had run their hands through it.

She advanced toward the front door with haste, and an acidic feeling settled deep in my stomach. Blake had hurt her. I met her half-way and grasped her shoulders before she bumped directly into me. She flinched when her gaze met mine.

"Jess, what happened? Did Blake hurt you?"

Her red lipstick was smeared all over her swollen lips, which could mean only one thing. They had been *kissing*.

"I hate him. He's the most horrible... I hate him!" she snapped through tears.

Mel drew Jess into a hug and remained silent as she held her. Kevin scratched his neck and shifted on his feet, glancing between them and me. I looked helplessly at Hayden, who stood aside observing us.

"I'll go talk to him," he said and marched over to Blake, who watched us from the distance with his arms folded over his chest.

"I'll chop that asshole into tiny parts and feed him to pigs," Mel hissed and caressed Jess's hair. "Did you at least kick him in his dick?"

Jessica pulled away from Mel and wiped the dark trails of mascara from her face, avoiding eye contact with us. "I want to go home. Right now," she mumbled. She moved to the entryway closet before we could stop her.

"Hey, you can't go home now! We're all drunk, so we can't drive," I told her.

"I don't care." She rummaged through coats and jackets.

"We can find a place to crash and go home in the morning," Melissa suggested, but Jess didn't even want to hear it.

"No, Mel. I need to go home right this second."

"Fine. Look, I'll find Steven and see if he or any of his friends are less baked than us, and we'll take you home, okay?" Not waiting for her answer, she darted away from us in search of her brother.

Jess pulled her jacket out, and I placed my hand on her shoulder. "Will you please stop and wait until Mel gets back?"

She refused to look at me. "I can't stay if he's here too. I need to go outside."

"Okay. Then we'll wait for Mel outside." I signaled to Kevin to look for his jacket as I tried to find my own. I sent quick texts to Hayden and Melissa to tell them we would be outside and shrugged on my jacket.

The outdoor quietude and fresh air were more than welcome, and I took a long inhale. A few people had gathered around the parked vehicles and chatted with cups, cigarettes, or blunts in their hands.

Kevin took Jessica in his arms and patted her head in an uncoordinated but heartwarming move. "It's going to be okay, Jess," he slurred.

I rubbed my cold hands together and blew on them to warm them. "What happened with Blake, Jess? Please tell us."

She separated herself from Kevin and sniffed, keeping her eyes on the ground. "We started kissing, and then he ruined it with an insult. He's so cruel."

I frowned. "What insult?"

"Why did, did, did you let him kiss you, Jess?" Kevin asked before she could respond to me, giving her an accusing stare.

She winced. "I know I was wrong, okay?! It's just that..." She grabbed her head with both hands and let out a loud groan. "I don't want to talk about it."

"How about you forget about him and have fun with us instead?" an unknown male voice asked.

A short, muscular guy leaning against a black Nissan nearby smirked at us, holding a blunt in his hand. His face was covered with scars that cut across his eyebrows and cheeks, and when he met my eyes, something unpleasant churned inside of me. Everything about him said he was bad, but then my gaze shifted to the tall Latino guy standing next to him, and that churning feeling tripled.

There was something in his stance and appearance that induced primal fear in me. He was calm—too calm—and his perfectly sculpted face hid his emotions. He observed us quietly with his hands in the pockets of his jeans, and I wanted to hide from his unnerving stare as fast as I could.

I caught Jess's elbow and motioned with my head at the house. "We should go."

The short guy straightened up and took the last drag of his blunt. He dropped it and put it out with his shoe. "Why are you leaving so quickly? Stay. We can show you a good time." He gave Kevin a dismissive glance. "You can leave, dude."

My pulse kicked up a notch, and I recoiled. I didn't want to know what their version of a "good time" was. I met Kevin's gaze and said, "Let's go."

I managed to take only two steps when the short guy grabbed my upper arm and stopped me. My heartbeat escalated. I pushed against him, but it had zero effect on him.

He chuckled. "Oh come on. Why are you so serious? We just want to have some fun, that's all." His breath stunk of marijuana and alcohol.

I tried to yank my arm away to no avail. My gaze locked with the Latino guy, who had approached us, and each cell of me urged me to get away from them.

"Let her go," Kevin shouted, pale as a sheet.

The short guy glared at him. "I told you to leave." He slid his lecherous gaze down my body and reached for my face. "I promise it will be worth your while."

"Get away from me!" Remembering a move I learned in my last Krav Maga class, I struck his chin with the heel of my palm. He growled in pain and released me, but I didn't stop there, stomping my heel over his foot before I darted away.

I shouted to Kevin and Jessica to move, but then Hayden stormed past me and lunged at the short guy, sending his fist right into his face.

"Don't touch her, piece of shit!" He struck his fist into the guy's stomach next before he could recuperate.

"Sarah," Mel shouted and pulled me to her as Steven and one of his friends skidded to a stop in front of us, shielding us.

The Latino guy shoved Hayden away from the short guy almost effortlessly. "Easy, Black!" he said, and I gaped at him. He knew Hayden?

Hayden staggered, but he caught himself before he fell down, glaring at him. "What are you doing here, Axel?"

Axel? That formidable guy was Axel? *No.* Of all the people we could've met here, it had to be him.

Axel's gaze skimmed over Steven and his friend, but he didn't seem alarmed by their presence in the least. Even though they were outnumbered, Axel looked like he was one up on us.

"We were just in the neighborhood, checking up on our old *amigos*, but who would've thought we would hit the jackpot? I was hoping to see you, Black." His smirk turned my stomach into knots. "Are you done playing sick?"

Hayden clenched his hands into fists, growing angrier with each shaky inhale. "The fuck you want, Axel?"

Axel's smirk dropped. "I said *easy*," his tone was condescending, as if he held some sort of power over Hayden. "We're going to leave fighting for our match." He inclined his head to the side. "Unless you're scared shitless and plan to duck out of it."

I wanted to move, say something, do *anything* that would get Hayden out of this situation. Hayden had barely been physically active at all, and his muscles definitely lost some of their strength. So if he was forced to fight against Axel, it would be an easy win for Axel, no doubt.

Hayden's face darkened. "I'm not a pussy, asshole."

"Now, now, *amigo*, *ya cálmate*. Why don't you watch your language in front of"—he looked between Hayden and me, connecting the dots—"*Tu novia?*"

If Hayden had been angry, he was hands down pissed off now, with his veins bulging out of his neck and temples. He pounced at Axel and swung his hand to punch him, but Steven wrapped his arms around him and stopped him.

"Hayden, no!" I let out and tried to move closer to him, but Mel and Kevin kept me in place.

"Are you crazy? You can't take him on now," Steven hissed at him.

The short guy chuckled as he looked between Hayden and me, deriving satisfaction from Hayden's condition. His cheek was swollen and bruised after Hayden's hit. "That's right, Black. Listen to your babysitters and don't mess with Axel, unless you want to end up in the box."

Axel's false laughter infuriated me, and my only comfort was the closeness of my friends. None of us moved as we watched the scene unfold in front of us. Hayden glanced at me, and fear cascaded over his eyes, twisting pain into my chest. As if he read my expression, Steven's friend shook his head at me, silently telling me not to make any problems.

"It's touching to see you care for a girl, Black. I thought you didn't have a heart. I guess we're less similar than I thought."

"Shut up," Hayden hissed. He struggled against Steven's grasp, who held him from attacking Axel.

"I'm glad to meet the girlfriend of the guy I'm going to beat to death." He shuddered with a playful smile on his face. His eyes rolled to the back of his head in a sickening display. "Just thinking about it gives me all kinds of shivers—"

"I'll kill you!"

Hayden managed to break free from Steven and jump at Axel with raised fist, but Axel easily dodged him, caught his arm, and pushed him against a car. His face switched from amused to deadly serious in an instant, and he pressed one arm against Hayden's neck and the other right against his ribs. Hayden barely managed not to voice his pain as he hunched. He grasped Axel's wrist to move his hand away, but he couldn't.

"Now let's get serious." Axel's voice dropped an octave, sounding sinister. "I don't care if you can barely stand. We're going to fight. If you still think you have a choice, I'm sure T will be happy to remind you where you two stand. Save your fuel for the match. I'd like to enjoy our fight before I end you, *amigo*."

Hayden sneered at him and moved to push him off, but Axel pressed harder against Hayden's neck and ribs, bringing him a fresh wave of pain. Hayden grimaced. He was at a disadvantage, but he refused to back down.

"You forgot our last match, *amigo*," he spat out the last word, and some of his spit landed directly on Axel's face. "Or do I have to remind you who won?"

Axel sneered. "You don't have the upper hand anymore, Black. I do. And I don't intend to lose this time."

He finally stepped away from Hayden and put on another creepy smile. "Now that we've finally settled this, let's go." He motioned to the short guy to follow him, and they went to their car.

I let out a shaky breath. They weren't going to fight now.

"Hayden!" I dashed toward him, and he pulled me into his embrace as soon as our bodies made contact. He was trembling, his arms holding me like I was going to disappear any second.

"Enjoy the rest of your night, Black!" Axel turned to us before he entered his Nissan and grinned, his gaze on Hayden and me. "And Happy New Year!"

Chapter 18

BILLY JOEL'S SONGS filled the sitting room in Raymond retirement home along with the constant chatter and laughter of the residents and their families. The atmosphere was cheerful, with so many happy faces surrounding me, but my mood remained low. I'd been this way ever since our encounter with Axel three days ago, when I realized Hayden had no way out of his match.

The fight was due soon, and as much as I talked to Hayden, I couldn't convince him to get out of it. A lot of money was riding on the game, and Hayden and Axel were some of T's best fighters, so there was no way he would let this golden opportunity slide. If Hayden cancelled it, he would suffer serious consequences, but he was holding out on what those were. This only played with my nerves more.

"Have you talked to him about getting out of the gang?" Melissa asked me in hushed whisper.

We stood next to a giant Christmas tree decorated with cute, hand-made ornaments made by the residents' grandkids. I'd taken one off and played with it in my hands to get rid of the restlessness that refused to leave my body.

"Yes." I looked at the wooden toy of a saint in my hand. "He wants to get out."

I was overjoyed when he told me this. The gang had given him an outlet for his destructive emotions through fights and racing, which helped him get over his daily hell, but he wanted to try his best to start fresh and find healthier ways of letting his emotions out now that he had me. This fight with Axel was supposed to be his last one, after which T would have to let him go. He wouldn't have to mix with that crowd ever again.

However, there was something he wasn't telling me. I was well aware that this fight was a high-risk for him, but there was more than that, and Hayden wasn't willing to talk about it.

"How will he get out?" she asked.

I shrugged, extremely frustrated. What were his options? Could he leave in one piece? "I don't know. He didn't want to talk about it. Do you know? Has Steven ever talked about it with you?"

She shook her head, her gaze on the residents slow-dancing in the middle of the room. "He never wanted to tell me how he joined them in the first place, let alone how to get out. I'm not sure if that's possible."

I whipped my gaze around to meet hers. I was terrified to even consider that option. "What do you mean?"

She looked away and shifted on her feet, and my heart plummeted to my stomach. "I mean that maybe his only way out is death."

The wooden figure slipped out of my hands and fell on the floor with a clatter, drawing attention from a few people close by.

"Is everything okay, sweetie?" one of them, Mrs. Zhang, asked me, stopping her reading to look at me over the rims of her glasses.

"Y-Yes. Everything is great."

She wasn't convinced. "You look pale."

Mel grinned and patted my shoulder cheerfully to ease the situation, but it was clear that her smile was fake. "She just has a hangover, Mrs. Z. You know how the kids are these days. We're getting drunk every day and act like monkeys whenever we can."

I frowned at her. A hangover? Of all things? "Mel," I hissed at her.

Mel flashed another fake megawatt smile at Mrs. Zhang, but it managed to persuade her because she smiled back at us and continued reading her book.

I pulled Mel away from Mrs. Zhang and the others and to the other side of the Christmas tree. I leaned to her ear. "You think there's no way out? He'll get killed?" I couldn't hide how distressed I was with my shaky voice.

"I don't know. I tried to find out since Steven never wanted to talk about it, but it's not that simple. I can't find any information about the gang on the internet, and the members aren't willing to share those things. I asked some of Steven's friends, but all I got from them was not to stick my nose into their business."

I couldn't breathe. I couldn't even move, sensing I was about to cry. If what Mel said was true, that would explain why Hayden was unwilling to talk about it. If it was impossible for him to get out or get killed if he tried...

No.

"Hey, Sar. Calm down." She caught my shoulders and willed me to look at her. "I didn't say that would happen for sure. As far as I'm aware, their gang is lower level, so maybe he can just distance himself from them, and in time they will forget about him. Or he can leave Enfield."

"That still doesn't change the fact that he has to go through Axel to get his freedom. You saw him, Mel. That guy is something else. Hayden hasn't fought for more than a month, and he only started training yesterday. Also, he can't overexert himself in his current condition. Fighting with a brain injury is extremely dangerous, and I'm afraid Axel will give him a fatal blow and—"

Mel wrapped her arms around me and held me tight against her. "It will be okay, Sar. Don't panic. We're just blowing this out of proportion."

"I don't know, Mel." I closed my eyes, battling against the incoming tears. I couldn't cry. Not here. "I'm trying to stay positive, but I'm so scared. I'm so, so scared."

"Sarah?" I heard Jonathan call me from the other side of the room, and I pulled away from Mel. I took a deep breath before I turned to meet his gaze. His eyebrows drew together when he spotted my ashen face. "Are you all right?"

He sat at the table playing chess with Adelaine, who was no match against him, as usual. They started dating a few weeks ago, and they got along more than well, which didn't surprise me. She was always the cheerful one, which contrasted his grumpiness perfectly, and it was plain adorable to see them together. I was happy for Jonathan. He needed happiness and love after he lost his wife.

"Come on," Mel told me. "Let's join them before he sees something's wrong with you. I'm sure a bit chit-chatting with good old Mr. J will calm you down."

I wanted to snap at her and tell her there was nothing that could calm me down, but I didn't want to take out my frustration on her. I followed her through the room and even smiled back at some residents, hoping my fake smiles weren't as transparent as I thought they were.

"Hey, Mr. J and Mrs. A."

Jonathan observed Mel with narrowed eyes. "I told you not to call us that."

Adelaine broke into a few embarrassed giggles, her hand covering her mouth. Today, she wore rouge that emphasized her full lips, and her long curly gray hair was put up in a bun, all for Jonathan's benefit.

"That's all right, dear. I love Melissa's nickname. It's so modern." She winked at Mel.

"Are you all right?" Jonathan repeated his question. His lips were pursed beneath his thick gray mustache as he studied me.

"I'm fine," I told him when Mel and I sat next to Adelaine. "I'm just a bit tired."

He pointed his finger at me. "You know you're not a good liar."

I glanced at Adelaine, uncomfortable because I didn't want to talk about my personal issues in front of her. I'd grown relaxed with Jonathan, and I could open up more to him now, but I wished we were alone.

"She's PMSing," Mel said loudly, and my face went extremely red. I wanted to strangle her. "So don't mind her."

Jonathan didn't even react to that, his completely serious gaze fixed on me. "Is everything okay with your boyfriend?"

Something twisted deep in me, and I hoped it didn't show on my face. "Everything is great."

He continued studying me like he didn't believe me. "I hope he treats you well."

My lips quirked up in a smile as I thought of Hayden's heated kisses and loving touches, but it didn't last long. I was supposed to be happy that I got to start a new year next to Hayden, but I couldn't forget about that fight. It was always in the innermost recesses of my mind, reminding me that my time with him could be limited.

"He treats me well. I'm just worried about our future."

He raised his bushy eyebrow. "You're worried about your future?" he asked. "Why?"

"Because sometimes it feels like only one thing could break us." I couldn't tell him that I was afraid for Hayden's life. "Like one moment we're extremely happy, but the next, everything falls apart."

He didn't respond immediately, taking Adelaine's bishop with his knight when he moved it from h3 to g5. "There will always be ups and downs. No relationship is linear. If it is, then it's not real." He switched his gaze from the board to me. "Love comes with a price, but it's worth paying."

"Gee, Mr. J. You're at it again," Melissa said with a grin. She twiddled one of Jonathan's captured pieces. "Wisdom at its best!"

He frowned at her. "You could learn something from it, insolent girl. Young people nowadays think they know everything, but they know nothing, especially when it comes to love. All they do is break up after one fight, not to mention all those divorces."

"How about you and your wife, Jonathan?" I asked him. I was still amazed that they had been married for more than fifty years before she passed away. "Did you have a lot of ups and downs?"

"All the time! That woman was stubborn as a mule. We fought a lot, but it was always worth it and we wouldn't have had it any other way." His face lit as he reminisced about the memories he shared with his wife.

"Jonathan is right," Adelaine said, a downcast smile on her face. "It was the same between me and my late husband. We always quarreled, but the connection we shared was one of a kind. You see, all relationships consist of fights, adjustments, and heartbreaks, but all that matters is that you two trust, love, and respect each other. You need to be ready to compromise because you can't expect to have a long-lasting relationship otherwise."

"I noticed how that boy looked at you," Jonathan told me after Adelaine made her move. "His emotions are raw and strong, and they aren't something that can disappear overnight. So instead of worrying about your future with him, think what you can do to make the present moment count."

I contemplated their words, remaining silent, but I was jolted out of it when my gaze fell on a familiar figure standing at the door. *Mateo.*

A sharp pain hit my chest. He entered the room and looked around for someone, presumably Jonathan. His curly hair was longer than the last time I saw him, reaching his shoulders, and his light brown eyes crinkled as he took in the festive atmosphere, paired with a small smile.

I whipped my head around. I wasn't ready for this. I wasn't ready to face him.

"Hey, Teo! Over here!" Mel called him, waving at him to get his attention.

Mortified of meeting his gaze, I stared at the chess board and told myself to keep it cool. I had to see him sooner or later, so avoiding him would only postpone the inevitable.

"This can be a good chance for you to talk with him," Mel whispered to me.

"I don't know, Mel," I gritted out, hating feeling this cornered.

"At least apologize to him." She stood up before I could answer her and bumped his shoulder with her fist when he stopped next to our table. "Happy New Year, Teo!"

Okay. *You reap what you sow, Sarah.* Mel was right. I couldn't pretend I hadn't said those hurtful words to him. I had to explain myself to him properly.

Blushing hard, I forced myself to look at him. His eyes were already on me, and his smile was gone, inviting my guilt back. He looked away from me and smiled at the others.

"Hi, everyone. Happy New Year."

So that's how it's going to be. I dug my nails into my palms. I couldn't really expect him to treat me any differently, now could I?

"Hello, Mateo. Happy New Year," I told him quietly.

I thought he was going to ignore me, but he returned my gaze and nodded, unsmiling. From the corner of my eye, I saw Jonathan observing us, the wheels turning in his head as he put two and two together.

"Why don't you take a seat, boy?" Jonathan asked him when Mateo remained standing. "We don't bite."

There were only two available chairs—one next to me and the other next to Adelaine—so it wasn't difficult to figure out which chair he would pick. He sat down across from me, avoiding even looking in my direction.

"I'm surprised you remembered your grandfather," Jonathan said when Adelaine made a move and captured his knight. "I heard you're never home these days, so I thought I would have to wait until next year to see you again."

Mateo grinned at Jonathan, but his smile didn't reach his eyes. "I'm here now, right? Better late than never." He glanced at Adelaine. "I have to tell you, you deserve a medal for putting up with my grandpa," he told her, and she giggled.

Jonathan glared at him, but the corner of his mouth twitched like he was suppressing a smile. "Respect your grandfather."

"Duly noted. So how are you? Did you beat everyone here in chess already?"

I squirmed on my chair as Jonathan answered. I didn't feel comfortable sitting here and listening to their conversation like everything was hunky dory. Mateo wasn't okay, and something told me it had everything to do with me. He'd never been this stiff in front of Jonathan, giving rather short, resentful answers.

Wimping out, I excused myself on the pretext of checking if anyone needed me and left the table. I felt Mateo's eyes following me, and I was unable to breathe, quickening my pace until I was out of the room and his sight.

Great, Sarah. You're pathetic.

I busied myself for the next hour with work, until Mel found me in the hallway on the second floor.

"Really, Sar? You're not going to say a word to him?" She gave me a sour look.

I shoved my hands into my jeans pockets. "I don't know what to tell him, Mel. It's so difficult, and it was embarrassing to sit there and listen to him talking—"

"You know what's embarrassing?" she interrupted me, looking at me with disappointment. "This." She motioned at me. "Running away like a little girl and sweeping all your problems under the rug." She shook her head and placed her hands on her hips. "You owe him an apology. I'm sure he'd appreciate it more than you think."

I looked away, pacing left and right. "I know, but you saw him, Mel. I'm not his favorite person at the moment, and I'm afraid he's going to brush off my apology and—"

"You don't know that, Sar. What if he does the opposite?" She ran her hand over her forehead. "Look. He's going to leave any moment now, so you still have time to talk to him. Even if he doesn't accept your apology, at least you tried. That counts." She looked over my shoulder at someone behind me and groaned. "And now I'm going to help Mrs. Crawford because she doesn't listen and walks all alone with her hip fracture. That woman will be the death of me."

She left to help Mrs. Crawford, who walked down the hallway using a walker, and I wished I had even the half of her strength and bravery. She was right. I was a coward, and I had to woman up and apologize.

After a few minutes of deep breathing and pep talks, I managed to encourage myself enough not to let this opportunity slip away. I headed to the sitting room and almost collided with him on his way out as he zipped up his jacket. I stopped before I got plastered against him. He snapped his eyes from his zipper to me.

"Mateo," I let out.

His face grew guarded, and he looked to the side. "Sarah. I didn't see you. Sorry about that." He was *apologizing* to me? I fisted my hands. I had to apologize right now.

He turned to leave, but I called his name again. Reluctantly, he faced me. "Yes?"

My face was terribly red, and my palms were sweaty, but I concentrated on letting the right words out. "There is no need for you to say sorry because it's not your fault. In fact, I should apologize, not you."

"Let me get this clear. You're not apologizing for almost bumping into me?"

My heart pounded extremely fast. "That's right. I'm apologizing for what I said when you came to see me in the hospital."

He raised his eyebrows. "Why are you apologizing? You told me how you felt, so what's there to apologize about now?"

I glanced away and told myself I could do this. I had to. "I'm apologizing for the way I said those things. It was hurtful."

He looked off into the distance, staying quiet, which made this a lot harder for me.

"I-I appreciate all you've done for me, especially that you came to visit me in the hospital. It's just that, due to specific circumstances, I couldn't let Hayden get the wrong picture about you and me. And I didn't want the situation to turn into something ugly. I didn't want Hayden or you hurt. But in the end, I hurt you. The words I said to you were too harsh, and for that I'm so sorry."

My words didn't make much sense to me, and my brain worked at full tilt to come up with the appropriate apology despite my poor communication skills and anxiety, but I came up short. I just hoped I'd managed to convey even a little how sorry I was.

In a barely perceivable move, he took a deep breath. He brought his gaze back to me. "Why are you doing this now? I don't need your pity."

I recoiled, and my cheeks burned once more. "I don't pity you. I just want you to know that I feel guilty for hurting you. I don't want that."

"So you're doing this so you can feel better? Why does it matter whether I know you're sorry or not? Either way, you want me to stay away from you."

I didn't let his sharp tone deter me. We couldn't quite wipe the slate clean, but at least I'd apologized.

"I'm not doing this to make myself feel better. I'm doing this so you'd know how sorry I am for reacting the way I did. I want you to know that I didn't hurt you deliberately. It was ugly, and even now I can't explain myself in the right way, but I hope you'll be able to forgive me one day. However, and I'm so sorry for this too, but at this moment, we can't be friends." I sniffed and took a step back. "I'm sorry."

There was nothing else I could say to him, so I might as well let him be.

"I wish you all the best in your life, Mateo. You deserve it. Happy New Year."

I spun on my heel, but before I could take two steps, he said, "Sarah, wait."

I stopped with my heart in my throat. I turned to look at him, wishing I could be done with this already. "Yes?"

He tucked his hair behind his ears and licked his lips. "I understand why we can't be friends because I'd feel the same as he feels. I wouldn't want you to be friends with him while you were still with me."

I didn't know what to say, surprised he would tell me something like this now.

"And about your apology, I accept it. I mean, I'm not okay, and I won't pretend that what you did didn't put me through a bad period, but I don't want you to feel guilty." He shifted his weight. "This is for the best, since I don't think I could stay friends with you anyway when you're with him. I'll be okay, so don't worry about me."

I hadn't expected him to say this, so now I had no good answer to it. He was actually accepting my apology. He wasn't mad with me, yelling at me, or anything of the sort. I didn't know if I should feel relieved or bad because he was being this nice.

"Thank you." I couldn't say anything else, abashed that he was forgiving me despite everything. "I'm going now. That's all I wanted to—"

"Is he good to you?"

I halted mid-step. "Yes. Hayden is amazing." His eyes exposed his true feelings, and I weighed my words. It didn't feel right to tell him just how happy Hayden made me feel, because that would be like rubbing salt in the wound. "I'm okay, Mateo. He's different, and things are going well between us. You don't have to worry about me."

He nodded and took gloves out of his pocket. "That's good to hear. Okay then. Happy New Year, Sarah. See you around."

For the first time today, he smiled at me, but he turned around before I could smile back. "Bye, Mateo."

I looked at his retreating back with a mixture of melancholy and hope that one day all of this would feel like a small bump in the road to be forgotten. Maybe all we needed was time that would allow us to heal. And one day, I was sure of it, he would find the right one for him—the one that would give him all he deserved and much more.

• • • •

AN HOUR LATER, I WENT to pick Hayden up from therapy. He'd agreed to let me drive his car, so I used it to get around. His smell lingered in the cabin, heightening my longing for him, so when he got into the car, I couldn't resist smashing my lips against his.

"You've missed me that much?" he asked when we separated from each other. His tone was playful, but there was no smile accompanying it.

"That much and even more. How was your therapy?" Luckily, Ms. Kishimoto wanted to see him even during holidays.

"Never better. I think I almost lost my voice from all that screaming at Kishimoto."

My forehead wrinkled into a small frown. "What happened?"

"She's trying to get inside my head too much. It's not helping me. I hate when she says she understands and nods—she *always* nods—but she doesn't understand a damn thing."

"Maybe she understands it as a professional. After all, she has a lot of experience with patients who have BPD."

"Still, I hate it. I hate her."

I put my hand on his, observing his profile as he stared at his lap. "She just wants you to get better. I'm sure it will be better next time."

"If there's going to be next time," he bit back, and I flinched. "I hate that place. I hate sessions with her. She's always so fucking calm and polite, and it's irritates the shit out of me."

I didn't linger on the nagging feeling in the pit of my stomach and focused on calming him down. I gave him a tight hug and kissed his cheek, holding him close to me.

"She told me there's a possibility that my BPD symptoms will decrease with age."

"Really? That's great!"

He didn't share my enthusiasm; his face remained stern when I leaned away to look at him. "Yeah. *Fucking great.* She mentioned she had patients whose symptoms became less intense as they grew older, but it's so hard to believe that because it feels like it won't ever end. It feels like it will always grip my throat and limit my freedom." He slid his hand down his face and clenched his other hand on his lap. "It's downright ugly."

"But if there is even the slightest possibility of that happening, we should be optimistic. You're already making huge progress, and that's what matters. I'm here, so you can always rely on me," I reminded him and ran the back of my fingers down his cheek.

"Whatever."

He looked unconvinced, his anger abiding, until I pulled him in another hug and he let his arms slide around my waist and hold me against him. A little while later, he managed to relax, and I started the car.

He turned on the car stereo, and the sounds of Breaking Benjamin filled the air as I accelerated down the road. We were having a movie night at his place, which was exactly what I needed to lift my mood. We slipped into a comfortable silence, and my thoughts went to an idea for the drawing I wanted to draw next. The sunset colored the sky in the most intricate way, and this awe-inspiring sight helped me with the setting I was going to use for my fantasy character.

I was about to park in his driveway when I remembered I hadn't told him about Mateo. I cleared my throat and shut the engine. I hoped my next words wouldn't rub him up the wrong way.

"I saw Mateo at my work today."

His face carried no expression when he met my gaze. "And?" he let out through his teeth.

"I apologized to him for being harsh that day in the hospital. He was always nice to me, so I wanted him to know that I didn't want to hurt him on purpose. However, I still think we can't be friends at the moment—"

"At the moment? So you want to be friends with him?" His tone turned sharp, and my hands turned cold.

"I don't want to be friends with him when he feels something for me. It would be nice if one day we can be friends without him harboring any feelings toward me, but if that's not possible, that's also okay. Life goes on, and I'm sure he'll move on sooner or later." His gaze remained hard, and I reached for his hand. "I don't feel anything for him anymore, Hayden, so you don't have to worry about that. I love you, and I only have eyes for you. And honestly, Mateo can't even compare to you. You're perfect. You're smart, beautiful, funny, and I feel great with you. I want everything with you." The ends of my lips rose in a tender smile. "I just don't want him to be hurt, that's all."

"Who cares about him being hurt?"

I tightened my fingers around his hand. "I understand that you don't like him, but he's a good guy. He doesn't deserve to suffer. He deserves to find someone who will make him happy."

He removed his hand from mine and crossed his arms over his chest. "Are you sure you don't feel anything for him? Because you defend him too much, and it's driving me mad!"

My heartbeat increased along with the tone of his voice. *No.* I didn't want us to fight over this.

"This doesn't have anything to do with that. I just want to make things right and have a clear conscience. I honestly don't care if I don't get to see him ever again. I apologized to him and told him we can't be friends, and that's it. He understood that and agreed it was better that way."

He didn't say anything for a long time, and I couldn't read his face because he was turned away from me as he looked through the window. He didn't even move, and my heart gave a lurch of fear. Would this distance us? Would he misunderstand this completely? Each heartbeat brought a fresh wave of pain that intensified with every second Hayden spent ignoring me.

"Please, Hayden. Believe me," I tried again. "There is nothing between Mateo and me, and I don't feel anything for him. You're the only person that matters to me, and that won't change ever." I placed my hand on his upper arm, wishing he would just look at me. "I love you. I love you so much, and I don't want to lose you."

I hadn't noticed when my tears started. I sniffed and wiped them off, but this didn't prevent them from stopping. He was too still.

"Please, believe me." I leaned my head against his shoulder. If only he would give away how he felt. "I love you."

He clenched and unclenched his hand on his lap, repeating this several times. I closed my eyes and snuggled closer to him, fiercely hoping my words would come through to him.

After what seemed like a couple of minutes, he moved and wound his arm around my waist, and I felt like my heart could burst with immediate joy.

"I'm so confused, and I don't know what to do." His voice was unrecognizable under the layers of despair, hoarse and deep. "I trust you, Sarah, but there's always that doubt. It's always telling me I'm a worthless piece of shit and you'll find someone way better than me."

I squeezed his shoulder. He had a long way to go until he learned to love himself. "Don't say that. You're my angel, remember? I can be myself only with you. Being with you is what makes me happy, and there's nothing more I want than that. I love you, Hayden."

He took my face in his hands, his eyes roaming over every inch of it. "I love you too, Sarah. I'm scared shitless that you're going to leave me. Please, don't leave me."

I cupped his hands with mine and smiled at him. "I'll never leave you. Never. My heart is only yours, you know that?"

His eyes smoldered, and he leaned in and put his lips to mine. His tongue grazed my lip before it slipped into my mouth, bringing intoxicating warmth that turned all previous coldness, fear, and pain into nothing. His fingers explored my neck in slow caresses that promised a long-awaited pleasure, and I clutched his jacket.

"You're mine. Just imagining some other guy having you... Fuck. I went through that shit already, and I don't want to go through that ever again."

"You won't. I don't want anyone but you." I caressed his cheek, lost in his fiery gaze. "It's strange. I was so sure you moved on when I was with Mateo, and as much as I tried to forget about you and grow to love him, I couldn't. I fought against my feelings for you, but it was pointless."

The look he gave me was incredulous. "You thought I moved on? There was no way I could've moved on. I couldn't stop thinking about you. I was reminded every single hour of you, and it was sickening. I hated myself for it, I hated you, and I hated the whole world. I wanted to drown my thoughts, so I did anything that would help me forget the reality that was killing me. Anything that would wipe out my memory of you, your skin, your lips... But. It. Was. Pointless."

He ran his thumb across my lips, observing them wistfully. "You don't know how painful it was to see him pick you up after school. To see you two *kiss...*"

I took his hand in mine. "It's all in the past. And his kisses never managed to make me feel the way yours do. They never made me desire something more." My fingers circled his palm, savoring the feel of his skin. "Mateo never managed to reach that part deep within me that always yearned for the kind of love that leaves you breathless and wanting more. The kind of love that makes you forget your reason and just feel. The kind of love I feel toward you."

Once more, our lips started a sensual dance, and we were taken to that place where no one and nothing existed but us. By the time we separated, the sky was completely dark, and the patches of clouds covered the stars.

"If we keep kissing, we'll never get to watch movies."

"I couldn't care less," he muttered and left another kiss on my lips before he moved away. "But you've been talking about the movie night for days, so you better get out before this turns into something else."

Chapter 19

THE NEXT TWO DAYS WERE a blend of trepidation and joy with Hayden's upcoming fight looming over our happiness. Hayden spent a lot of time working out with Masen and Blake to regain his previous fitness level, but it seemed impossible. T was getting more impatient, so the fight was going to be scheduled pretty soon, way before Hayden could be fully ready.

Hayden didn't want me there, because it was dangerous and the fight could take a turn for the worse, but I couldn't just stand aside and wait for him without knowing what was going on. It took a lot of convincing, but I managed to get him to agree to let me be there for him, determined to stay with him through everything.

I put the finishing touches to the drawing I'd been working on for hours and opened my Instagram to post it. It was of a girl in a school uniform standing in the rain in the middle of a magical forest, and thanks to some new brushes I'd used in Photoshop, I was able to emphasize the twinkling lights that adorned its dark background.

I uploaded the picture and replied to a few comments that poured in, when Hayden's text arrived.

"We're done training for today. Can you come to my house in twenty? I want to take you somewhere."

Huh? Where did he want to take me?

"How should I dress?"

"Wear a sexy dress and high heels."

I frowned at the text. I failed to get the drift of it.

His next message popped up on my screen right away.

"We aren't going to a ball. So dress however you want."

Would he ever run out of sarcasm? I rolled my eyes and typed a new message.

"As my master commands."

"I taught you well. ;)"

My laughter filled the room as I moved to change my clothes. I left my room fifteen minutes later and slowed my steps when I noticed the door of my mother's room was wide open. As I passed next to it, I found her lying in her bed and flipping through the pages of some magazine with a bored look on her face. She was supposed to get the casts off her legs in a week, and like a kid, she was getting more impatient to function on her own each day.

I had to take my hat off to Lydia for staying positive and patient with her all this time. She managed to get along with her and keep her away from alcohol most of the time. She even tried to convince her to go to AA. At first, Patricia didn't want to admit her addiction, refusing to even think about Lydia's suggestion, but the next day, I heard her say she'd decided to join it after all, which was a huge step for her. For her sake, I hoped she would finally get a hold of her life.

"I'm going out," I told her and continued down the hallway, not expecting her to answer me.

"Again?" she asked, and I halted before I reached the stairs.

"Yes. Again."

"Going back to Blacks' house?"

What was her problem now? "Yes," I gritted out. "Why do you even ask?"

"You spend more time there than here these days. Does that have anything to do with Carmen's son, Hayden? Are you two good friends now or what?"

The tone of her voice set my teeth on edge. I reached her doorway and met her questioning gaze. "Hayden is my boyfriend."

She raised her eyebrows, and blush covered my cheeks. I hated when she looked at me like this, like I was worthless. "Your *boyfriend*? Hayden Black?" She whistled. "Nice. First his brother, now Hayden."

My eyebrows furrowed. "What are you talking about? Kayden was never my boyfriend. He was my best friend."

She waved me off. "That's just semantics. Either way, you know how to catch them. It's obvious why you waste your time on them. Blacks are super rich."

I bridled at her horrible implication. "What do you want to say? That I'm with Hayden because of his *money*?"

"The apple doesn't fall far from the tree, does it? You're not the Virgin Mary. I should've known you'd try to find a good catch sooner or later."

"Let me get this straight. You think I'm a gold-digger?"

Her lips curled into a disgusting, condescending smile. "Of course you are. All women are gold-diggers, but some just hide it better." She winked at me. "It would be nice to have my daughter married into a rich family, so I completely support you. I can already imagine all the benefits."

I couldn't believe her. What the hell was she thinking?

"Now listen here." I stomped inside. "I'm not like you, and I will never, *ever* be like you. You're a disgrace to mothers and women. Just because you want an easy way out of your problems, it doesn't mean the rest of us think the same way. You disgust me."

Her smile fell. "Shut your mouth! Don't you dare speak to me like that!"

"I will speak to you however I want because I'm sick and tired of you! You don't control me or my life! Unlike you, I'll have my future the way I want it if it's the last thing I do. Soon, I'll be out of this house and I won't have to see you ever again."

"Oh, so now we're so brave? Now that the little girl has found her rich boyfriend, she's all tough? Wait until he dumps you. You'll crawl back here in no time."

And just like that, as I stood unmoving watching her, all my anger diminished. I pitied her. This was why she would never get anything out of her life. She was full of negativity and resentment that kept her down. I was tired of being at the bottom. I had no intention of staying there any longer.

"Thank you, Patricia." I threw a small smile on my face as I retreated out of her room. "You're just giving me more motivation to get out of here and make something out of my life. Seriously, thank you. Whether Hayden 'dumps' me or not, I'll never stop fighting for something better—something that's not being stuck here with you. And soon, all of this"—I motioned between her and me—"Will just be a faint memory that's not even worth remembering." I spun on my heel and headed to the stairs.

"If only Thomas hadn't left you half of this house, I would've kicked you out a long time ago!"

I shook my head, already going downstairs. So she was resorting to this? Truly pathetic.

"Yeah?" I shouted back. "Well, it's too bad my grandfather messed up your plans."

She cussed a blue streak, but I tuned her out, putting on my jacket and shoes. I was out of the house in no time.

She was so terrible, but at least there was something good in that—she taught me how *not* to live my life.

Pushing the thoughts of her aside, I rang Hayden's bell and let excitement take over me.

Carmen opened the door and gave me a warm, welcoming smile. "Hello, dear." She embraced me.

I stiffened, unaccustomed to being this close to her, but then I felt myself relax and returned her hug. I wasn't fully comfortable with it because I needed more time to get used to this new relationship between Carmen and me, but I was gradually getting there.

"Hayden is upstairs."

"Thank you."

I climbed up the stairs wearing a gigantic smile, but that smile disappeared when I saw the door of Kayden's room was open.

What was going on?

I padded to his room and peeked inside, wary about what I might find... My pulse skyrocketed when I spotted a tall form next to the bookshelf. He flipped through the pages of *One Piece* in his hands, and I couldn't even begin to understand what I was seeing.

Oh my God. *Kayden?!*

I stopped breathing as my eyes went over his profile, but the moment of confusion passed as quickly as it came.

He wasn't Kayden.

Closing my eyes, I took a deep breath. *Silly me.*

"Hayden." My wobbly legs carried me inside. I looked around Kay's room, realizing just now that he'd come in of his own accord. "What's happening? What are you doing here?"

He turned around to look at me, his face blank. "Hey." He closed the manga and put it back in its place on the shelf.

He met me half-way and pulled me into a kiss. The memory of our last time together in this room flashed through my mind as I molded myself into him. How things had changed... Now, his hands held me like he never wanted to let me go, cocooning me with his warmth, and each passing second was full of love and need that brought us closer to each other.

We separated slowly, gazing affectionately at each other. This was the softest kiss he'd ever given me.

"What was that for?" I asked, dazed.

His rapt gaze studied each line of my face. "Unstaining memories."

My pulse sped up once more as the meaning of his words sank in. "What do you mean?"

"All that bullshit about staining your memories keeps bothering me." He brushed a strand of my hair off my face. "It's high time to fix that. I don't want to remind you about all the abuse I put you through right here. I don't want you to go through anything like that ever again. So it's time to create some new memories that can stay with you forever and erase the old ones I made."

I didn't know what to say. Before I could even form a sentence, he stepped away and looked around the room with sorrowful eyes. "After so much time, I'm finally able to come here."

He went over to Kayden's telescope and brushed his fingers over it. "I'm finally able to step inside his room without feeling horror or switching back to that dark period. I'm finally able to handle this trigger."

My chest went tight with relief. He was healing.

I came from behind him and hugged him. "Does this mean that you moved on?"

He covered my hands with his. "Not quite, but it's much better now than it was before."

"And how do you feel now, being in his room?"

He caressed my hand with his thumb, and the seconds passing in silence intensified my anticipation of his answer.

"*I miss him.*" His whispered answer touched me profoundly, and a dull pain spread through my chest. Our mutual grief shaded our world in darker tones. How I wished Kayden was here—to smile and make his dreams come true.

"His room brings me a raw pain that I hope will stop one day." He snorted. "It's ironic. I couldn't stand him for so long, and I often thought my life would be so much better without him, but now that he's gone, I miss him more than I ever had."

He turned around and took my face into his cold hands. My stomach knotted at the sight of his red eyes and face twisted with lament. "This room is another reminder how quickly a person can die, and nothing can ever bring them back," he said. "They're never coming back."

He cupped my cheeks and held my gaze. "That's why I want to go with you to a special place today. I need to unstain all those memories and make new ones."

"A special place?"

"Yes. I want us to visit Kayden's grave. There's something important I need to tell you."

• • • •

HEAPS OF SNOW HAD ACCUMULATED on the ground around the headstones, attuned to the gray sky that held no promise of sunny weather. The cemetery looked gloomier than ever, but this time no feelings of loneliness or desolation followed me as Hayden and I walked hand in hand.

The times had definitely changed.

We stopped at Kay's grave, and I bent to put fresh flowers into a pot, flicking my gaze to Hayden's epitaph.

> *"Breaking into pieces, bleeding so deep,*
> *wishing I was the one who went into eternal sleep.*
> *You'll never be forgotten, you pure soul,*
> *you left a crushing emptiness, you left an immense hole.*
> *Rest in peace, my dear brother, and sleep tight,*
> *know that I'll always love you with all my might."*

"I never told you how beautiful these lines are," I said and straightened up, taking his hand into mine.

A slight curve of his lips revealed regret. "These words are more beautiful than anything I'd ever told him when he was alive. He never got to hear anything like this from me."

"He knew. I told you about the way he spoke about you. You weren't on good terms and couldn't find common ground, but that didn't take away from the fact that you loved each other."

He went down on his knees and sat on his heels. I joined him, shivering when the cold from the ground permeated through my jeans. He wrapped his arms around me and pulled me closer to him to warm me up.

"Thank you." I leaned my head against his shoulder as we gazed at Kay's headstone.

"I felt so distant from him that sometimes it didn't feel like we were family. This will sound weird, but I could never be who I really was with him."

"Do you know why?"

He shook his head. "I could never get over the animosity I felt toward him. It was always there, especially because I knew our mother loved him more. Just like everybody else. No matter what I did, I always took second place."

He inhaled a long breath and started making random patterns with his finger in the snow.

"I always blamed him for being in the spotlight and the most successful in everything. And I *hated* when he played down his success and acted like we were equal."

I didn't know what to say to that. I didn't have siblings, so I didn't know what that rivalry was like.

"I think that each of you were good in the things you liked. For example, Kayden was clueless about writing. He always asked for my help when we had to write essays, but you have a way with words, and I'm always amazed how good it is."

"Yeah? Even now it's hard for me to believe that. I feel that if he were still alive, he would be way better than me at everything."

I snuggled closer to him. "I don't think so. Besides, I wouldn't ever compare you. Both of you are different and unique, so it's pointless to compare."

He didn't say anything for a while, letting the wind do the talking in our newfound silence. I deliberated on his words. Would things have been different if Carmen had given undivided attention to both brothers?

"I often wonder what he would be like if he was alive," he said suddenly. "Would he still be a nerd? Would he start smoking? Would he get to work for NASA?" He chuckled, but it was a dry sound that tugged at my heart. "Would we ever get closer?" He turned to look at me and palmed my face with his icy hand. "Would he still have feelings for you?"

I averted my gaze, a bitter feeling coursing through my stomach. "I often wonder the same things," I muttered.

He took a deep breath, looking like what he was about to say was too personal. "All that time, I acted like you were the only one to blame for that night, when I actually blamed myself the most."

He dropped his hand from my face, and his jaw clenched. I thought about his diary entry and the guilt he carried all this time, which was devastating. I caught his hand.

"I read what you wrote in your diary. How you thought it was your fault. Hayden, it wasn't your fault, and you never deserved to die. Kayden made that choice. I refused to believe that for a long time, blaming myself, but it's true. He *chose* to save you."

Slowly, he met my gaze. "For a long time, I felt I didn't deserve to be saved. Sometimes, when I looked at this in the mirror"—he pointed at this scar—"I thought how unfair it was that I only got this. It hurt so much looking at it and remembering that moment."

Tears collected in his eyes as he studied the epigraph, and a pang shot through my heart.

"But there's also something else," he continued. "Everything is twisted in me. I'd blamed Kayden for saving me that night, but if he hadn't done that, I would've never experienced what I now have with you... So here's the irony: I'm actually grateful to him." His raspy whisper was so quiet, so powerfully painful. "And I'm grateful that it wasn't you who died that night."

A dull ache lodged in my chest. "Grateful?"

He fisted his hand against his lap. "Back then, I loathed him for sacrificing his life. I loathed myself for not avoiding that car. But it was the easiest to loathe you. I let all that hate consume me and turn me into a monster, and it took me a long time to see that by punishing you, I also punished myself because I couldn't be happy when you were suffering." A tear escaped his eye, finding its way over his cheek to the snowy ground. "But you've become so precious to me, and I can't bear losing you. So yes, I'm grateful. And that brings me to what I wanted to tell you today."

He wiped off his tear briskly and turned to face me, catching my hands into his.

"I was thinking a lot about it after I woke up from the coma. All that time I blamed you for your careless mistake, thinking that we could control everything. But mistakes happen. Hell, I made so many mistakes I know them the best. Now that I've made the same careless mistake that led to my accident, I saw how unfair I was. I thought I would never forgive you, but then I realized there was nothing I should forgive you for."

I raised my eyebrows. "Wait. You don't blame me for Kayden's death anymore?"

He nodded. "I don't. It wasn't your fault. Yes, you didn't pay attention, but if that driver hadn't driven so fast, maybe there wouldn't have been an accident." He looked at our connected hands. "And you said it yourself. Kayden chose to save me, just like I would've if the roles were reversed."

My heart beat loudly in my ears as I watched him close his eyes and take deep breaths. I was on the verge of tears.

"It's fucking stupid that I needed to go through another accident to see this. It's so stupid, and I'm so embarrassed I can barely look you in the eyes, Sarah. I was blind and judgmental, but I can finally overcome my toxic thoughts and see the whole picture clearly." A melancholic smile took shape on his face as he brought my hand to his lips and kissed it softly. "I can finally get over how he died and accept it."

I pressed my hand against my heart that pounded harder. "I... I feel so relieved." My voice turned shaky. "I thought you'd never forgive me for that..."

A smile unfurled across my face. This meant so much to me. He wasn't blaming me for his death anymore. He'd *accepted* it.

"Thank you for telling me this... Thank you."

I pressed a kiss on his scar and hugged him. His arms wrapped around me instantly, bringing me warmth and a sense of security I relished in.

"I forgave myself, but I needed these words," I told him. "I needed them so much, and now it feels unreal." I moved to look at him, and a tear slid down my face. "This feels like a dream. It isn't a dream, right?"

He smiled. "No. It's not a dream."

His eyes glistened with sadness as he looked at Kayden's headstone, which contradicted the smile on his face. "I forgive you, Kayden," he whispered. "I forgive you for leaving me. I forgive you for making that choice. I hope you can forgive me for destroying Sarah's life."

Oh God.

"I hope you can forgive me for torturing the person you cared for. I hope you can forgive your brother for being a horrible human being."

I whimpered, more tears rolling down my cheeks.

"From now on, it's time to start making it up to Sarah." He looked at me, and his smile grew bigger. "It's time to unstain her memories, like this one."

He cupped my cheeks and kissed me with an intensity that reminded me of the day of Kayden's death anniversary, when we shared our first kiss. However, everything felt different this time, and my lips parted for him immediately as our bodies molded together and his touch carved into my skin. My heart picked up speed, expanding with euphoria.

"Our first kiss," he said into my lips and pressed his forehead against mine. "It was real. It wasn't a part of my revenge. It was something I'll never be able to forget, because for the first time, I felt so alive. For a moment, I felt *complete*. And it meant something to me, even though I stupidly ruined it."

He pressed his lips on mine again and pulled me up so that we both stood on our knees, embracing. Just like back then, I felt flutters in my stomach that grew stronger when he moved his lips over my cheek and neck, kissing the spot right below my ear. Completely warmed, I clutched his jacket when he pulled away to look at me.

"I want you to remember this. I want you to remember how much I love you. Not all those bad memories but this." He brushed my lower lip with his thumb. "Only this."

I smiled. "Thank you for this. It does help me heal."

He pulled me into another embrace and nestled my head against his shoulder. The wind had picked up, and a flurry of snow colored the snowy background with more shades of gray and white. I shivered when a few snowflakes ended their journey on my face.

"How did you know that Kayden liked me?" I asked. "Did you two talk about it?"

His hand caressed my back up and down. "I knew it from the moment it started. It was so obvious he didn't even need to confirm it to me. It was your birthday."

Wide-eyed, I drew away to look at him. "My birthday?"

He nodded. "I'd just come back home when I saw you two in your drive-way."

I thought about that day. I had a huge fight with my mother, who came off her night shift so drunk she forgot it was my birthday. I remember being hurt that she didn't even make me a birthday cake. She slapped me, and I rushed out of the house in tears with no destination, but Kayden saw me from his driveway and stopped me.

"Sari? Are you okay?" Kayden asked me.

I sniffed. "It's my mother."

He frowned at the mark my mother had left when she slapped me. "Your cheek is red. What happened?"

I hugged myself and recounted our fight, looking to the side. "And there I was, thinking she would at least make me a birthday cake for a change. Is that too much to ask? Is her love too much to ask for?" I sounded pitiful, lonely.

My eyes filled with tears again, and something shifted in Kayden's gaze. I could discern an unusual softness I'd never seen before as he inspected my face, and I didn't know what that was for. It almost seemed like he was seeing me for the first time.

"Come here," he said after an extended moment of silence and pulled me into a hug before I could move.

I stiffened, surprised by this unexpected body contact. Kayden rarely hugged me, and it always lasted for a short time. This hug, however, lasted for a much longer moment, and his arms held me too close to him for comfort.

"Kay?"

"It's going to be all right." He pulled away only to brush his fingers over my red cheek. "Does it hurt much?"

My heart started pounding at the way he touched me. These last few moments felt more intimate than they should have, and I couldn't wrap my head around it. I had to take a step away from him, breaking the contact.

I shook my head. "Not really."

He grimaced. "I hate to see you like this. I'll go talk to her."

"No, don't. It's not worth it."

"Of course it's worth it. It's your birthday, and she shouldn't treat you that way."

"I know, but I don't want to deal with her any more today. Let's just drop it."

He gave me a long look, which only made me more uncomfortable. What was going on with him?

It was almost on the tip of my tongue to ask him why he was being different, when he grinned and said, "Okay then. I'll take you somewhere so we can celebrate."

He placed his hand on my shoulder in what was supposed to be a comforting gesture, but all I could think about was Natalie. I was sure she would totally get the wrong picture if she was here. She flipped her lid when she found out Kay and I ended up in his room during Kay and Hayden's birthday party, refusing to believe that I just dozed off and he left.

I was about to put distance between us once more, when Hayden's voice reached us from behind.

"Why don't you kiss while you're at it?"

I twirled around to find him in their driveway. He wore a snarl, his hands fisted on his sides, but for the first time, his glare wasn't directed at me. It was directed at Kay, and a strange understanding settled in his gaze.

"You got it all wrong," Kay said. "I was just—"

Hayden's eyes darkened with hate. "Spare me your bullshit. I don't want to hear it." His gaze lingered on me, giving a glimpse of hurt, but it was gone as soon as it appeared, and all that was left was a promise of more pain to come before he stomped off into the house and slammed the door shut.

My heart twisted, and I met Hayden's gaze. He hadn't bullied me since that night in Kayden's room, giving rise to hope that maybe he would finally leave me alone for good, but that hope crashed when he returned to his old ways at school next day.

"You were so mad when you saw us," I said.

"I was mad because you managed to get him to like you. I was furious with you both, but I was also jealous. So jealous. I even thought I had some stupid right on you because I liked you first."

I glanced at Kay's headstone, thinking how different he was that day. He took me to a diner and spent most of the evening just staring at me, and I was so weirded out I wasn't able to see it for what it was. The next day, he acted like his usual self, and I was all too glad to forget the sudden, temporary change in him.

"I never knew. I wasn't even aware of his feelings until he told me he liked me the night we kissed in the Nepaug state forest... Knowing I liked you made everything more difficult for him."

He stood up and brushed off the snow from his knees. "Kayden is one of the reasons why I'm trying hard to make every moment with you count. And that's another thing I wanted to tell you."

I got to my feet. "Yes?"

"I want you to pack a few things because we're going away for the weekend."

Oh. A whole weekend.

I grinned. "A romantic getaway?"

"You can call it that, yeah. It's going to be very 'romantic.'" The way he looked at me told me exactly what kind of things he had on his mind, and my body flushed instantly.

"Where are we going?"

"We're going to Vegas to get married."

I erupted into laughter, seeing right through him. Of all things... "Right. And I'm the pope."

"Exactly." He smirked. "The place is a surprise. All I can say is that it's special for me, and you'll see why. But before that, we'll visit the Nepaug state forest."

I cocked my head to the side. "Really? Why?"

His eyes were ardent as he closed the distance between us. "Because I'm unstaining memories, baby. I want to make every moment count."

Just as he pressed his lips on mine, a voice hidden deep within me came to the surface, bringing horrible pain with it.

Now that I thought about it...

His words and actions seemed just like goodbye—like terminally ill patients who wanted to make the most out of life before they were gone.

As if he'd already given up on life, not believing he would survive the fight.

His phone chimed, and he pulled away to take it out. My heart pounded heavily against my chest when I saw his face turn dark after he read the message.

This is a bad sign.

"What's going on?"

Instead of answering me, he handed me his phone. I had to take a deep breath before I looked at the screen, terrified of what I might see...

"The rematch is on next Sunday at the usual time. Old Murphy's warehouse. Be there or else."

Chapter 20

WE WERE HALF WAY TO the Nepaug state forest when the snow started falling heavily, and I had to switch on the wipers of the rented Land Rover. The whole landscape was stark white, and the fog reduced visibility, so I made sure to drive very carefully and slowly. This didn't stop Hayden from commenting every few minutes to slow down, his jaw flexed like we were going to die any moment.

"For someone who likes living dangerously, you sure are scared now," I told him when we reached Hartford.

"Yeah? It's one thing to do it myself, but quite another to give you all control," he growled, staring at the road ahead.

I sighed. I wished there would be at least a little sunshine to brighten this day and my mood. I'd been feeling down ever since we returned from the cemetery yesterday.

I was supposed to let go of all bleak thoughts and focus on the upcoming weekend with Hayden, but it was hard knowing this could be our last chance to make happy memories together. Our happiness was tainted with the knowledge that our time together could be limited.

"I miss driving. I just don't understand why I can't drive. I feel fine."

"We can't risk it. You know that."

He fidgeted on his seat and rested his head against the window. I gave him a side-glance. I guessed this was as good time as any to tell him what Carmen told me this morning.

"Your mom offered for me to move to your house."

He straightened up, and our gazes met briefly before I returned my attention to the road. "She did?"

"Yes."

I let my mind wander off to the moment with Carmen in the kitchen.

"This house feels different when you're here, dear," she told me as she put *dirty plates into the dishwasher after breakfast.*

Her friendliness thinned the wall I'd put between me and her, and I felt more relaxed with her, which built a stronger connection between us. She was more energetic and healthy-looking these days, and she stayed home to take care of Hayden, determined to make things right between them and stop working so much at the hospital.

"I enjoy being here. It's much better than being trapped in my own home."

She turned to face me; her earnest expression was an overture to her next words. "I thought about this a lot, and I wanted to talk with you about it. Both Hayden and I love having you here, and I understand how hard your life with your mother is. I tried to talk to her before and told her to get a grip on her life and treat you better, but it was like talking to a wall."

I gaped at her, touched by her gesture. "You did? You talked to her?"

"On a couple occasions, yes. But your mother is something else, which is another reason why I want to propose something, Sarah."

My mouth went dry. "Yes?"

"Your eighteenth birthday is in less than two months, and you'll be able to leave your house then if you want. So I want you to come and stay with us."

The significance of her words prevented me from finding the words easily. She perceived my silence as reluctance, so she was quick to assuage me.

"You don't have to pay for anything, if that worries you. We don't use the nursery, so you can stay there. We'll just refurbish it the way you want it." I still couldn't say a word, my heart expanding with gratitude. "I don't want you to feel pressured, dear, so you don't have to answer me now. But think about it, okay? You're family now."

"So what do you think?" I asked Hayden after I recounted our conversation and he remained quiet for a long time.

He brushed his fingers across my cheek, and I glanced at him. I was met with a slight curve of his lips. "I'd love nothing more than that." He pulled his hand away. "But it bothers me that I don't know what her motive is now."

"Motive?"

"Yes. Don't you think it's too much of a coincidence that she's inviting you to move with us just when she's trying to get in my good graces? I don't want her to string us along."

My heart squeezed. "I understand your mistrust and what you say is plausible, but I don't think she has an ulterior motive. Hayden, she helped me a lot these last few weeks, especially during your stay in the hospital. She never asked for anything in return, and I can't help but feel grateful. I never had something like this with my own mother. It feels unreal, only, it isn't, and I don't know how to repay her. She offered to let me stay in your home for *free*. That just shows how amazing she is."

I cast another glance at him and bit into my lip when I noticed his pursed lips. He didn't trust her, so it would be difficult for him to even begin to see her in a new light.

"Your life with her was hard and disappointing, and that's putting it mildly. If I was in your place, I probably wouldn't want to have anything to do with her too. But I'm speaking from the perspective of someone who sees how much she's hurting right now. I do see she's changed and feels guilty for favoring Kayden, and this is me saying this—someone who doesn't believe others easily, just like you."

I exited the highway and continued through the city to Route 44. Out of the corner of my eye, I saw him run his hand down his face.

"I don't know," he said. "I don't know anything. I've been trying to impress her for as long as I can remember, but I always received the same disappointed look. I never knew why I wasn't good enough for her, and it was killing me day by day. I thought that if my own mother couldn't accept me, how could anyone else?" His voice was strained, and it was painful to hear yet another testimony of the scars he bore from his childhood.

"She told me she's accepted you, but you need to hear this from her. If you can let her explain herself... Maybe it will be easier for you to forgive her. I don't know." I exhaled loudly. "Her apology is late, yes, but better late than never. At least she's trying, unlike my mother, so that counts for something, right? Just think about it."

He began tapping his fingers against his thigh, staying silent for quite a while. Just as I decided to drop the subject, he said, "I'll think about it."

I grinned. "That's great."

"I said I'll think about it. I didn't say I'd forgive her, so wipe that smile off your face," he bit back. As a response, I pecked a kiss on his cheek, and he twisted to look at me. "What was that for?"

"If you keep sulking, I'll keep kissing you," I said playfully and looked at him when he didn't say anything.

He crossed his arms over his chest. "Some days, I wonder if you're crazier than me," he muttered.

I chuckled. "We're a perfect match, right?"

"A match made in hell," he mumbled back, definitely in the mood for arguing.

"Well, hell is hot, and since I hate the cold, I like the sound of it," I retorted cheerfully just as I turned onto Route 44.

I could practically see him rolling his eyes. "Whatever." He uncrossed his arms and started tapping his fingers against his thigh again. "I don't trust her and I'm not sure if she really likes you or has hidden intentions, but let's say I'll give her the benefit of the doubt. Anyway, it's good she asked you to move to our house because I wanted that all along." He covered my hand on the gear shift. "So? Will you move to our house after your eighteenth birthday?"

My pulse accelerated. I never thought the day would come when I would be given the opportunity to leave the toxic confinement that was my home and live with Hayden and his mom. In a way, everything was happening fast, and it sounded so good it almost felt like an illusion, like it would slip from my hands any moment.

Then again, I wanted this so much. I already spent most of my time in their house, so what would be the difference?

"I have to admit that even though our houses are right next to each other, it feels like I'd be moving to another part of town." I said this in a cheerful tone, but I couldn't stop my voice from trembling. I hadn't even noticed that my hands had started to sweat.

"No need for you to be scared, Sarah," he said, and his mellow voice soothed me. "I'll take care of you and make you feel at home. Please, say you'll move to my house. Please."

I licked my dry lips. I knew this was important for him as much as it was important for me. I would be making a huge leap of faith, but I chose to believe in the positive outcome of my decision.

"Okay," I replied excitedly. "I'll move to your house after my birthday."

"Yes!" He fist bumped the air and left a kiss on my cheek, grinning. "You'll see. Everything is going to be all right."

And in that moment, despite what might or might not happen in the next couple of days, I fully believed him.

• • • •

HALF AN HOUR LATER on foot, we reached Kayden's and my clearing. Several inches of snow covered the ground, making our trek more challenging, but unlike me, Hayden didn't mind it. His mood had improved since I agreed to move to his house, and he kept teasing me about my red nose and cheeks, using every chance he got to throw snowballs at me.

"How can you be so happy when it's freezing?" I complained, hugging myself. My chattering teeth were more proof of how terribly cold I felt. As if following a cue, a strong gush of cold wind hit us, and I grabbed Hayden's arm, pressing myself against him as close as possible.

"I'm happy because you're funny. You're acting like you're going to die any moment."

"You're such a sadist! What if I die from hypothermia?"

"We won't be here long enough for you to get it, so stop being overdramatic."

The surrounding leafless trees swayed under the surges of wind, bathed by a few rays of sunshine that had fought their way through the clouds. It was the only source of colors and warmth in this dreary landscape. Hayden headed for the patch of ground that was less covered with snow and pulled a waterproof outdoor blanket out of his duffel bag.

He placed it down and cleared the snow off the ground before he gathered some rocks and made a small platform out of them. Then he pulled firewood out of the bag and placed it on the rocks.

I grinned as I watched him start a fire, fascinated. He reminded me so much of Kayden, who made fire each time we stayed here overnight. "You thought about everything."

"Of course I have. I wouldn't want you to 'die from hypothermia.'" He sat down when he finished and opened his arms, inviting me to come. "Come here. I'll keep you warm."

He didn't need to tell me twice. Letting my backpack slip down to the blanket, I rushed into his embrace. He pulled me up on his lap, making me straddle him, and kissed me. A surge of warmth coursed through me when my lips parted and his tongue darted out to meet mine. His arms wrapped around my waist and held me close to him.

His lips continued their journey along my jaw, and I tilted my neck to give him better access. I dug my fingers into his shoulders when he sucked the spot below my ear, much warmer than just a couple of seconds ago.

"Your skin is so soft," he muttered and pulled my knitted scarf a few inches down so he could kiss the hollow of my neck.

He palmed my backside and pressed me against him before he claimed my lips again, and I let out a small moan. I couldn't resist moving against him, rocking my hips to meet his.

I was all hot and breathless when I pulled away to sit next to him a few minutes later.

"I told you I'd keep you warm," he said and snaked his arm around my waist.

I touched my swollen lips, impressed all over again at how good of a kisser he was. "I never doubted your tactics."

His laughter filled the air, and I grinned, satisfied that I made him laugh.

We lapsed into silence, and our gazes set on the clearing sky. The clouds had floated away, and the sun shone brightly, doing wonders for my mood. The firewood popped and crackled with flames dancing in an upward spiral, which soothed me and warmed me enough against the occasional gusts of wind.

"Sometimes, I wish the brain was like a computer memory," he said. "We'd be able to clear any data we want and replace it with new information." He glanced at me. "You'd be able to completely forget about that evening I brought you here and remember only today with me."

I gazed off into the distance, thinking about this. I was amazed he'd wanted to do this for me—to replace the old memories with new ones, which helped me heal.

"I really appreciate what you're doing for me. This place already feels different because you're different too."

He ran his gloved fingers down my cheek. "You know that it was never real? Pretending I was going to rape you that night, threatening to steal your virginity... It was all just to get into your head. I never meant to do it."

"I know."

He curled his fingers into a fist. "I'm so sorry."

"It's okay." I took his hand in mine. "I'm not going to lie; what you did that night in the forest felt all too real, but I know you're regretting it, and I know you wouldn't hurt me."

I brushed my lips against his, speaking the truth of my words through this sweet kiss.

"You're not that old Hayden who instigated fear in me. You make me feel happy and loved, and that's all that matters to me now."

He drew away with a smile. "That's good."

"I'm curious about one thing, though."

"Yes?"

"You knew exactly how to reach this place back then. How do you know about this spot? Did you visit it before with Kayden, or did he tell you about it?"

"Actually, this was my dad's favorite spot."

Oh. My lips parted at this unexpected revelation. Kay never told me this. He mentioned he liked this spot on the small hill because it had a perfect sky view, but he didn't say how he'd found it in the first place.

"Whoa. I never would've imagined that."

"Dad used to bring Kayden and me here. Those memories are vivid in my mind, like everything happened just yesterday. Carmen brought us here a few times when we were in elementary school, which helped me memorize the way."

I intertwined my fingers with his. Kay hadn't been able to tell me anything about their dad since he didn't remember him, so I was all the more curious about him.

"I always wanted to ask you about your dad. Do you remember what he was like?"

A shadow of a smile flickered across his lips as he directed his warm gaze at the sky. "He was the best." His whispered words carried deep longing, and I couldn't look away from his face, captivated by its rapt expression. "He always played with us and took us outside. He never got mad at us, and he was always so... Full of energy."

He placed a kiss on my forehead and drew me flush against him. A flock of birds flooded the sky, creating formations that captured our attention in a short moment of silence.

"Kayden and I were completely different from each other even then. Kayden was shy and didn't want to be separated from our mother, while I was hyperactive and wanted to be the center of everyone's attention. Dad called me his little adventurer because I liked to explore and do things I wasn't supposed to do."

"Like what?"

"Like climbing to the top of a cabinet to reach the toy I wanted to play with at preschool."

I burst out chuckling. "What?"

"Yeah. They used to keep some toys on top of a really high cabinet. We had limited time for playing, but I was bored and I wanted to play with that toy. There was a drawer next to it, so I got on it first and then climbed to the top of the cabinet."

My chuckles turned into laughter. "What did your teacher say?"

He snorted. "She nearly had a heart attack. She started yelling at me and called other teachers to help her to get me down. Carmen was so angry with me and wanted to punish me, but dad... Oh man, he cracked up when he heard about that. He was laughing about it for days. He even told me he was proud of me."

I traced his jaw with my finger. My chest swelled with bitter pain, hurting for Hayden who lost his dad so young. "It appears that Carmen and your dad had different parenting styles."

"You can say that again. She was always so strict. Take our diet, for example. She prohibited us from eating chocolate and snacks most of the time, but dad allowed us to eat them whenever she wasn't there to keep an eye on us, promising to keep that as our secret."

He smiled for real now, and his voice turned more unsteady the further he went down the path of memories.

"I loved him so much." His teary eyes landed on my face. "I was his favorite, and only he and I knew about this. Once, he painted with me on his lap, and I remember him saying he loved me the most. I used to spend a lot of time there, watching him paint... I even used to dream about becoming like him one day."

His face fell, and the first tear slid down his cheek before he turned his face away from me and wiped it away.

"Hayden, come here." I hugged him and brought his head against my shoulder.

"I miss him, and it hurts so much. Why did he have to die? Why did I have to lose him?"

I closed my eyes to stop the tears and placed my chin on top of his head. "Carmen told me about that day. How you found him." I felt him tremble, and I hugged him more firmly. "I'm so sorry that you had to witness that."

"It's fucked up." His gravel voice sliced my heart, and my tears spilled out. "I opened that door expecting him to be working on his latest painting and be covered in paint like usual. Instead, he was lying still on the floor covered in blood."

My heart leapt up. I didn't want to interrupt him, so I kept quiet.

"I thought it was paint." He let out a sorrowful chuckle, which felt like a punch in the gut. "I knew something was wrong, but I thought he would open his eyes and explain why there was so much red paint around him. Only, with every step I took, I saw more and more paint around him, and it was so dark red it couldn't be paint. Its smell hit me, along with the realization. That wasn't paint and he wasn't going to open his eyes."

My face was wet with tears that I shed silently; my arms held Hayden like I would never let him go. His trembling grew stronger.

"There was so much blood," he whispered, breaking another piece of my heart.

"Shh. Don't think about it."

He straightened himself up to look at me, allowing me to see his tears, and it was too painful. "Sometimes I hate him so much. Why did he leave me? He said he loved me, so why did he leave me?"

He clutched my jacket as his sobs started, and I reached for him again, pulling him back into my embrace.

"There are times when people are too lost in their darkness to consider the consequences of their choices," I told him. "He loved you, but he was broken."

"Did he really? Everything is a mess. I'm a mess. I doubted he loved me too many times, because if he did, he wouldn't do that. He wouldn't be gone."

Now that I knew his real feelings regarding his dad's death, I was able to fully understand why he was so angry with Kayden for choosing to save him and angry with me for indirectly contributing to that. He felt abandoned because, in his mind, the people he loved left him, which was heightened by his disorder.

"He loved you," I repeated. "He loved you so much, but his pain blinded him. His pain and darkness played with his mind, clouding everything good in his life, until the only thing that mattered was the way out."

His fist hit the ground. "If only I went there earlier he would be alive. I would be able to save him..."

I thought about his last diary entry, which I'd read this morning. He mentioned he regretted not saving him. "No, don't say it like that. It's not your fault."

"But—"

I cupped his face and made him look at me. "Don't. I blamed myself for so long, but the truth is you can't blame yourself for someone else's decision. Just like Kay made the decision to save you, your dad made the decision to end his life. So please, don't blame yourself."

Another silence ensued, interrupted only by our sobs as we held each other. I couldn't erase his abandonment issues and pain, but I'd prove to him time and again that he wasn't alone. I wasn't leaving.

"Both you and I suffered a lot, but now we have each other, and we'll heal piece by piece together," I told him after a while. He was much calmer now, and his tears had dried up. "One day, it's going to be easier for both of us. We won't be weighed down with regrets and pain. We'll come out of this stronger."

He held my gaze as he stroked my cheek, and I leaned into his touch. "You're so special to me. You always manage to create the light that leads me out of my dark mind."

His lips moved across my cheek, bringing color to my cheeks with tiny kisses on my cold skin. Sadness was gone from his eyes and replaced with softness that melted me.

"So now you know about my dad and how I knew about this place. He had another favorite place, and that's where we're going now. He used to take us there often."

I cocked my head to the side. "Oh? And that is?"

The corner of his lips curled up. "A log cabin in a nearby mountain area." He tilted his head toward me, only a few inches separating our lips. "It's a nice place. You'll see." His warm breath caressed my skin before he kissed me and wiped away all my thoughts into a sweet oblivion.

• • • •

BY THE TIME WE REACHED the cabin, which Hayden had rented for the weekend, it was already dark outside. We barely spoke when we entered the place, and my excitement grew more intense because I knew this was it. Hayden and I were going to have sex.

I sat down on the couch and silently observed Hayden build a fire in the fireplace. The room was dim; the only source of light was a lamp in the far corner. More than ever, I was aware of the way his muscles contracted after each move and his delectable body I wanted to kiss and touch. His arms never seemed more muscular or stronger than now—those very arms that were going to hold me as we crossed the last step to becoming one.

I glanced around, feeling a wave of gratitude toward him for bringing me to a place that contained some of his most precious memories. It was furnished with simple furniture and a few decorations that gave it life and emitted comforting vibes.

"Will you stop being a breathing corpse?" he said when the fire came to life and he turned off the lamp. The room got darker, illuminated only by the flames that formed the most intricate shapes.

"Breathing corpse?"

"You haven't moved from that spot at all. Come on. Get off your ass."

"If this is your version of foreplay, I have to tell you that it doesn't work," I replied playfully, watching his lips quirk up in sudden amusement.

"You finally learned that comebacks exist. Congratulations." He clapped his hands, and I rolled my eyes, standing up to help him with the blanket.

We placed the blanket over the plush carpet in front of the fireplace, and I reached inside my backpack for Pringles and bags of Cheetos and Doritos. I sat next to him and rested my head against his shoulder when he wrapped his arm around my waist.

"Are you cold?" he asked me.

I opened the bag of Doritos and reached inside. "No."

"What do you think about this place?"

I popped a Dorito into my mouth before I passed the bag to him. "It's nice and cozy. I can't wait to see what outside looks like in the morning."

"We'll take a look around tomorrow." He took a few Doritos and stuffed them into his mouth. "I just love everything about it. It's special for me because every time I think about it I remember all the fun I had with my dad. I feel peaceful when I'm here."

"Thank you for bringing me here. It does feel special." He responded with a barely visible curl of his lips, captivated by the flames twirling in the fireplace. I took my backpack and pulled out his diary. "I finished your diary this morning."

He glanced at the diary in my hand with a glimpse of insecurity on his face. "And what do you think?"

I flipped the pages to his last entry. I wanted to tell him so many things. "That you're capable of the most beautiful things. You always want to give love and fight against the negative thoughts. This last entry..."

I started reading it aloud:

"There are so many things I regret in my life, but if I had to make a list with the top five things I regret, this would be it:

1) Not showing up sooner and saving my dad

2) Not avoiding that car

3) Not doing anything as I watched Sarah fall down those fucking stairs

4) Strangling Sarah

5) Not being the "normal" twin

Maybe if I were normal, I would have a chance at normal life.

And I would make Sarah happy."

I looked at him. "It doesn't matter whether you're 'normal' or not. I love you for who you are. Now, after everything, I feel like all these things helped us because they enabled us to learn from our mistakes. I always thought mistakes were bad, but if I make no mistakes, how can I hope to change? Mistakes are there to help me learn, gain experience, and overcome setbacks, so I can become better and stronger in the future. So I can become better me one day. Just like you. All of this led you to who you are today. So those aren't necessarily completely bad things."

He watched me wordlessly, his face remaining blank as he reflected on my words. "You should form your own philosophy," he finally said. "It could be called Boring People To Death."

I pursed my lips. "And you should stop being so addicted to sarcasm."

He smirked. "Never. That's my daily drug."

"I thought I was your daily drug."

"You're like the cheapest kind of drug."

"Ha ha. Not funny."

"Then why are you smiling?"

It was hopeless. I was grinning like a fool.

He took his phone out. "I want to show you something." He tapped on his screen a few times, sitting on his heels. "I want to get a new tattoo, but this one will be the most special. I'm going to put it right under your tattoo."

The flickers of excitement unfurled through me. "A tattoo of what?"

"It's about you and me. Here. Check it out."

He handed me his phone, and I read his note.

"You're bullied,
forever ashamed.

I'm pained,
feeling the same.

We're damaged,
together as one,

Because our storm

always precedes the sun."

I raised my eyes to meet his gaze filled with need, finding my home again. "Hayden, this is beautiful. How did you think of this?"

He shrugged. "I just thought about the things that define us—those bad things that led to something good in the end."

I moved so that my knees touched his and placed my hand on his. "I love it. Together we're managing to conquer everything. Despite every storm."

He nodded and took his phone to place it on the floor. "Together as one."

I inched closer to him. My heart beat fast as we looked at each other, our breaths mixing together. "And we're better together. I love you, Hayden Black."

The fire reflected in his eyes, his lips only a breath away from mine. "And I love you even more, Sarah Decker."

Our lips connected, and he pushed me down on the blanket, hovering above me. I explored his mouth with great intensity, wanting much more, and pressed my fingers into his shoulders that tensed under my touch. He buried his head into my neck and moved his hands underneath my sweater, sliding them delicately up my waist before he cupped my breasts over my bra. I squirmed with need.

"Are you nervous?" he whispered above my lips, his eyes dark.

"Not anymore."

He broke into the most beautiful smile and pulled my sweater and undershirt off, leaving me only in my bra. Blush covered my cheeks, but I didn't want to hide from him this time, letting him see every inch of my uncovered skin freely.

His warm fingers skimmed over my ribs on their way to my back. He unclasped my bra and tossed it aside, drawing away to take in my naked upper body. His fast breathing matched mine.

"You're beautiful," he said huskily, watching the rapid rise and fall of my breasts. He took them in his hands and kissed each of them, giving extra attention to two hard nubs that rose to meet his lips. "The most beautiful girl."

I threw my head back and moaned, lacing my fingers into his hair to keep him close to me. His hands and mouth made love to my skin, cherishing every curve and crevice. His hot kisses brought heat to my insides and cloud-ed my mind as he moved to take my jeans off.

I rose up on my elbows with only my panties covering me. Any feeling of insecurity I might've had was erased under his loving eyes that roamed all over me. The way he looked at me made me feel like I really was the most beautiful girl, and more than ever, I needed us to become one.

"It's not fair. I'm here naked, and you're completely dressed."

He smirked. "So what are you going to do about it?"

Sitting on his haunches, he let me undress him, following my every move as his breathing grew heavier. My eyes drank in his chiseled chest, abs, and tattoos, which were emphasized by the shadows that danced across his skin in the dimly-lit room. I fumbled with the zipper of his jeans, brushing his erection before I stopped to cover it with my hand. This was the last straw for him, apparently, since the next moment, he took off his jeans and boxers in one swift move and pushed me back to the blanket.

"It's funny," he said and planted a feathery kiss on my neck.

"What's funny?"

"How only one touch from you can turn me into this." He supported himself on one hand as he leaned away to look into my face, his expression full of lust. "I want to give you everything and take everything from you. And I want it right now."

He continued kissing me as he settled himself between my legs and start-ed grinding against me. Blood hummed through my veins with anticipation as I ran my hands across his strong chest. He was my undoing, and there was no going back. I cupped his cheeks, looking at him pleadingly.

"Then do it."

He groaned. "I will. But first..." He repositioned himself, kneeling as he held my thighs wide open.

I let out a breathy moan when his lips skimmed over my stomach and moved even lower. "Hayden?" I grabbed his head when he kissed the spot right above the edge of my panties. Everything in me was desperate for the kiss that was far more intimate than anything.

"I want you to feel good," he replied hoarsely and took off the last piece of my clothing, exposing me completely to him.

The world stopped to exist the moment he lowered his head and did exactly what he'd said. My body fed on the addictive sensations that coursed through me, and I couldn't stop calling his name over and over again, amazed that he was doing this to me—amazed at how *good* his lips and tongue felt on me. And then my pleasure reached its peak, and the love for this beautifully imperfect guy washed over me in powerful waves. He was my *everything*.

"You're so fucking beautiful," he said when he pulled away to look me in the eyes.

Blissed out and quite speechless, I watched him reach out to his duffel bag and grab a condom package, never breaking our eye contact. He ripped it open, and my chest tightened in excitement. We were really going to do it.

"Do you trust me?" he asked me and positioned himself in between my thighs.

"Yes."

He ran his hand through my hair. "I'll make sure it hurts as little as possible." I nodded and grasped his shoulders, mesmerized by the incredibly soft look in his eyes.

In one emotion-charged moment, he entered me and brought his lips to mine as he slowly worked his way inside of me. His tongue swept into my mouth, distracting me from my discomfort with its rousing strokes, and my heart pumped stronger, fueled by our love and need.

"Does it hurt?" His voice was strained, showing just how much he was controlling himself.

Did it hurt? Not really. I'd expected an intense pain, but what I felt was rather dull, and it gradually diminished the longer he remained inside.

"No." He still didn't move. "Um, you know..." I blushed. "You can move now." I bit into my lip. "Please."

His lips twisting into a ravishing smile, he began a steady pace that brought me rising pleasure, removing all the traces of the uncomfortable ache. No words were spoken as he showed me just how much he loved me, all those broken and misplaced pieces of our past gluing together into a clear picture of unity and devotion. Everything finally came into its place.

Our hearts beat in unison as we savored each other. I slid my fingers down his back and pulled him closer to me. His lips were hot and fiery on my neck as he increased his pace, which doubled my pleasure, making me create sounds I'd never thought I was capable of.

"You're amazing, Sarah. So amazing," he gritted out, beads of sweat sliding down his temples.

He brought my arms above my head and intertwined his fingers with mine. His lips matched his urgency, moving his body with mine in complete harmony, and once more my world exploded into potent pleasure that was heightened by the connection I shared with him, leading me into pure happiness.

"I love you," we said almost at the same time, right before he came, hugging me close to him.

Later, we lay naked on the blanket in our afterglow, entangled together in an embrace. His fingers trailed my waist as he gazed adoringly into my eyes, which reinforced the powerful thread that held our imperfect hearts connected together. The crackling sounds of the fire completed the romantic atmosphere in the otherwise quiet room.

"How do you feel?" he asked.

"Like I want to do it a million times more with you." He chuckled. I stroked his cheek and jaw idly with my finger. "And you?"

His arms tightened around me. "I feel so high."

"So I'm your best drug after all." I planted a kiss right over his heart.

"Definitely."

I started making various shapes on his chest, gazing at each one of his tattoos. "I never knew it could be like that."

I could practically see him smirk above me in all his smugness. "Yeah? That's nothing, baby." He tipped my chin and made me look up at him. "I'll show you much more. The whole night."

My cheeks burned, but I decided to turn this into a joke. "And the whole day. And the whole weekend."

He pursed his lips together as if he was about to burst into laughter. "Insatiable much? Consider it done. I brought enough condoms."

With an enormous smile, I closed my eyes and nestled against his chest, memorizing this moment forever. Just like he'd written before, we were two dysfunctional pieces that would find their way to become whole again.

He was the half that made me whole. He was the one that accepted all of me and made me a better person. He helped me realize I should always go on and fight to be stronger despite all the seemingly insurmountable hurdles in my way.

And I would cherish this night forever—the moment we crossed the last part of the bridge that separated us, embracing all of us.

The night we were together as one.

Chapter 21

NEXT SUNDAY ARRIVED too fast, ending the almost honeymoon-like days Hayden and I spent together. Hayden kept to himself the whole day, spending most of his time training for the fight. Luckily, Carmen was at work because if she were here, she definitely would've noticed something was wrong. She didn't know what her son would go through tonight, and I didn't know how to feel about it.

A tiring blend of emotions stayed with me all the time, and fear was the most dominant among them. Hayden and I didn't speak much, especially since he didn't want me there, but I refused to change my mind and stay home.

Blake arrived two hours before the fight in a rented Jeep. He was going to drive us to the warehouse, which was an hour's drive away from Enfield, and Masen would wait for us there. Very few words were exchanged between us before we set out, and the silence in the car grew suffocating. I wished I had the right words that could break the tension.

"You won't separate from Blake and Mace even for a second," Hayden said and turned around in the passenger seat to look at me. "Got it?" We'd gone over this a dozen times already, but I nodded. "Try to be as invisible as possible. Keep your eyes open. And don't even try to interfere in the fight for any reason."

I gave him a hesitant nod. The last "rule" was the most difficult. I just had to stand there and watch him get beaten, but that was what I'd signed up for.

"After tonight, this all ends, right?" I asked, hoping they couldn't hear how shaky my voice was. A ball of nerves tightened in my stomach. "You won't be part of that world anymore?"

I didn't miss the brief look he and Blake shared. "If everything goes well tonight, I'll be out," Hayden answered and turned back to the front.

I caught Blake's gaze in the rearview mirror. His face was expressionless. "What?" I asked him.

"I still don't understand why you had to come with us. You don't want to be around those people and see those things."

"I want to support Hayden."

He held my gaze a moment longer, before he shrugged and focused back on the road. "You do understand that you can't say a word about this to anyone?" His tone was condescending. "Absolutely no one."

I crossed my arms over my chest. "I know. And it's not like I even want to."

"Good. Because it's more than enough that you're involved in this. We don't need anyone else involved too."

I gave him a sideway glance. "I know, Blake."

Slowing down, he drove off the road and into a forest, following a path that could easily be missed in the dark.

"This warehouse is in a forest?"

"Yes," Hayden replied.

"Why the warehouse? Why not that place you fought at the last time?"

"For safety reasons. If fights were only held in one place, the cops could easily find it," Hayden said.

"Tonight's fight is special because of all the money riding on it, and only the people from T's inner circle are invited to watch," Blake interjected and swerved to the right, which led us down a much narrower path. "So T arranged it at a lesser known place. We don't want 'uninvited guests.'"

"What would happen if the police discovered that place?" I asked.

"For one, we'd all go to jail," Blake replied. "But since T and his lapdogs have connections with the police, they would get out in no time and then..."

"Then what?"

"Then you wouldn't want to be free, because you'd wish you never got out of jail once T was done with you."

Chills ran through me. "Is he that influential?"

"Yes, he is," Hayden said. "How do you think he managed to keep his large circle secret all this time?"

"How did you hear about them if everything was done in secret?"

Hayden and Blake glanced at each other again, and I wondered if they were going to deny me this answer.

Finally, Hayden said, "It's not that hard to figure out some things when you know the right people." I waited for him to add something else, but he didn't.

Ten minutes later, thick trees gave way to an open area that housed a huge, rundown warehouse. Blake's headlights cast a light on a glimmering surface in the distance.

I peered at it. "Is that a lake?"

"A swamp," Hayden answered, and I chewed my lip nervously. I didn't like the sound of it.

At least twenty cars were parked near the entrance to the warehouse, which was surrounded by burn barrels that provided enough light in the dark forest. Some people had gathered near them, talking in groups, and it took only one glance for me to see they looked tougher and more dangerous than the lot at the place Mel and I visited that night.

Their faces painted a picture of a rough life, and I didn't even want to imagine what kind of things they had experienced. I hoped not to cross paths with them ever again after this night.

Blake parked right next to a red Jeep, which was the same model as ours. Masen was sitting on its hood, talking to Steven and some other guys as he smoked.

"We'll come in five," Hayden told Blake. Blake nodded and went to join Masen and the others.

Hayden got out and hopped next to me in the backseat. The tinted windows hid us from the guys, so when Hayden jerked me toward him and kissed me, I fully responded to him, unleashing the burning need within me that begged me to keep him as close to me as possible and never let him go.

Threading his fingers through my hair, he tugged it to tilt my head backward. His lips moved to the hollow beneath my ear, giving me the most ardent kisses ever, and I clung to him like he was going to disappear into thin air any moment.

"Remember, don't leave Mace and Blake," he said into my neck, keeping me flush against him. "You won't talk to me or stand next to me once we're inside. Don't try to stop the fight or do anything crazy." He pulled away to look at me. "Do you understand?"

"Yes."

His scorching hot eyes fell on my lips, and he kissed me again, but this time it was a bruising kiss that perfectly portrayed just how desperate he was. He drew away and grabbed my face.

"You're going to stay strong. Okay? You have to, even if I die."

I grasped his wrists right above his hand wraps, feeling like I was going to start panicking any second now. "Hayden—"

"No." He shook me once, demanding my attention and compliance. "Listen to me. You won't do a single thing. Even if I'm beaten to death on that floor, you won't interfere."

I bit into my lip. I wanted to cry, but I'd promised myself I wouldn't fall apart in front of him. I wouldn't make this any more difficult for him than it already was.

"You won't die," I told him. "Stop saying that because you won't die." I pressed my fingers into his arms, holding him tight. "You'll survive this fight. I believe in you."

His gaze turned so soft I was barely able to breathe under the intense emotions it provoked in me.

"I love you." He threaded his fingers through my hair again, his moves hurried and fervid. "I love you so much." He left kisses all over my face, each more despairing than the previous one. "Thank you for everything, Sarah. Thank you for everything you've done for me."

I frowned at him. "I love you too, but don't you dare act like this is goodbye. This isn't goodbye. You're going to be fine."

His eyes reflected deep sadness and regret, telling me this could very well be our last moment together.

"I love you," he repeated and removed my hands from him. "I could tell you so many things right now, but we don't have time." *No. I hate this. I don't want this.* "Just remember I'll always love you. Stay strong."

He got out of the car before I could do anything to keep him with me any longer. I shook so hard that I wasn't sure my legs would be able to carry me. For a few minutes, I just stared at my lap, trying to pull myself together.

We'd spent so many heart-warming moments together this last week, but now it seemed like all of it had passed in a fleeting second, and it wasn't nearly enough. Nothing would ever be enough.

The passenger door opened, and Masen popped his head inside. "Any moment now, Sar, if you haven't chickened out and want to stay in the car."

His taunt ruffled my feathers, which was exactly what gave me the strength to move and avoid breaking.

I got out of the car and closed the door. "I won't be a nuisance, Masen."

I looked around for Hayden, but he was nowhere in sight. Only a few people were left outside, and some of them had their eyes on me, making me feel like I was sticking out by a mile. A shiver that rolled down my spine had nothing to do with the exceedingly cold weather, and I had to remind myself once again that I was doing this for Hayden and wasn't going to give in to fear.

"Hayds is inside with Blake and the others," Masen said. "Come on. The fight will start soon."

He surprised me when he put his hand on the small of my back and ushered me forward. I frowned at him and removed his hand from me.

"No need to push me around. I can walk by myself."

He cast me a quick smirk. "You've finally grown some balls. Nice."

He walked ahead of me so he couldn't see the glare I sent him. My anger was short-lived, replaced with pure dread the moment we stepped into the warehouse. I was intimidated by its vast space that was filled with a foul smell, broken glass on the floor, and piles of bricks and other debris. Burn barrels had been lit all around, contributing to the sinister atmosphere of the semi-dark space, but what chilled me to the bone was a big, round cage in the middle. It was surrounded by people who looked all too excited about what was going to transpire soon.

"A cage?" I asked Masen, unable to mask the fear in my voice.

Masen's gaze landed on me for the briefest moment before he turned his face away, but I managed to catch distress in his expression. "Tonight's fight is different. It could get more brutal than usual."

"What does that mean?" My voice was high-pitched.

He stopped and turned around, and I halted abruptly, almost bumping into him. I winced when I met his hard gaze.

"It means you have to keep it together. Don't make this difficult for Hayds." He shook his head. "This place is dangerous, so I don't know what you're doing here, but since you're already here, you're going to toughen up. No crying, no whining, and no interfering."

Without waiting for my response, he moved around me and pushed me forward with his hands on my shoulders. He was close behind me as we headed over to Hayden and the other guys. I was well aware of how right he was, so I had to do better than this.

The refuse crunched as I stepped on it. My eyes went to the faces around me that wore nothing but menacing intensity. I was done for if I made even one wrong move. I scooted closer to Masen, but I walked with my head held high, putting on a brave front.

I stopped across from Hayden, drawing attention from the guys next to him, but he didn't look at me. He talked to a guy whose scowl was enough to make me think twice about looking at him again. Blake and Masen engaged in conversation with Steven and two girls who packed more muscles than Mel and I together, and I felt out of place. Nobody said a word to me, acting like I was invisible.

I tried catching Hayden's gaze, but he hadn't looked at me even once, which twisted my insides with anxiety. More than ever, I felt like we were running out of time, and I felt like any gaze could be our last...

Keep it together. It's going to be all right.

Masen and Blake suddenly shifted their attention over the heads of the crowd, and I followed their gazes to an older man approaching us. He was accompanied by Miller and the other two guys who checked up on Hayden at the hospital.

The whole group grew silent as they stared at the man. I had no clue why, because out of all people here, he looked the least dangerous and powerful. Moreover, he looked like everyone's favorite grandpa.

He was in his late fifties or early sixties, with a black mustache and trimmed black hair that had only a few gray strands near his temples. He had an average height and body, and he was dressed like he was attending a formal dinner in a navy suit, polished shoes, and a tie, but it didn't scream "power." It screamed "out of place." On top of that, his lips were curled in a smile that could be easily interpreted as friendly.

Nevertheless, all eyes were on him as if he owned the place and all these people, and I knew he was T.

"It's good to see you, boy," he said to Hayden with an accent, but I couldn't pinpoint it. "For a moment there, I thought we'd need to have a serious talk."

How could he induce such fear with his words when he looked and sounded so benign? Hayden didn't even blink as he looked him in the eyes, showing no sign of insecurity.

"I understood what's at stake the first time we talked," Hayden replied coolly, and T's gaze hardened with displeasure briefly.

"Good. That's good." He patted Hayden's shoulder. "You know you're one of my favorite fighters, so I'd be disappointed if you let me down tonight."

"Don't worry, T. You'll get your money."

T's smile held no sincerity. "Good boy. I'm sure you'll give the crowd a good show, as always."

He glanced around at the people surrounding him, and my stomach turned over when our gazes met. I fisted my hands in my pockets, hoping he wouldn't ask who I was or what I was doing here. Did he know I was Hayden's girlfriend? After a long moment, he looked back at Hayden.

"I'll ask you one more time. Are you sure about tonight? You want out?"

Determination was written all over Hayden's face. "Yes."

"You know the consequences, son. As much as I'd hate for that to happen, you know how this goes."

I looked between Hayden, Masen, and Blake, trying to find the answer to his cryptic comment, but I found none. I grew more fidgety when I noticed how edgy they were. No one dared to say a word.

"I know," Hayden replied.

T nodded. "All right then. Good luck." He patted Hayden's shoulder once more and turned to leave, sparing me a glance before he and his thugs blended in with the crowd.

"Are you sure about this?" Blake asked him.

Hayden's eyes met mine for a second. He nodded to Blake and took off his jacket. "Yeah."

My heart swelled, and I wanted nothing more than to hug him and take him out of here. The distance between us now seemed like miles.

"Okay, everyone! It's showtime!" the announcer said from somewhere near the cage, and the crowd cleared to let Axel through.

He was dressed the same as Hayden—a black tank top and black sweatpants, despite the low temperature—looking completely unfazed. He had less muscle than Hayden, but he seemed agile. The people cheered and called his name repeatedly, but his face remained expressionless on his way to the cage. One of T's guys searched his body for weapons and let him pass after the quick inspection.

"Good luck, bro. You can do it," Masen told Hayden and slapped his back.

"Good luck," the other guys said, to which Hayden only nodded, his expression serious.

Finally, his gaze landed on me and lingered, and something in his eyes burned slowly. I thought he was going to approach me and take me in his arms, but he did neither.

He leaned to Blake and muttered something into his ear I hardly discerned as: "Don't let go of her if I win."

What?

Before I could ask what he meant by that, he looked at me and mouthed, "I love you."

"Hayden...," I let out, pressing my nails into my palms. I was cold, and my heart rate wouldn't go down. I mouthed the same words to him as I did my best to maintain the encouraging smile. My world crumbled when his face fell for a brief moment, revealing his fear and pain, and it ripped me. *No.*

He wasn't supposed to fight. He wasn't supposed to go through this and risk his life. I was so scared!

I made a step toward him without thinking, but he turned around and headed to the cage.

Masen shot his hand out to grab my arm. "Stay put," he hissed into my ear.

I couldn't utter a word as I watched Hayden walk to the cage, and each second brought more pain.

The guy who had frisked Axel did the same thing to Hayden and let him pass once he was done. The crowd became louder, and everyone gathered around the cage in rising anticipation. I spotted T through the fence on the other side of the cage. He never took his eyes off of Hayden and Axel, who moved to the center of the cage, staring each other down.

We got closer to the cage, and I was thankful for my height that allowed me to see over the heads and shoulders in front of me. There was something comforting about having Masen and Blake next to me, which was strange since they weren't on my list of favorite people.

"Why so serious, Black?" Axel taunted him, a ghost of a smile on his lips.

"Fuck off," Hayden bit back.

The announcer closed the door to the cage. "Okay. You know the rule. If you're unresponsive for fifteen seconds, you're out. All techniques are allowed, and you can hit anywhere," he said loud enough for everyone to hear him. "Have fun!"

Have fun? Was he serious? He jumped off the steps that led to the cage and joined the crowd, announcing the beginning of the match.

Before I could even prepare myself for imminent violence, they pounced and swung their fists at each other's faces. Axel dodged Hayden's hook with ease, which couldn't be said for Hayden, who swayed after Axel's fist caught his jaw. The difference in their speed was evident from the start; Axel was much quicker and nimbler as they circled each other.

He didn't stop, managing to catch Hayden's face more times than I could count. Hayden slumped against the fence and barely managed to avoid Axel's next blow when he ducked and darted behind Axel.

Axel was fast, spinning on his heel and swinging his fist at Hayden's already battered and bruised face, but Hayden blocked it with his forearm and punched his cheek with his other hand. Axel staggered, which Hayden used to land a flurry of quick punches all over his abdomen.

The crowd was ecstatic. The pungent smell of blood and sweat spread through the stale air, and nausea swept over me as I watched them hit each other mercilessly.

"Come on, Axel!" spectators cheered him on.

"Get him, Black!" others said. "You can do it!"

Axel fell down, and Hayden came at him, but he swayed, which Axel used to trip him with his leg. Hayden crashed down to his stomach and had just enough time to turn to his back and shield himself when Axel straddled his waist and began throwing punches at his head.

No. Get up, Hayden. Get up!

He managed to catch Hayden's cheek, and his head pounced against the floor, causing a cracking sound that turned my stomach. *No, no, no.* This was bad.

Hayden seemed so stunned he could barely raise his arms to deflect Axel's hits.

"He's only blocking him," Blake said.

"He isn't fighting like usual. Not good," Masen added, creating a whirlwind of panic in me.

No way. This couldn't end like this!

Axel landed his next hit right into Hayden's left ribs, and a heart-shattering scream filled the warehouse. "You can't win, Black."

He struck again and caught Hayden's right ribs. Another scream pierced the air, breaking my heart into thousand pieces. Each inch of me begged me to do anything to save him. But I couldn't do a single thing.

Axel's fist caught Hayden's nose with a crunching sound, and Hayden cried out. I pressed my hand against my mouth. The cheers and boos blended together, and everything indicated this was the end...

"It's time to finish this," Axel said and raised his fist.

I reacted on impulse. "You can do it, Black," I screamed, blind to everything and everyone but the guy my heart beat for. "You can do it! So fight back!"

Hayden moved his head to look at me, his eyes half-closed and swollen. I could hardly recognize him with his broken nose gushing so much blood that it turned his face into a repulsive image.

Axel pressed his forearm against Hayden's throat and cast his gaze at me, blood trickling down his cheeks in gruesome trails. Hayden clawed at his arm to separate it from himself, but his move was sluggish and ineffective.

"You can do it!" I repeated. "You can win!"

Axel made a smile that felt like a kick in my gut. "Look at her. Cheering her pathetic *novio*. Maybe I can play with her once I'm done with you? Have some fun?" He pressed his forearm harder against Hayden's throat, almost strangling him. "Die, *hijo de puta*."

Defining seconds ticked off, and everything slowed down as I waited for something to happen. Just when I thought that this was it, some switch flipped inside of Hayden, and something changed in him. His eyes flashed with rage, bringing my hope back to life.

"No," Hayden gritted out through his bared teeth, gagging as he struggled to push Axel away from him. "*NO!*"

Too quickly to comprehend, he struck him into the throat with the heel of his hand and elbowed his groin. Axel bent and automatically reached for his crotch, howling in pain.

Hayden used that moment to roll Axel to the right with a roar that showed how painful and strenuous that move was, but he didn't stop as he positioned himself between Axel's legs. He pinned his arms against the ground and started kneeing him into his groin, ruthlessly hitting him again and again.

Axel groaned and almost freed himself when he pushed against Hayden's hands, but Hayden grabbed his hair and used all his force to slam his head into the ground. The contact emitted a loud crunch, and terror replaced all joy I'd felt at seeing Hayden turn this fight around.

Axel lost his consciousness immediately, but Hayden hit his head against the ground one more time before he stood up. He extended Axel's arm, held his wrist, and smashed his knee into his elbow, managing to break it.

I couldn't swallow past the constriction in my throat. The puddle of blood spreading under Axel's head got bigger, and its smell violated my nostrils.

Looking like he was on the verge of passing out, Hayden did the same thing to Axel's other elbow and kicked his waist a few more times before he finally moved away from him. He groaned as he swayed on his feet.

"Axel is down! Black wins!" the announcer said, and everyone turned delirious, chanting Hayden's name triumphantly.

It was *over*. It was finally over.

Our gazes barely met before he collapsed to the ground, falling on all fours.

"Hayden!" I took a quick step forward, but a hand wrapped around my upper arm to keep me in place. I looked over my shoulder and found Blake shaking his head at me.

"Don't move."

"What? Why? He won. The fight is over, and he needs our help."

"It isn't over."

"What? What do you mean?"

The announcer entered the cage and encouraged the crowd to keep cheering with his arms raised high in the air. He stopped above Hayden, who sat on his heels with his head hung low.

"Good job, Black," he told him, kneeling next to Axel. He checked his pulse and nodded to T. "Still alive."

"Take him out," T ordered, and two guys got in the cage to pick up Axel.

Hayden didn't move from his spot or raise his head. His blood dripped from his badly injured face, and it was frightening. He just stared at something on the ground as he tried to catch his breath.

I tugged my arm, but I couldn't set myself free from Blake's grasp. "Let me go," I hissed at him. "What are you doing? Why don't you go and help him?" I looked at Masen, who also didn't move, and his stony face only added to my anxiety. "And you too," I said to him. "You're just standing here, doing nothing."

"T isn't done with him," Blake told me.

I frowned. "What's that supposed to mean?"

"It means he's still not out," Masen said.

"But he fought Axel and won. What more does T want?"

T got in the cage and stopped right above Hayden. "For the sake of old times, I'm giving you one last chance," he said loudly. "Are you absolutely sure you want out?"

Slowly, Hayden tore his gaze from the floor to T. "Yes," he replied in a quiet, hoarse voice.

The mass started booing. T inhaled deeply and looked over the spectators until his gaze stopped on me, stealing the air out of my lungs. I didn't dare move. Fear gripped my throat when it dawned on me that he could use me against Hayden as part of some sick punishment.

His face didn't reveal anything when his gaze moved from me and continued scanning the crowd until it settled back on Hayden. "All right. Since this is what you want, this is what you're going to get. *If* you survive."

I snapped my head at Blake, all hairs rising on the back of my neck. "What does that mean?" I asked him, but I didn't get to hear his answer because the crowd booed even louder, and I turned to see two guys enter the cage.

"Pick him up and take him outside," T told them. "We're going to settle this next to the swamp."

My panic rose too fast. "No! What are they doing?"

"He's going to get jumped out," Masen said. What? No!

"That can't be possible!"

"Those are the rules," Blake responded. "We all got jumped in, so now he has to get jumped out."

Out of all possibilities, getting jumped out was as frightening as receiving a bullet in the head. It was equally fatal. Even if he wasn't terribly injured, his chance of surviving would be virtually nil because many members of the gang would beat him until they were satisfied.

"But he's terribly hurt! They're going to kill him!"

Even though he could barely stand, Hayden didn't protest when T's thugs pulled him to his feet and dragged him out of the cage and through the unsatisfied mass. He turned his head to look at me, and a piercing pain coursed through my chest at the sight of his desolate eyes. He held my gaze, telling me so much through our silent connection, yet too little because our eye contact was too transient. The only words he formed were, "I'm sorry."

Everything in me told me this was goodbye, and a crippling fear blasted through me, tearing me apart.

"Hayden!" I headed toward him, but Blake was too strong; he pulled me back and flush against him, limiting my movements. "No! Stop! Let me go!"

"Calm down! Don't make this worse for him," Blake hissed.

Now I understood what Hayden meant earlier when he told Blake not to let go of me if he won. The people moved toward the exit, whether to witness whatever was about to happen or join it, I didn't know.

"How can you be so cold? He's your friend, but you don't care that he's going to die," I yelled hysterically at Masen and Blake, ignoring glares from Steven and the others.

"Who says we don't care?" Masen exploded. His face went completely red with rage, and his blue eyes turned the angriest I'd ever seen them. "What the fuck do you think you know about us? You don't know anything, so stop saying bullshit! We don't want to make things worse for him. If we interfere, we'll make T angry, and you don't want to make him angry because knowing him, he'll decide that Hayden's punishment for leaving the gang will be death! He can even hurt you."

I had nothing to say to that, shocked to the core.

"Why are you wasting time on soap operas?" Steven asked. "Let's go."

He turned around and walked away, followed by Masen and the other guys. Blake grasped my shoulders and made me look at him.

"Either you'll stand aside and keep quiet, or I'll have someone make sure you stay in the car. Your choice."

Defeated, I nodded, and my body went numb. It was over. I was going to lose him, and there was nothing I could do. *Nothing.*

"I understand. I'll stay quiet and won't interfere."

I wasn't aware of our short walk to the crowd who had huddled near the swamp. I wasn't aware of what the spectators were saying, the sounds, or anything but Hayden, who was surrounded by a group of at least ten people.

Pain solidified in me as they pushed Hayden's head into the water and held him there for an abnormally long period of time. Pain intensified and spread through every single inch of me as they pulled him out and beat the living daylights out of him, covering each part of his battered body with their punches and kicks, even after he *passed out*. Pain turned my world into nothing as they lit a cigarette and pressed it over his arms and waist, marking him forever with horrendous evidence of barbaric violence.

I had no idea if he was still breathing as he lay on the ground unconscious. I had no idea how long the torture lasted. I had no idea if he'd lost too much blood, watching it flow out of him in abundant amounts. I had no idea how I was able to just stand and watch these monstrous acts, which were ingrained in my mind forever.

And then it was over. The guys dispersed and left him alone, but I couldn't move. As I stood there, seconds ticking and ticking, I knew that any possibility that he survived this had been destroyed.

Blake, Masen, and the others ran to him, but I still couldn't move. Destructive darkness enveloped me into its powerful shell, threatening to change me forever.

And the world turned into everlasting nothing.

Chapter 22

End of February

Third period dragged on, and I had a hard time keeping still. All I wanted to do was leave, so when the bell rang, Kevin and I were the first people to head out of the classroom, glad to put the tedious lecture and our dreary teacher behind us. Students filled the sunlit hallway in a flash, and the clash of noises and voices enclosed us.

For the hundredth time, I checked my phone for any message from Hayden, but I found none. I wondered why he hadn't replied to my last text, which I'd sent thirty minutes ago. I typed a new text.

"Are you coming to the cafeteria?"

I send him the message and returned my phone to my pocket, searching for a glimpse of his tall form.

"Is Hayden okay?" Kevin asked me, avoiding eye contact.

I noticed the blush on his cheeks, which manifested almost every time he mentioned or saw Hayden. We all knew he had a crush on Hayden, as much as he tried to pretend he didn't, partly because of me. It wasn't easy for him since he was torn between Hayden and Jess, whom he also liked. On top of that, I wasn't sure if he was okay with his sexuality; he acted like he still didn't fully accept his attraction to both women and men. We'd never had a good opportunity to talk about that.

I shrugged. "I don't know. He didn't reply to my last message."

"S-So he finally got the casts removed?"

"Yeah. He said, and I quote, 'Long live freedom.'" I half smiled, but it quickly diminished as I remembered all the times he complained about them and acted like a petulant child because his movements were limited and he was in terrible pain. He'd been through a lot.

After so many days, Hayden had finally recovered from the life-threatening injuries he suffered that dreadful night last month. I couldn't quite remember what happened after Hayden got jumped out, because shock erased most of my memories of the rest of that day. Only luck kept Hayden alive.

There was no other way to describe how he'd survived the trip to the hospital and the immediate surgery for a collapsed lung in such a lifeless condition.

He had broken ribs, a fractured skull—that luckily didn't lead to brain damage or make his old brain injury worse—internal bleeding, a broken arm and leg, countless cigarette burns, a broken nose, and so many bruises that turned most of his body into an appalling painting of violence. Even the doctors were surprised he'd survived, considering that his life was hanging by a thread when he arrived at the hospital.

Now, the only thing that remained were new scars, which reflected the grim reality of the world Hayden had been a part of for a long time. But not anymore. After that day, Hayden was officially out of T's gang and free to live his life the way he wanted without worrying about debts or twisted retaliations.

Out of the two, Axel suffered bigger consequences. We'd heard he suffered from serious memory loss and couldn't fight anymore, so T didn't have much use of him. Whether Axel would face jumping out or something else was yet to be seen, but I didn't care. All that mattered was that it was over.

We found Mel near her locker. She talked to a group of freshmen, carrying a stack of pamphlets with her, which was nothing unusual for her these days.

"Trying to snatch more followers?" I asked her with humor in my voice when she approached us, but her face remained serious. She looked like she was ready to kick some butt.

"I'm seriously losing my mind here. If I offered them free tickets to a Justin Bieber concert or the latest iPhone, they would be all over me. But nooo. Who cares about students' wellbeing? Who cares about making this place better? Who cares about countless silent victims of bullying when they live their lives so blissfully ignorant, caring only about gossip and latest trends? Fricking morons."

Kevin and I glanced at each other, wearing equal smiles. She was definitely born to be an activist.

We were all surprised when Mel announced she wanted to join student council and try to make a difference before the end of the year. The council's previous vice president was in the hospital and would be out of school for quite a long time, and Mel managed to get the position.

Since then, she was all about promoting her anti-bullying campaign, ask-ing students to join it to improve the school. It went without saying that principal Anders and Mel were at each other's throats. She called him her arch nemesis aka "The Uneducated Swine And Pain In The Ass."

"Take it easy, Miss Vice President," I told her and patted her shoulder. "That's nothing new."

"Yeah, that's nothing new, but if we keep turning a blind eye to what's happening in our school and how corrupt our administration is, the bullying is going to continue, and I'm tired of dealing with all of those sick bullies on my own."

"Melissa, the savior!" a guy passing next to us shouted. A few students standing close by snickered.

Mel grabbed a pamphlet from the stack she held, crushed it into a ball, and threw it at his head. "Do us a solid and cut off your tongue!"

The students around us burst out laughing, enjoying the drama a little too much. Melissa was something else, all right.

"Don't worry, Mel. I'm sure your campaign will be a s-s-success," Kevin supported her.

"Yeah," I agreed. "By the time you're done, the principal will have to quit."

"He better," she said. "Because I won't stop dragging the media into this until that swine breaks and moves his fat, hairy ass out of that position."

We'd just rounded the corner on our way to the cafeteria when Jessica came from another hallway. My lips moved to form a smile, but they stopped when I noticed her ashen face.

"Jess?" Kevin asked her, reaching her. "What's wrong?"

"I just got detention." *Oh?* She pinched the bridge of her nose. "The 'best' part? I have it with Blake."

I raised my eyebrows. "What? How?"

Her eyes downcast, she fiddled with the ends of her hair. "I threw Blake's phone on the ground and broke its screen in U.S. history because he kept ha-rassing me while I was trying to talk to Marcus Robinson. You know Marcus? The guy who asked me out last week?" We all nodded. "So now Ms. Gentry wants to punish us both."

Mel looked at her like she couldn't believe her own ears. "You threw his phone? Damn, girl, that's savage." She whistled. "I mean, that's something I'd do for sure, but you? Are you sure you're the same old Jess and not some evil spirit that possessed you?" She waved her arm at her, acting like an exorcist. "Begone, evil spirit! Begone!"

My snort turned into a chuckle, but it didn't last. "I thought Blake stopped bullying you. He's been ignoring you ever since the New Year's party, so what's this about?"

She pursed her lips together. "Probably because he's a jealous jerk." At that, her whole face turned red. "Well, he's definitely acting like one. He sits right behind me in U.S. history! Today, he didn't stop picking on me and taking embarrassing photos of me, and it was degrading, especially in front of Marcus. So I don't know how, but I just snapped. The next thing I knew, his iPhone was on the floor with a broken screen."

"He is s-so awful!" Kevin exclaimed. "Why can't he just s-stop?"

"Because he's a sick moron, and I wish I could smash his head against... Against... Actually, any hard surface will do," Mel said. "Hopefully, this school will finally install cameras and make harsher punishments for bullies like him after my campaign."

"At least you fought back," I told Jess. It was amazing that she'd won against the fear that had confined her and fought for herself. "That's got to count for something."

She didn't share the sentiment. Based on the frown lines on her face, I didn't need to ask her to know she was afraid of Blake's reaction.

"If you want, Hayden can talk to him and—"

"No," she interrupted me, her eyes widening. "Don't." She placed her hand on my shoulder and sent me a pleading gaze. "Please."

I nodded. I didn't like this in the least, but I'd respect her wishes.

My phone chimed when we reached the lunchroom, and the corners of my lips kicked up when I saw Hayden's name on the screen.

"Come to the cafeteria patio. I have a surprise for you."

My smile widened, and my heart beat faster in rising excitement when we entered the cafeteria. Hayden loved to surprise me with various gestures and gifts once in a while, but today was special, as he'd said, so he wanted to make sure it was unforgettable for me. This morning, I woke up in his bed to a red rose and chocolate pancakes, which he made for the first time, and I still couldn't get over how sweet that was.

I noticed students flocking together outside the cafeteria, and some of them pointed at something. My legs carried me out faster. The cold air wrapped around me, leaving me short of breath, and I was thankful for the sun that warmed at least a bit of my body.

I faced the wall everyone was staring at and gasped at the huge black spray-painted letters, which were written for the whole world to see:

"HAPPY BIRTHDAY, SARAH DECKER.
I <3 YOU.
HAYDEN BLACK."

"This is amazing," I breathed.

"He's something else, all right," Mel said next to me. "He just *has* to break a few rules and vandalize a building, right?"

I couldn't reply, struggling to find the right words to express how elated I was. People turned to look at me, pushing me into the spotlight once more, but this time there was no shame or nervousness knocking on my door. This day was getting better and better.

"Happy birthday, Decker!" a guy from across the patio shouted, grinning at me.

"Happy birthday!" a girl close to me said.

As if on cue, all the students wished me happy birthday one by one, and all I could do was stand awkwardly and gape at them. It was like I'd entered a completely different reality, and I tried to grasp the fact that I was the center of attention, but not for the wrong reasons. For once, it was a good reason, and my chest felt so warm.

"He's so romantic," Jess said.

Arms enclosed me from behind, and warm lips touched my cheek. "Happy birthday, gorgeous," Hayden said seductively into my ear before I turned my head to look at him.

Subconsciously, my eyes passed over his now-crooked nose, two small scars that marred his left cheek, and his old scar on his temple. Not even these anomalies could spoil the beauty that entranced me each time I looked at him.

Our lips met, and I melted in his arms as our tongues flirted with each other. The kiss started out slow, but then it turned more desperate, and it didn't matter that there were so many pairs of eyes on us. I'd been so close to losing him again, and the agony had been unbearable. So, I returned his kiss with everything I had. Each new day with him felt like a gift, and I wanted to make the most of it, cherishing each moment more than ever.

Slowly, we pulled away, but we stayed transfixed on each other in a tight embrace. I didn't need to look to know phones were aimed at us, and I could already imagine a new meme that would refer to what some people called us these days: Romeo and Juliet as high school sweethearts. East Willow High students were overdramatic, no doubt.

"Thank you, Hayden." I cupped his face and kissed his lips a couple more times, beside myself. "Thank you, thank you, thank you! You're full of surprises today."

"Everything for my girl. Here." Hayden opened his jacket and pulled me inside of it, wrapping it around me. "I don't want you to get sick just because you forgot to wear your jacket. *Again.*"

"Thank you. But won't you get in trouble with the principal?"

He'd skipped midterm exams and spent many days out of school, but luckily he'd managed to take makeup midterms and apply to the computer science major at Gateway Community College in New Haven. Additional setbacks that could hinder his chances of college admission were the last thing he needed right now.

He tapped my nose. "Don't worry about it. He's supposed to procure another donation from Carmen, so he won't be a problem."

I opened my mouth to comment on how terribly corrupt Anders was, when Steven entered my field of vision.

"Smile for the camera, lovebirds," he said in a high-pitched voice, imitating a girl. "Say cheese with macaroni!"

The shutter clicked, and I cringed at how awkward the moment was. Masen, who stood next to him, burst into a fit of chuckles, holding his own phone as if to film us.

"Hey, don't do that!" I told them with red cheeks. "Don't ruin this."

"This is going to be my birthday gift for you, Sar," Masen answered and took a step closer to us to film us at a different angle. "I'll even edit it if you want and make it a little steamier, if you know what I mean." He winked at us, and I looked at Hayden. He was smirking.

"And there he is," Mel said in a bored voice. "Sex freak. I wonder how any girl can jump in bed with you when your brain *and* dick, I'm sure, are the size of a seed."

"Why don't you check it out, since you can't stop thinking about the size of my dick?" His eyebrows scrunched together. "Actually, don't do that. I wouldn't want your satanic face anywhere near my dick. Preferably at least a mile away."

"Mr. Black!" Principal Anders bellowed, and the horde of students stepped aside to let him and a few teachers come through. "What is the meaning of this?!" He pointed at the letters on the wall.

"See," Masen started. "We usually say 'happy birthday' when it's some-one's birthday." A short round of unanimous laughter prevented Anders from responding to Masen's mocking. "And 'I heart you' means 'I love you.' We say that when we—"

"I know what the words mean, Mr. Brown! You have the audacity to ridicule your principal?"

"That's what you get when you're a stupid, crooked, ugly swine," Mel muttered under her breath.

Masen raised his hands in the air. "You asked for the meaning, Mr. Anders. I just wanted to help you."

"Silence! This has gone too far! Black! I don't allow students to vandalize school property, and you've crossed the line!"

Mel looked like she was having a hard time keeping her amusement in check, her hand pressed over her mouth as if she was going to explode into laughter any moment. Anders sliced her with his eyes, his black mustache twitching in anger that built up in him fast.

"You have something to say, Miss Brooks?"

Melissa was completely unfazed. She returned his gaze with a conde-scending smile. "Just that you should be an actor. You would be great! Not an A-list one, of course, because not even a child would fall for your theatrics, but it would definitely suit you better than this job."

Anders's pudgy cheeks inflated and reddened, his chest rising and falling in an erratic tempo that bordered on comic. "That's it! To my office, Brooks!"

"Now you've done it, sis," Steven said and shook his head at her. "Your big mouth will get you snuffed one day."

"Do you have to do this now, of all times?" Hayden asked Anders with a bored expression. "It's her birthday, and you're exaggerating."

"Mr. Black! I don't want to repeat myself. To my office." He looked at me, and for a confusing moment, I thought he was going to actually wish me happy birthday, but he only nodded at me and turned to leave. "All of you! Enough of this circus! Back to the cafeteria!"

Melissa and I looked at each other, both of us trying our hardest to suppress our laugh. Some things never changed.

"Will he ever get tired of repeating himself?" Hayden asked me, his face deadpan.

"I don't think so." I cupped his cheeks. "Are you sure you're going to be okay?"

"Yeah. I've visited his office so many times it got old ages ago. I'll be okay."

A shiver raced through me as the cold seeped deeper into me. I placed a soft kiss on his mouth.

"Thank you for the gift," I whispered into his lips. "I love it."

"It's nothing, baby. But I'll give you the real gift tonight." Redness crept up my cheeks at the double entendre in his words.

"There's more? But you've already done so many things for me today."

"It's never enough. Now, come on. Let's go inside before you freeze your ass off."

• • • •

I LOOKED AROUND MY almost bare room. Its empty walls brought me a bittersweet mix of sadness and joy, confirmation of a huge step I'd made in my life. I turned eighteen today, so I was able to leave the place I called home for the past three and a half years and design my future the way I wanted. The first step toward brighter days was to move to the Blacks' house.

The drawings I'd created over the years and plastered on my walls were now in a big box I carried, about to be put in the room that was ready for me. I'd already moved my art supplies, along with my desk, chair, graphic tablet, laptop, and a few more items that had given this room life.

Nostalgia rushed through my veins, whispering about those moments of happiness I'd experienced in a room that was my buffer against the cruel world. The playful irony of life never ceased to amaze me. I lost the security I'd had here, but I gained a person who offered me so much more, despite the conflicting past we shared, and it colored my world with brighter shades of hope, joy, and love.

"Are you going to miss it?" Hayden asked, breaking the silence.

I turned around to face him and eyed the huge box of books he held. "A little bit. After all those years my mother and I spent moving from one place to another, we finally got a place we could call ours, but it wasn't enough for her. It wasn't enough for her to change herself and lead a better life."

He stepped closer to me, gazing at me softly. "You sure you're okay with leaving her?"

I nodded. "Yes. It feels liberating. I'll be out of her toxic reach. I've been foolish all this time, thinking that just because she was my mother she would change the way she treated me, but I was wrong. Just because she's my biological mother, doesn't mean she's my mother for real. So instead of letting her break my heart continuously for the rest of my life, I'm better off without her."

A smile took shape on his face. "I'm proud of you. You're my fighter."

My heart contracted with pure joy. "Thank you."

I connected my lips with his and deepened the kiss, relishing in the feel of his tongue against mine for a few moments.

"Let's go. We're finished here."

Giving one last glance to my room, I followed Hayden out and closed the door behind me. I wouldn't be coming back here anymore, having agreed to spent the next few months at Hayden's place until we moved to New Haven and started college.

I entered the living room and braced myself for the farewell talk with Patricia. This last month, we barely spoke to each other, and we led separate lives. She'd completely recovered, so she was back to work and her ordinary life.

She didn't need Lydia anymore as her caregiver, but they stayed in contact as friends, which was surprising, to say the least, because Patricia wasn't good at making friends. As far as I could see, Lydia was a good influence on her, since she helped her manage her alcohol addiction, following her to AA meetings and cheering her up during crises.

I lowered the box on the coffee table and crossed my arms over my chest as I faced her. She was reclined on the couch, her eyes fixed on an episode of Game of Thrones.

"I'll be leaving now."

There wasn't even an inkling of interest on her face as she looked at me. "Okay. Do you want my blessing?"

I clenched my jaw as Hayden tensed. He put the box on the floor and came to stand next to me.

"And look at you. Her prince in shining armor," she jeered at him. "Ready to ride into the sunset with her."

"Stop it," I told her before Hayden exploded and unleashed his fury on her. "I don't want to fight. We've done that more times than I can count. I just want to tell you I won't be coming back anymore. I hope you'll take care of yourself."

She brought her attention back to the TV screen. "Yeah, whatever. You can drop the act and leave already. Wouldn't want you to waste your time here."

If I was the old Sarah, her sarcasm would have sliced me deep and left me to bleed in anguish over the mother I'd never had. I would spent hours thinking there was something wrong with me since not even my own mother loved me, and I would despise myself, with no way of accepting who I was.

The new Sarah knew this wasn't about me. This was about her and her inability to give love to her child. She'd never accepted me just because I was a "mistake," as she'd said, and her interest in me went as far as how much she could use me. So, I was over her, on a path of self-acceptance and self-love I'd denied myself for too long.

"You're right. I'm wasting my time here trying to act civilized and mature. In the end, it changes nothing. Goodbye."

I moved to pick up the box and head for the front door, but the way Hayden looked at her stopped me, making hairs stand up on the back of my neck.

"I thought my mother deserved a medal for being the worst mother of the decade, but you're something else."

Patricia rose to her feet. "What did you say?!"

Hayden gave her a disdainful look. "You have a great daughter. She's a sweet, compassionate, and smart girl who's achieving amazing things—more than you'll ever achieve—but unfortunately she had to live with a person who shouldn't even be called a mother."

The veins on her temples popped, and an ugly sneer pulled at the corners of her mouth. "How dare some spoiled brat speak to me like this?!" She fisted her hands by her side, her face red with rage. "Out of my house! Now!"

Hayden didn't even blink; he wasn't intimidated by a long shot. "You don't deserve her. You don't deserve her wasting even a second more of her time on your sorry ass. And I'm glad as hell that she doesn't have to see your fucking face anymore."

"Out! Now!"

He took a step closer to her. The menacing expression on his face was unnerving, but Patricia didn't get the hint. She stared him down, and I sensed she was about to slap him or worse.

"I'll make sure you don't hurt her ever again. I'll protect her so you won't ever be able to reach her. But if you even try..." He took another step toward her, and Patricia swung her hand at him. He grabbed her wrist before she could hit him and got into her face, his eyes as cold as ever. "You'll regret it. So you better think twice before even speaking to her. You got it?"

She let out a shriek of frustration that grated on my ears, and my stomach lurched with tension that could only be resolved when we were out of this house. This phase of my life was over, so the sooner we got out of here, the better.

"Let her be," I implored him. "Let's get out of here."

Patricia yanked against him and brought her other hand to hit him, but he stopped her again and pushed her back to the couch before he backed away from her. "You better stay in your lane and don't mess with Sarah."

A slightly diabolic glint to his eyes sent a strong message, and she recoiled for the first time, finally understanding that Hayden didn't issue empty threats.

"What are you waiting for?" Her voice trembled, and she looked between him and me with wide eyes. "Out!"

I took Hayden's hand. "Let's go. We have nothing else to do here."

He let me pull him away from her, but he kept his gaze on her. "Yeah. Let her rot here all alone, for all I care." The anger in his eyes dissipated when he met my gaze and leaned in to leave a kiss on my forehead. "Let's go, baby."

I watched her a few seconds longer, reflecting on how far away we were from each other. This was exactly like three years ago. She didn't even remember it was my birthday. This was just another push for me to leave her in the mud of her negativity and resentment and head for more positive things in my life.

I didn't feel empty or remorseful when I stepped out of the house I'd called home. No, I felt free. I was free from the suffocating shackles that had held me captive for as long as I could remember.

A huge smile came to life on my face. I felt like skipping as my legs led me to the Blacks' house—my new home—and a place where I'd created some of my most precious memories with Hayden and Carmen during these last few weeks.

After Hayden's fight, Carmen didn't want to be separated from him. She tried her hardest to help him in any way she could, especially when he was discharged from the hospital and had to spend several days in bed.

It was difficult to explain to Carmen why her son had suffered life-threatening injuries without mentioning T and his gang, but I did my best to make her believe Hayden had gotten into yet another street fight. She was furious and threatened to sue Hayden's attackers, and only after Hayden swore to her that he wouldn't end up in such a mess again, she decided to let it slide for the last time. Barely.

Hayden still wasn't okay with everything that had happened between them, but he was starting to accept her, which could, hopefully, help rebuild their trust in the future.

Carmen had definitely changed. She'd abandoned the woman who was deep in her work as a way to escape reality and showed more affection to

Hayden than ever before. She wasn't chained to the hospital anymore, and she was slowly getting used to life free of ceaseless work.

Hayden and I had also changed. The crushing pain I experienced the moment I thought I lost him brought me reinforced strength to deal with anything that could come our way. I met every low with more determination and patience than before, resolved not to let our darkness or insecurities undermine all the progress we'd made so far. Hayden was allowing me to be there for him whenever he got pulled into his dark world, and we'd started couples counseling. It helped us open up more to each other and learn how to deal with our arguments and misunderstandings in a healthier way.

I also started cognitive-behavioral therapy to treat social anxiety, accepting Ms. Kishimoto's suggestion to let one of her colleagues work with me. I was making small steps because I had yet to get over feeling exposed and vulnerable whenever I shared my thoughts. I needed to get rid of the urge to build a shield around me. But even so, being able to talk about my issues was comforting. It pushed me closer to a life in which I wouldn't be controlled by my anxiety or fear of socializing with others and letting them closer to me.

"Come here," Hayden told me when we entered his house and he put the box with my books down. I lowered my box next to his and allowed him to pull me against him.

"I'm okay," I told him as I buried my head into his shoulder. His pine tree scent engulfed me, and I breathed it in. "I knew something like that would happen."

He threaded his hands through my hair. "You're worth a lot, Sarah. Just remember that I'm always here for you." His soft lips brushed across my cheek. "You're not alone. You have me."

I nodded and squeezed his jacket as my lips got closer to his neck. "I know. And you have me." I planted a kiss below his jaw. "I love you."

"I love you too. I love you the most."

We found Carmen in the kitchen slicing pieces of the chocolate cake she'd made for me. "There you are," she said with a dazzling smile. My heart pumped with joy because she was doing this for me.

She'd made me a birthday cake and even bought me a present—a white gold jewelry set with a necklace, earrings, and a bracelet. I didn't want to accept it, shocked that she would buy something so expensive for someone who wasn't even her daughter, but she didn't want to hear it.

There were no words to express how this woman made me feel. I'd gained a person who truly cared for me even though we weren't connected by blood.

"Let's eat cake together," she said.

Unlike before, Hayden didn't protest. He wasn't quite himself, but he also wasn't angry with her, eating his cake and responding in normal tone of voice whenever she asked him something.

I observed them silently, feeling the urge to grin. They were my family now. Somehow, we found our way to each other and this moment filled with peace, love, and a promise of better days.

Hayden met my stare. "What?"

I smiled and took another bite of the delicious cake. "I'm just happy. Sitting here like this feels amazing."

He lowered his fork and ran his hand across my cheek, gazing at me warmly. "We'll have many more moments like this."

Carmen's eyes twinkled with affection. "I'm so happy for you two. There is nothing I want more than to see you both smiling and happy."

My heart skipped a beat at her words. *Family.* I was becoming emotional too quickly.

"Thank you for accepting me, Carmen. You've done a lot for me, and I can't ever repay you."

"There is no need to repay me." She covered Hayden's hand, to which his body went rigid, but he didn't move away. She offered him a calming smile. "You brought joy back to this house. You helped my son, and you brought a smile back to our faces. We're truly lucky to have you."

She placed her hand on mine across the table and held both Hayden and me. The way she looked at me—so tenderly—brought happy tears to my eyes.

"Happy birthday, sweetie," she said. "May all your dreams come true."

My vision blurred, and I sniffed, closing my eyes. My dreams were already coming true. Just half a year ago I couldn't even imagine I would be this happy surrounded by people who showered me with love, but here I was. And it was just the beginning.

"Okay. Enough with this sentimental crap," Hayden growled and thrust his fork forcefully into his cake. "You're going to drown us with your giant tears."

I shook my head at him. A wavering smile settled on my face. "I love you too," I replied jokingly and leaned in to kiss his cheek, memorizing this wonderful day for good.

Today was, for sure, my best birthday ever.

Chapter 23

"HE BOUGHT YOU THE LATEST iPhone?" Mel asked me incredulously, trying hard to be heard over the live music that blared through the house.

A local rock band, Hawks and Roses, was currently playing a cover of "Radioactive" by Imagine Dragons, which had the teenagers in the living room in a frenzy. They were old friends of Hayden's, who were making a name for themselves doing local gigs and posting their original songs and covers on YouTube, and they came to play tonight for Hayden's and my birthday party.

Since Hayden didn't celebrate his birthday more than two weeks ago because he was still recovering from his injuries, we'd decided to celebrate it together. Carmen had gone to spend the night at her friend's house, but not before she made us promise we wouldn't trash the house.

I was uncomfortable about this whole birthday party notion at first, since I'd never thrown one, let alone with people who had bullied me. However, everyone had been nice to me so far, and I didn't know what to make of it.

"He said it was not only my birthday gift but also a gift for getting into Yale."

"What did you say?"

I sighed. "I said I'd go back to working as his cleaner if I had to accept such an expensive gift."

Mel chuckled and took a swig from her cup. "I bet his reaction was priceless."

"Not really. He just reminded me that my old LG was on the verge of dying a painful death because of all the damage it had suffered, mostly because of him." I hadn't been able to say anything to that. After all, he *was* responsible for damaging my phone. "So now he wants to compensate with a new phone."

"Th-Th-That's amazing," Kevin said, pushing his glasses up the bridge of his nose, and glanced away. "He's s-so thoughtful."

"I just wish I could buy him something expensive too. All my gifts are pretty cheap compared to his."

"I'm sure he doesn't care about that, Sar," Jess told me with a smile and pushed her curls from her face.

Just like me, she was dressed in a tight dress that reached her mid-thighs. It was completed with high heels and a multi-layered necklace with heart pendants.

I glanced at the cute silver bracelet with flower charms that adorned my wrist. It was Melissa, Jessica, and Kevin's birthday present. "He said the same thing. He doesn't care what it costs, but still, I want to surprise him sometimes."

"Maybe you can soon," Mel said. "You started doing commissions, and you're doing great so far."

Her words weren't far from the truth. I had a lucky start when I announced I was open for commissions to my followers. Many people had contacted me, much to my disbelief, and asked for drawings of their pets or themselves, and I was overwhelmed with such a positive response. For once, I was able to earn money doing something I loved. I was getting closer to making my dream of becoming a professional artist come true, and the feeling was indescribable.

"I hope so."

The band started playing another cover song from Imagine Dragons, which caused a new wave of excited shouts and screams. More teenagers joined the others who were already dancing.

"Okay, let's dance," Mel said and motioned to us to follow her.

"I'll stay here a bit longer because my feet are killing me in my heels," Jess said.

"I'll stay with her," I told them and took a seat with Jess on the couch. "Have fun."

Mel saluted us and shimmied across the floor with Kevin tailing her. Amused by her childish antics, I looked across the living room to where Hayden sat with Masen, Blake, and Steven. Our gazes clashed. I turned completely hot when his eyes raked my body. His sensual lips quirked up into a seductive smile before he took a drag of his cigarette and sent the smoke twirling up in the air.

"Sometimes I envy you," Jess told me.

"Why?"

"Because you have someone who looks at you that way." Her blue eyes turned soft, gazing between Hayden and me like she was awestruck. "You can see from a mile away how much you love each other."

I smiled back at her. "You'll get that one day too. You'll have that person who will look at you the same way Hayden and I look at each other."

"How?" Her brows furrowed, and she blushed. "I'm stuck."

"What do you mean?"

She glanced at where Hayden was sitting. I followed her gaze to Blake, who was talking to a girl next to him. "I made a mistake. I knew it was dangerous to let him get under my skin. And I *really* hated him. But then I saw a different side of him, and before I knew it, I was trapped. I hate it. I hate him for doing all those cruel things to me, but I can't help but want to know what is behind it. What is the reason for his behavior?"

I studied Blake as I thought about her words. Strangely enough, it felt like she was describing Hayden and me. "A different side to him? What did you see?"

She fiddled with her thumbs on her lap. "He has a past. Something obviously troubles him because, if you haven't already noticed, he's like a ticking bomb ready to explode. He's always so angry, and I..." She glanced at him again, biting into her lip. "I saw him *crying* once."

I raised my brows. This was just like the day I saw him and Hayden together, when I fell for Hayden.

"Where did you see him?"

"In the school gym. I was walking past it when I heard sobs, and I went in to see what was going on. He was sitting right under the basketball hoop, calling some girl's name and crying." She chugged her beer. "That's when I started noticing him for real, and I grew curious about him. Like, what makes him tick? Why is he a bully? How is he such a good friend to Hayden but treats the rest of us like dirt?"

I took another sip of my beer. I felt lighter and warmer. "And now you like him?"

"And now my heart beats faster when he's close to me, but it's not in fear. Not entirely. But now we have detention together, and I don't even want to think what will happen on Monday."

Oh Jess... "When you kissed him on the New Year's Eve, how did you feel?"

Her eyes glazed over as she stared at one spot on the ground, and her lips curled into a tiny smile. "It was breathtaking, Sar. I felt lost in him so easily, and the scariest part was that I wanted more." She let out a sigh. "I messed up, right?"

"Did he say how he felt that night? Does he like you?"

She shook her head and chuckled bitterly. "No and no. There's no chance he would ever like me."

I placed my hand on her shoulder to make her look at me and offered her a smile. "I thought the same about Hayden. I thought it was impossible to have a love that was born out of hatred, but love is resilient. It can surprise you in many ways and empower you even when you're at your lowest. It can illuminate even the darkest of places."

Hayden and I had managed to reach a place where we were free from prejudices, hatred, and dark thoughts that allowed pain to spread. We were allowed to heal piece by piece, becoming better people.

So many people weren't able to change. So many were completely lost in their toxicity, hurting others to bring themselves up, and it only continued the chain of hatred that destroyed everyone.

"I didn't used to understand how some people weren't aware of how powerful hatred could be. They lash out, hurt others, and destroy their lives without even realizing that harboring such hatred could be even worse than death. It's like you're slowly dying, but you never die, tethered to a world full of darkness and pain. Some people just don't understand, and they continue to hurt others until maybe one day they see the other side of the coin. They see just how much pain they've inflicted. And maybe, just maybe, they regret it and want to change.

"But after seeing Hayden's struggles, I understand that too often we're so lost in our pain to consider other people's pain, and we do what helps us get through another day, what *we* think is right. It's horrible, dark, and twisted, because abuse is never justified, but sometimes lines can be so blurred we don't even realize how awful our actions are until it's too late.

"So, maybe one day Blake will realize his mistakes and start to change. He may accept you despite all his previous actions. And then it's up to you whether you want to forgive him or not. I'm sure that if that time comes, you'll find your own answer."

She remained speechless, her eyes wide as she stared at me.

"What?" I asked, turning red.

"You're so amazing, Sar. Your words... They're just *wow*. I admire you so much."

My blush intensified, and I looked sideways. I downed my cup. "Thank you, but it's nothing, really."

I looked over at Hayden, and my pulse sped up when he smirked at me and beckoned me with a quick motion of his hand to come to him. I stood up and swayed. Alcohol was definitely working its magic.

"Why don't you join Mel and Kevin while I talk with Hayden?"

"Sure." She giggled. "Kevin totally looks embarrassed out there. He definitely has two left feet."

I glanced at Kevin and chucked at his clumsy dance moves. "Yeah. And Mel doesn't help." I grinned. "She's had so much to drink that she doesn't even notice."

"I better help him before he runs away." She winked at me and ambled away in their direction.

Hayden's eyes blazed as I approached him through the throng of teenagers blocking the way, scanning all of me. When I reached him, he yanked me toward him, and I fell sideways into his lap. His arms wrapped around me to hold me close to him.

"If you only knew what you're doing to me right now," he said into my ear and nibbled my earlobe. "That dress fits you too well."

"Maybe you can take it off me later?" I flirted back.

He groaned and squeezed my butt. He traced my neck with his warm lips, and I had to bite into my lip to stop myself from moaning. "If you keep talking like that..."

"You two can't stay off of each other," Steven slurred from the other side of the couch. "You've completely changed him. Now he's a pussy." All the guys except Hayden laughed.

"That's not true!" I defended Hayden as he frowned. "Hayden is Hayden, and that will never change."

Blake cocked his head to the side. "What's that supposed to mean?"

All eyes were on me, but that didn't prevent me from pouring my thoughts out, encouraged by the alcohol in my system.

"It means that Hayden will always be that unique, smart, brave, and talented guy who's ready to do anything for the people he loves. Yes, he has a lot of flaws and he's far from perfect, but I'd pick him over everyone else any day."

I cupped Hayden's cheek and looked earnestly into his eyes. I whispered the next part so only he could hear me, never looking away from him, "I'll always glue back his broken pieces and shower him with love. I'll always pick him up whenever he falls."

He was spellbound, telling me so much with his gaze and a subtle curve of his lips. I felt so high on him.

Steven's clapping burst our bubble. "Wow. That's a devoted girlfriend! Where can I find one?" His words were rich with sarcasm. "Can someone give this girl a Nobel prize for devotion?"

Hayden stretched his arm over Blake who sat next to us and punched Steven in the shoulder. "I'll make you eat those words."

"Hey!" Steven recoiled, rubbing his shoulder. "You really don't hold back, do you? I was just joking, all right? It was so emotional I even had a tear coming out of my eye." He sniffed and wiped away a non-existent tear.

Hayden hit his shoulder again before Steven could even react. Steven jumped up and glanced at Masen as if looking for support.

"Keep talking and you'll be eating through a straw," Hayden growled at him.

"We don't need any more visits to the ER, thank you," Masen replied with an amused smile.

Blake snorted. "That's true. I've seen enough of that hospital to last me a lifetime."

"Joking aside, you two look good together," Masen said.

I hadn't expected such honesty from Masen, whose serious face spoke of respect and approval. Before my surprise could wear off, Blake managed to intensify it by saying, "True. You make him happy, so we give you our stamp of approval."

My eyebrows winged up. "Geez, you're not our parents," I replied, masking just how happy their words made me feel. The guys around us let out a spurt of laughter.

Hayden nuzzled my neck and gripped my waist with his hands, which gave me an idea.

"Let's dance," I whispered into his ear.

He groaned. "I don't dance."

"Oh come on. We've never danced, and I really, really, really want to dance with you."

"Nope."

"Please! Just this once and I'll never ask you to do it again. Okay? Pinky promise?" I offered him my pinky. "Pretty please?"

He ran his hand across his face, and another groan left his lips. "Come on. Let's get this over with." He pulled me to my feet, standing up.

"Pussy whipped," Masen sing-sang and raised his thumbs up at us.

Hayden slapped the back of his head. "Do you want to be kicked out? Shut your trap."

Masen was about to reply, but Hayden flipped him off in his face and pulled me away to the band, who was taking a break between songs.

"Since you want to dance, I might as well give you my last gift now."

"Last gift? But you've already given me more than enough and—"

He tapped my nose. "Didn't I already tell you it was never enough?"

He let go off my hand and moved to say something to Cameron, the lead singer. Cameron nodded to Hayden and turned around to his band members. "Okay, guys. 'Everlasting Black and White' is next."

Goosebumps erupted all over my arms when I heard the title of the song. That was the title of the poem Hayden wrote for me when I was in the hospital after the incident with Josh.

Hayden took my hand again and led me to the dancing crowd.

"Hayden? Is that the poem you gave me?"

Stopping, he turned around and placed his hands on my hips, drawing me closer to him. "I called them some time ago and offered to give them my lyrics for one of their songs. I wanted it to be my gift to you, so I've reworked some lines."

Cameron approached the microphone and cleared his throat, drawing attention back to him before I could even express my surprise.

"The next song is a rock ballad, and it's our new song. It's the lead single from our debut album Bleeding Promises, which will come out at the end of the year. We hope you'll like it."

"You rock, Cam!" a tall girl with glasses standing close to Hayden and me shouted, staring at Cameron with adoration.

Cameron smirked at her, and I could guess he was making her and the most of the female population here swoon. "Thanks, sweetheart." He sent her a kiss before he turned his attention back to all of us. "You'll be interested to know that the lyrics were written by one of our hosts tonight, Hayden Black! This is for you, Sarah." He looked directly at me and winked. "Happy birthday!"

I pressed my hand against my pounding heart, melting under Hayden's hands that held me against him. The keyboard player started the melody, which was followed by the mellow bass. They created a slow-paced emotional intro that gradually progressed into the first verse, and Hayden moved slowly with me. Our bodies swayed in unison to the beautiful melody that stole my heart from the first note. Cameron's deep voice filled the room, charged with emotion.

"A long time ago, he was my only light,
Until you arrived and brought more dark.
The night he left brought havoc and pain,
Erasing my love. Making me insane.
Completely insane.

Without you I'm lost,
But with you I'm crushed,
You're my everlasting sorrow
And my sweetest rush.
I hurt you, and my heart and bones break,
Suffocating me, drowning me in a never-ending ache.
A never-ending ache.

The hole in my heart paved road to despair,
And brought out my eternal nightmare.
But then you reached me and gave me peace,
And now you're the light that heals me.
You uplift me.

Without you I'm lost,
But with you I'm crushed,
You're my everlasting sorrow
And my sweetest rush.
I hurt you, and my heart and bones break,
Suffocating me, drowning me in a never-ending ache."

The bass guitar grew louder, building tension that led to a soul-stirring climax, and Hayden stopped dancing. His hands on the small of my back held me flush against him as he gazed at me, and my heartbeat turned erratic.

"So now that you know all my highs and lows,
And now that I know I can't let you go.
It's time to say goodbye to hate and pain.

You're my next reason to be happy (I'm here to stay).
You're my next smile (I'm here to stay).

No more pain, no more doubts.
No more pain, no more doubts..."

The music quieted for a few moments, and Hayden crashed his lips against mine. I brimmed with joy, at the tower of happiness Hayden created in me.

"Without you I'm lost,
But with you I'm crushed,
You're my everlasting sorrow
And my sweetest rush.
I hurt you, and my heart and bones break,

And now after everything
I'm burying all that hate..."

Hayden tilted his head back to see my reaction and traced my waist with his hand as our warm breath mingled.

"After everything we've gone through...

...You're my only fate."

The keyboard took over, carrying the last notes of the powerful, mesmerizing ballad that took its place in our minds and hearts. The song finished, and everyone started applauding, but I could barely move.

"This was..." *Phenomenal.* My voice broke, and I took a deep breath.

The intensity in his gaze created a throbbing ache in my chest that grew stronger with each heartbeat. "This was what?"

"So beautiful. Hayden, everything you do is so beautiful, and I can't believe how lucky I am to experience all of this with you." I grabbed his cheeks and planted a kiss on his lips. "You know how much I love you?"

Before he could answer me with a kiss, Mel clamped her hands on our shoulders and got into our faces. "Such a devoted boyfriend, right? Count on him to win a girl over with a song." She wiggled her eyebrows at me and patted Hayden on his shoulder. Her glassy eyes and slurred words gave away just how drunk she was.

Hayden rolled his eyes. "Your breath stinks. Get away from me."

She burst into laughter. "Ha! That's a good one! You stink of cigarettes, but you don't see me complaining."

"But I'm not the one who's getting in your face. Now stop touching me."

He stepped aside and pulled me next to him. My grin grew bigger as I watched their banter. Their relationship had changed a lot this past month. Melissa enjoyed teasing him, but she wasn't bitter anymore, and Hayden didn't get angry by her remarks anymore. Or at least not much. They had accepted each other and became more understanding of each other's characters, even though they were like water and oil.

"That song was so emotional!" Jessica squealed. Her arm wrapped around Kevin's as she rested her head on his shoulder, clearly having trouble keeping her balance. "I just love the lyrics!"

The corners of Hayden's lips curved up. "Thanks."

"Maybe Hayden can create lyrics for your songs," I told her, glancing between Hayden and her. Jessica played guitar and sang her own songs, and it would be amazing if Hayden and Jess could combine their talents.

"Th-Th-That's a good idea!" Kevin bobbed his head excitedly. "Th-That would be an amazing collaboration!"

Mel scratched her neck and sneaked a glance at me. I knew exactly what she was thinking about. Him having a crush on both Jess and Hayden was so complicated that none of us knew how to react to it. If only Jessica could respond to Kevin's feelings, then maybe Kevin could get over Hayden.

"I'd like that," she said in her tiny voice; her cheeks were covered with a deep shade of red. "But you don't have to do it if you don't want to."

"Why not? It could be fun," Hayden told her.

"Thank you."

"Don't mention it."

I smiled at Jessica. It was amazing to see Hayden getting along with my friends, and we could all have a fun time together. However, the same couldn't be said for Blake and Masen, unfortunately. They didn't go out of their way to bother them, partly because Hayden had asked them not to, but that didn't mean Jess and Mel would become their favorite people any time soon. This led to many awkward situations that made me feel like I had to run interference.

This didn't matter tonight, though. As I looked at Hayden's and my friends, I felt happy that we could all gather and celebrate my birthday. Maybe we all had some differences that couldn't be solved at the moment, but at least we'd made some progress compared to only several months ago. Hayden and I had changed, so maybe they would change for the better too.

It was almost midnight when the doorbell rang, announcing more people. Hand in hand, Hayden and I reached the front door, and I opened it to reveal the girls from the cheerleading team, math club, and one girl from my writing club. They had apologetic expressions on their faces.

"Hello," they said almost simultaneously.

Anna, the cheerleading captain, stepped forward and handed me a basket filled with cosmetics. "Happy birthday."

I stared at the purple bow wrapped around the handle, surprised by their gesture. "Thank you. Come in."

I stepped aside to let them in, but they didn't move. Anna glanced sideways and tucked a strand of her hair behind her ear. Hayden and I looked at each other, both confused by their odd behavior.

"What's going on?" Hayden asked them.

Anna shifted on her feet, meeting my gaze. "We wanted to apologize."

My jaw almost dropped. "Apologize? What for?"

She tucked another strand of her hair behind her ear and looked at the dark skinned girl next to her, who was a member of the math club.

Mia, if I remembered her name, cleared her throat. "We want to apologize for how rude we were before. We treated you poorly and talked behind your back." Her eyes went to the ground, and she cleared her throat again. "I was one of the people who created memes about you."

I stood stock-still as erratic thoughts rushed through my mind. I didn't know what to say.

A girl from my writing club stepped to the front. "We were so stupid back then. We didn't like you, and we helped spread nasty rumors about you, but it was so wrong. We were so wrong."

Another girl from the cheerleading team shifted closer to me. I remembered seeing her at Josh's and Natalie's trials about two weeks ago, when they were finally convicted for their crimes.

"I'm so sorry." She glanced at Hayden, twisting her hands together. "After Kayden died, I helped Natalie Shelley and Christine Thompson spread the rumor about you being a 'murderer.'" My pulse jumped, and I glanced at Hayden, who looked at her without a single trace of emotion on his face.

She licked her lips. "Natalie and I used to be friends... Actually, I wouldn't call us friends, but we had similar interests, and I knew her better than some. She hated you so much. She and Josh were obsessed with you, but back then I didn't think it would get *that* serious, if you know what I mean." She chuckled dryly. "Anyway, I was so wrong, and it's good to know both of them are going to spend many years in prison."

My eyes darted from one girl to the other as I thought of what to say. This was surreal.

"I..." I glanced at Hayden looking for anything that could help me find the right words, but he was impassive as he stared at the girls. "I'm not sure what to say."

"I know we sound strange," another girl from the math club said. "We were thinking about this a lot, and we knew we couldn't just come here and pretend everything was okay. We had to apologize to you. That's the least we can do."

"We're not the only ones who feel this way," Anna added. "We talked to other people as well, and they feel the same. We're all sorry." She directed her gaze at Hayden. "I hate to admit this, but we also didn't want to go against Hayden. The whole school knew you were enemies, so we just followed his opinion blindly. We didn't even bother to consider if we were being fair or not."

My throat clogged up, and I had to clear it twice to be able to say anything. Slowly, confusion gave way to gratitude. Their words were like an ointment on a deep wound, and I hoped in time that ointment would enable the wound to fully heal.

People had started treating me better these last few months—much better than I'd ever thought could be possible. I could finally come to school with a self-esteem that wasn't as bruised as it was after years of insults. I was finally able to live my life free from acts that had been nourishing my social anxiety and turning me into someone who was afraid to have any social contact.

I felt a sense of hope that the future would bring me different, *better* things. A part of me had been terrified of going to college only to get bullied again, but I didn't want to let my insecurities drag me down. Everything was going to be all right.

"But what changed your mind?" I asked them.

"Honestly?" Anna asked. "What Josh and Natalie did to you. It was wrong, and you even saved Hayden, which was amazing. No, amazing doesn't cut it." She bit into her lip. "We're ashamed for assuming bad things about you."

"We know it may be hard for you to forgive us, and it's okay if you don't, but at least know we're sorry," Mia said with a timid smile.

I could guess how difficult it was for them to come and say this, especially in front of Hayden. He hadn't said a word, standing next to me with his hands stuffed in his jeans pockets, and I wondered what he was thinking. I looked at each girl one more time.

I could be hostile toward them and decide to hold a grudge, but I wanted to be better than that. I wanted to do what was best for me, and that was to forgive them and the rest of the school, who clearly didn't know better. Maybe not knowing how wrong they were was punishment enough. Maybe one day they would learn and have to live with themselves. They would have to look themselves in the mirror, knowing they had hurt someone, but that was on them.

I knew what I was going to find in my reflection—self-acceptance and peace.

"It's okay. Thank you for coming here and telling me the truth. And I forgive you." The girls cracked huge, sincere smiles.

More weight lifted off my shoulders, and I could see my past and future in a brighter way. I needed this. I needed to forgive so I could move on. I was healing, far away from that scary, lonely place that only brought pain.

"And I think you should come inside because it's freezing here," I said.

Their laughter followed me as I motioned to them to come in. I looked at Hayden, whose lips had yet to move from that stern line they formed a few minutes ago.

"Is everything okay?" I asked him.

He nodded. "Let's go upstairs." He headed toward the stairs without waiting for my response.

I closed the door and went after him, carrying the basket. I glanced into the living room when I passed and noticed Kevin, Mel, and Jess dance together like there was no tomorrow. Everything about this day was perfect.

No matter what tomorrow might bring, today was all I needed, and I would remember it forever.

Hayden surprised me when he headed for Kayden's room and went inside. My heartbeat went haywire.

"Hayden? What are you doing?" My voice came out shaky. I stepped in and looked around the dark room as memories of Kayden rushed back to me.

He closed the door, drowning the cacophony of voices and sounds of Coldplay's love ballad coming from downstairs. He moved to Kayden's bed, leaving the room dark.

"I just wanted to come to where it all started for me. To the spot I fell for you." My stomach swooped.

He sat down on the bed and looked up at the ceiling. I brought my gaze up and met the myriad of tiny stars that shone brightly in the dark. It evoked the clear image of the night in Kayden's room when I confused Hayden for Kayden. Kay had never gotten the chance to take them down, which left a bittersweet reminder of his adorable personality.

I went over, placed the basket on the floor, and lay down next to him, assuming the same position as on the night of their fifteenth birthday. Silence enveloped us as we observed the stars that held a special meaning for us.

"Countless tiny spots that confuse me instead of giving me any answers," Hayden began reciting my words, never taking his eyes away from the stars. "Whenever I think about all that unlimited space, I feel overwhelmed. The more we learn about it, the more we see that we know nothing. It's scary how tiny, so tiny, we are compared to it." His hand covered mine. "Just the way I feel about you."

He turned his head to look at me, allowing me to see the mesmerizing softness in his eyes.

"You know how much I love you, Sarah?"

I nodded and interlaced my fingers with his. My pulse was racing, and my breathing grew uneven under the potent rush of love that had consumed me.

"It's good those girls apologized to you. That's the least all of us can do. They were right. We've done a lot of shit, but I was the one to blame the most. It was wrong." He looked away. "I felt powerless, confused with my life, my feelings, my fucking mind. I was so frustrated and unable to contain all that anger in me. So I lashed out. I lashed out at my family, at you, at the whole world. It was only a temporary fix that didn't lead me any closer to my salvation."

He brought my hand to his mouth and kissed it, meeting my gaze. "But you pulled me out of that dark place. You were there for me, even though I didn't deserve it, and I don't think I'll ever be able to explain to you what that means to me. You were my wake up call. You gave me the strength to fight against that dark part of me."

I glanced back at the stars. My mind replayed all those twists of fate that had separated us. Maybe our love had started with hatred and misunderstanding, but we managed to reach the mutual trust and respect that allowed our love to bloom.

"I was so stupid," he continued. "I couldn't even understand myself. I thought you were to blame for what was happening to me, like you were responsible that I was a mess, but it was never about you. It was never about anyone but myself. So now I'm learning to live with myself after everything I've done to you."

"You've changed, Hayden, and you keep changing. You're doing good things now. It's true that you can't erase the past, but you can make sure you lead your life better and make people happy from now on. You can use the past as a source of strength and motivation to work harder on being a good person."

I closed my eyes and took a deep inhale. There was something special about being in Kayden's room like this. It felt like he was here giving us the strength we needed. My lips twisted into a smile when I focused on the stars again. Kay would definitely be proud of Hayden and me now.

"I don't regard our past as completely bad," I said, admitting what had been on my mind for some time. "I told you before that mistakes can help me become a better me. So, all those scary and difficult days have made me who I am today; they made me stronger. They made me strong enough for anything that may come my way and gave me confidence to deal with it. They helped me build a thicker skin and realize I was much, much stronger than I've given myself credit for."

I raised my hand to touch his cheek, gazing at his perfect face. I could look at him for days and it wouldn't be enough. My thumb brushed over each scar in a languid caress.

"If anything was different, maybe I wouldn't be who I am today, and I wouldn't have you. Maybe you and I wouldn't be able to overcome all those things that dragged us down. Maybe you wouldn't be who you are today. We've lost Kayden, but we managed to find a path in the darkness that led us to this moment today. We've come a long way."

I sat up and cupped his cheeks. "Our past is in the past. We can bring it up countless times, but it won't change anything. So no more 'what ifs.' From now on, let's live our lives without regrets."

His unwavering gaze stole my breath. "You're right, oh wise one. I, your devoted and enlightened follower, accept your mighty philosophy." We broke into chuckles.

"You had me worried," I joked. "You haven't said anything sarcastic so I thought there must be something wrong with you."

He flashed a smile at me and kissed the top of my nose, inching closer to me. "Don't worry, baby. My sarcasm works 24/7. Just like my—"

"Yeah, I know," I interrupted him and burst into another fit of chuckles.

My laugh ebbed away when his expression turned serious. His glimmering dark brown eyes told a tale of love and devotion as they skimmed over my face. He threaded his fingers through my hair and pressed my hand right over his heart.

"It will be difficult," he said. "And we'll probably have lots of ups and downs, but we didn't go through all of this for nothing. You're my fate, Sarah, and I'm not giving up on it for anything." His heart pounded hard beneath my palm, matching the rhythm of my own. I was so madly in love with him.

"That's right," I said and pulled him in for a kiss, needing his lips on mine.

Our kiss deepened and our worlds intertwined—together as one—our hearts beating in sync under the stars that symbolized Kayden and us. I was home.

"Because after everything we've gone through," I quoted his lyrics, holding his joyous gaze. "You're my only fate."

Afterword

IMPORTANT BPD DISCLAIMER:

Hayden isn't a representation of all people with BPD, and this author's intention wasn't to portray this disorder or people with BPD in a negative way. Each person with BPD is different and may react differently in the same or similar situations. Hayden is just one person with this disorder whose own life circumstances played a role in some of his actions.

• • • •

THE TITLES OF SARAH and Hayden's story hold a special meaning. Hayden's condition is borderline personality disorder, or BPD. The first letters of *Bullied, Pained, Damaged* spell BPD.

• • • •

IT FEELS LIKE JUST yesterday that I wrote the first draft of *Damaged*, and now almost three years later, I can finally say Sarah and Hayden's story is complete. While I'm happy they got their conclusion, it feels bittersweet because I've been living with these characters for so long, and a part of me wishes I didn't have to let them go. But they will live on in these pages and hopefully in your hearts. They will live on as a reminder that everything is possible, and even the greatest darkness can contain a flicker of light that can lead us on the right path toward happiness.

Just like Sarah said, their love started on a ground filled with hatred and misunderstanding, but they managed to heal the spoiled soil through mutual trust and respect. They showed us that, even after many ups and downs and numerous bumps on the road, it's possible to find solace and inner peace, overcoming all obstacles and becoming stronger and better in the process.

So never give up and stay strong, no matter what. Life may bring you darkness and try to drown you with despair and sorrow, but you only lose the moment you give up. Don't stop. Fight. Life can be as colorful as you want it to be, so keep going and keep fighting. Whether you're bullied, struggle with mental illness, or feel like the whole world is against you, always believe in yourself because you're special. You are you, and no one can take that away from you.

• • • •

SARAH AND HAYDEN'S roller coaster journey may have ended, but the *Bullied* series continues. Stay tuned for Jessica and Blake's story in book four, *Trapped*, and Melissa and Masen's story in book five, *Scarred*.

Acknowledgments

A LOT OF PEOPLE HAVE helped me make this come true, and as always, I feel like words can't express enough how thankful I am.

To Caitlin Tipping, Casey Laura Dickson, and April Skylynn: thank you for being some of my most amazing readers. I can't thank you enough for your huge support and enthusiasm all these years.

To my most wonderful ARC team: thank you for helping my books reach more readers. I appreciate your dedication and effort so much.

To all bloggers: thank you for spreading the word and for your time. I'm super grateful to you for all your reviews, graphics, and promo posts.

To Jess and Kat: you two are simply amazing. Thank you!!

To my editor Bethany: you make my manuscripts polished and so much better. Thank you so much.

To Jo and everyone from Give Me Books promotions: huge thanks for your hard work and for making my writing journey so much easier.

To Evil Bunnies, my Facebook reading group: thank you for being so awesome and for caring so much for my stories and characters. I'm always amazed at how enthusiastic and supportive you are.

To Rasha: you're the most amazing guy anyone could wish for. Thank you for your immense support and for your beautiful covers and graphics.

And to you, my dearest readers: thank you so much for your constant support and for reading my books. You will always hold a special place in my heart.

About the Author

Vera Hollins is the author of the *Bullied* series, which has amassed 40 million reads online since 2016. She loves writing emotional, dark, and angsty love stories that deal with heartbreak, mental and social issues, and finding light in darkness.

She's been writing since she was nine, and before she knew it, it became her passion and life. She particularly likes coffee, bunnies, angsty romance, and anti-heroes. When she's not writing, you can find her reading, plotting her next book with as many twists as possible, and watching YouTube.

Read more at https://www.verahollins.com/.

Made in the USA
Monee, IL
09 April 2021